CW01468441

Man Vibes

MASCULINITIES IN
THE JAMAICAN DANCEHALL

Man Vibes

MASCULINITIES IN THE JAMAICAN DANCEHALL

Donna P. Hope

Ian Randle Publishers
Kingston • Miami

First published in Jamaica, 2010
Ian Randle Publishers
11 Cunningham Avenue
P.O Box 686
Kingston 6.
www.ianrandlepublishers.com

National Library of Jamaica Cataloguing-In-PublicationData

Hope, Donna P.
    Man vibes : masculinities in the Jamaican dancehall / by Donna P.
Hope

    p. : ill. ; cm.
    Bibliography : p. - Includes index

ISBN 978-976-637-407-5 (pbk)

1   Masculinity in popular culture   2. Dancehall (Music) – Social aspects -
Jamaica
3. Reggae music – Social aspects – Jamaica   4. Sex role
I. Title

781. 646097292   dc 22

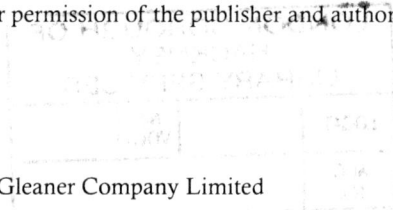

Cover image courtesy of The Gleaner Company Limited
Cover and book design by Ian Randle Publishers
Printed and bound in the United States

To the memories of my father, Lloyd and my grandfather, Wilbert. And to the lives of my mentor, Rupert, my brother, Trevor, my son Bertland and my life partner Marlon, whose 'Man Vibes' hold centre stage in my life.

CONTENTS

Preface

My interest in gender and the terrain of masculinities in Jamaica has been influenced by my experiences. Hindsight is always 20/20 and now from this vantage point, I recognize that my upbringing as the younger and female of two siblings by a single mother in the rural town of Linstead, in the parish of St Catherine, Jamaica, was radically ungendered. My mother, a strong, Black woman whose background was in the farming communities of deep rural St Catherine, had no pretensions towards what I would later learn were artificial and socially constructed forms of gender, so it was natural for me to play marbles in the yard with my only sibling and elder brother. It was also natural for me to join the group of local boys during their bird hunting quests in the wooded areas that were close to our home, and it was natural for me to climb trees and play makeshift cricket. At the same time, I was also good at playing house and had my own collection of dolls, miniature cooking pots and utensils and could sew a mean seam or two. As I grew older, particularly during my mid-20s, many people took great pains to inform me that I was 'a different kind of woman' – to this day I am still working out the hidden meaning in that statement. As time passed, I found the social company of men much more compatible with my own identity, and would often be found in the midst of large groups of men, for example at the community barbershop, debating on social, political and sexual issues. This process of un-gendering that began with my early socialisation has led me to question the ideas that underlie the rigid constructs that underpin the construction of gender in Jamaica, in particular masculinities, as my own interactions with men have been marked by ambivalence, discord and mystery.

For many years I tried to reconcile my paternal abandonment with my fantasized concepts of strong, responsible, powerful men epitomized by the 'knight in shining amour' images gleaned from the countless hours I spent as a child reading European fairy tales. Needless to say, as I stepped into adulthood, these fairy-tale images grew increasingly tarnished. My variegated encounters with men in a variety of settings and relationships including my first academic mentor's unswerving support and calm patience, and my teenaged son's increasing ambivalence, fed my desire to understand what underlay the multiple ways of being masculine in my own society. Was there one way of being a man in Jamaica? How was a real Jamaican man actually defined? The impact of the lives of several very different Jamaican men on my own life, coupled with my earlier work in dancehall culture provides the foundation for this work on Jamaican masculinities and dancehall culture. Indeed, I continue to spend countless hours researching, writing, teaching and debating on dancehall culture. A significant percentage of this time is also spent enjoying the entertainment that dancehall provides. I consider myself specially blessed to have the opportunity to conduct my academic research around an area that also provides immense cathartic release from the stresses of daily living.

During the period of my initial research on Jamaican dancehall culture, which culminated in a Masters of Philosophy in Government (Political Science), I discovered that despite earlier claims for dancehall's awesome capacity to empower women and act as a site of feminine transgression, the dancehall was rigidly bounded by patriarchal mores which privileged the masculine over the feminine.* Over time, my continued research began to point to the fact that dancehall culture was an ideal space from which to examine and theorize on Jamaican masculinities because dancehall's lyrics, performances and discourses represented performances of several masculine roles as dancehall masculinities in and of themselves.

Note

* Hope, Donna P. *Inna di Dancehall: Popular Culture and the Politics of Identity in Jamaica*. Kingston: University of the West Indies Press, 2006.

ACKNOWLEDGEMENTS

This work is the organic output of my doctoral work and represents the support and guidance of many individuals whose contributions have been invaluable and upon whose personal and professional support this work is founded.

My colleagues in the Cultural Studies PhD programme at George Mason University in Virginia, including Robert Carley, Jaafar Aksikas, Chris Sutch, Sean Andrews and Ludy Grandas contributed their time and support both professionally during the doctoral leg of this journey. My advisors Roger Lancaster and Cindy Fuchs gave unstintingly of their time and expertise throughout our relationship before and during this work. The encouragement, guidance and patience of my dissertation Chair, Paul Smith, cemented this academic relationship into a truly wonderful partnership which continues.

The Fulbright Foundation provided me with a generous Fulbright Scholarship for the two years of my coursework at George Mason and the Cultural Studies Program at George Mason University for providing me with a Graduate Assistantship during my last year in the USA during which I began working on the early stages of this work.

In the summer of 2002, my mentor Professor Rupert Lewis and his wife Maureen Warner-Lewis told me that I had to begin this journey, even though things were falling apart. I thank them for their firm belief and support during the darkest hours of this journey. Plenty 'Big Ups' to my friends and colleagues Ansel Bather, Chris Charles, Pat Saunders, Lorna Thomas, Paul Kenyon, Mabel Smith, Claudette Sterling, Pierre Davis, and Dalton and Donna Ebanks for your encouragement, support and numerous phone calls and emails, particularly during my time in the USA.

To the dancehall massive and crew your unquenched and unquenchable drive to produce and create multiple images on multiple stages continue to provide researchers and writers like myself with a never-ending supply of data and information from which to level various debates and theories about Jamaican life and society. Big up to the Sting Crew, Missa Laing, Missa Mac, Heavy D and DiMario McDowell. And to all dancers and dance crews too many to mention.

My friends deserve special thanks for their long-standing support and encouragement throughout this process. My deepest gratitude to my long-standing friend and supporter Selena Rose-Sortie who facilitated the necessary photocopies, faxes, supportive calls and visits and putting her money where her mouth is. Jennifer White-Clark and Trevor 'Fabbie' Clark, your constant support and words of encouragement have provided backbone for this work. And to my friend and colleague at the University of the West Indies, Mona, Lloyd Waller who has been a constant companion throughout the process of the PhD even while we existed on different continents, to the place in our journey where we now reside in the same city – thanks!

To Latoya West, Christine Randle, Ian Randle and the entire IRP crew my gratitude and respect for your professional and personal efficiencies during this very taxing process. I trust you have found the fruit well worth your efforts.

And throughout all things, family remains my most important resource. Always. Nuff respect and love to my brother, Trevor for opening my eyes to Jamaican masculinity and for being there through the years. To my late mother, Edith Elizabeth Henry, a poor Black woman from the rural working classes of Jamaica whose dreams and love of words are my legacy and who always believed that I could – Mama, I love you beyond words. My son, Bertland, whose *Man Vibes* and cyberspace jaunts bring comfort and joy especially when the workload gets heavy. And last but certainly not least, my gratitude overflows for the gift of my friend, muse and husband, E. Marlon Marquis for your unselfish support and unswerving loyalty, intense discussions, midnight counseling, cups of tea, and back rubs throughout the entire process that has given life to this work. You give me wings.

INTRODUCTION

Jamaica is a postcolonial, Anglophone Caribbean society with a population of 2.7million people.[1] For over two decades, Jamaican has been in a state of social, political and economic flux driven by local and global factors. This state of flux continues to wreak multiple and varying effects on the lives of women and men, as well as on the rigid class structure that continues to be the main source for ranking status and personhood in Jamaica. Within this context, Jamaican popular culture remains organically tied to and influenced by its political and economic interaction, as well as by the vagaries of socio-economic and class orientation. Since its development as a form of popular music culture, dancehall music culture has consistently weighed in on the social and political contestations at work in Jamaica.

Since the early 1980s, dancehall music and culture has remained the most pervasive and persistent manifestation of Jamaican popular culture. Yet, since Cooper's celebratory feminist focus on eroticism in her textual and lyrical analyses of Jamaican dancehall culture,[2] book-length analyses of dancehall culture in Jamaica have remained sparse (Stolzoff, 2001, Cooper, 2004, Hope 2006, Stanley-Niaah 2009). In this regard, Norman Stolzoff's (2001) work on Jamaican sound system culture and dancehall music culture stands as a critical watershed in analyses of Jamaican popular music culture, not only because of his passion and participant-observer strategy, but also because his position as a white, foreign, outsider in this Afro-Jamaican, working class space replicates the e constraints and tensions that characterize the Jamaican socio-political landscape. Only a white foreigner would have been willing and brave enough to view dancehall music culture as an area worthy of serious, indepth, ethnographic study and would have been able to access the resources to transform this passion into a seminal work at that time.

In *Wake the Town*, Stolzoff uses his ethnography of Jamaican sound system culture to argue that dancehall music culture is an organic phenomenon that arises from the underbelly of Jamaican society. For him dancehall music culture both mediates and reproduces, and challenges and generates the Jamaican social order. He sums this up in his politically loaded statement that 'A dancehall artist's ability to succeed outside the customary channels of education and wage labour threatens the hegemonic definition of human accomplishment established in Jamaican society' (p. 17). He points towards the role dancehall plays in tackling the hegemony of Jamaica's middle classes.

Cooper's *Sound Clash* (2004) is a collection of ten articles which, as outlined in the 'Introduction', and the first chapter titled 'Border Clash', aims to defend dancehall culture and propose that there is more to it than many critics believe. In so doing, Cooper replicates some of her earlier literary-based work on the metaphorical readings of violent lyrics in dancehall. She uses feminist theory to argue that dancehall culture provides female empowerment through masquerade and role play, and that female artiste Lady Saw's explicit sexuality emerges from or is an extension of a West African tradition of female empowerment, contained in sexuality rites. The other articles which compose *Sound Clash* range from a discussion on the war metaphors and motifs in dancehall culture as postcolonial critique and culture clash, to the proposition that dancehall's use of language represents a border clash between competing moral codes in Jamaican society. This clash motif reverberates in dancehall culture's engagement with the social, political and gendered structures of power in Jamaica and, in this work, is intertwined with dancehall culture's response to, and engagement with, Jamaica's hegemonic masculinity.

My first book *Inna di Dancehall* represented the research and work completed in a graduate thesis in the Department of Government at the University of the West Indies, Mona in 2001. This work is built on a personal, anthropological perspective and traces important themes in dancehall culture. In *Inna di Dancehall*, I argue that the creators and consumers of dancehall take control of their own representation, tackle traditional power relationships and exercise some level of social, cultural, political and economic autonomy in dancehall. As a result, I explore the socio-political meanings of Jamaica's dancehall culture and provide an account of the power relations within the dancehall and between the dancehall and the wider Jamaican society. The book, therefore, gives the reader an unmatched insider's view and explanation of power, violence and gender relations in Jamaica as seen through the prism of the dancehall. The negotiation of identity in dancehall is viewed in relation to society at large so skin bleaching or 'browning' reflects European beauty standards and race/colour hierarchy and homophobic lyrics imitate Jamaican masculinities and femininities. *Inna di Dancehall* reorients early feminist debates around dancehall to position actors firmly within the scope of patriarchy, while confirming the expansion of modes of activity for women in dancehall, arguing that dancehall culture is in fact a mirror of the country's traditional patriarchy and historic racial values.

Today's dancehall is a montage of multiple and overlapping discourses that reflect and refract the essence of Jamaican life in the current era. While early dancehall was limited by the availability of distribution networks and viable publishing deals, contemporary dancehall takes flight on the wings of digitized pathways and high technology highways. The explosion in technology has ripped dancehall from its limited spaces and flung it far and wide in all its extreme and often debatable forms and formations. The essence of this explosive exposure opens new avenues of opportunity for those involved in the creation of 'things dancehall' including music, lyrics, riddim, style, fashion, and dance. Yet, it also exposes dancehall's harsh Jamaican underbelly to international scrutiny. Many of dancehall's very location-specific themes traverse international boundaries to be consumed and interpreted in places that are so far removed geographically, socially and cultural from their original site of creation that meanings are transposed, transformed and oftentimes lost in translation. The nearly two-decade long controversy with dancehall's extreme anti-male homosexual discourses is a stark example of this.

This transfer of dancehall's active cultural and social energy is married to the urge of many Jamaicans, who live in the shadow of the dancehall, to be made visible within the spaces that were created out of this desire for a modicum of visibility and a foothold on the precarious ledge of existence bequeathed to many ordinary Jamaicans via the workings of the country's social hierarchies. This existential urge to 'become' in the very act of visibility, documented in my early discussion on the Videolight Syndrome,[3] has evolved considerably with the rise and democratic availability of new forms of technology such as cellular telephony, digital cameras, computer technology, internet connections with their ubiquitous social networking highways – e.g.

Facebook, MySpace, Twitter, Hi5 and YouTube, – and the ability to market oneself created by these and other internet and telecommunications modes.

While dancehall and its contemporary manifestations are certainly not limited to the foregoing, and is indeed continually evolving, the varied discourses that play across its stages historicize dancehall culture as a late-twentieth to early twenty-first century, urban, Jamaican cultural product, predominantly created by black Jamaican men and consistently supported by both women and men locally, regionally and internationally. An important characteristic of dancehall's dominant male creators is the fact that a significant majority of these men hail from the inner cities of Kingston, St Andrew, and St Catherine and their class of origin is predominantly within the lower- or working-classes. In this regard, the role of women and the redefinition of femininity in the patriarchal space of the dancehall have received some critical academic attention (Bakare-Yusuf 2006; Cooper 1990, 1993, 2000 & 2004; Page 2003; Skelton 1994; Tafari 1994) while discourses of masculinity in dancehall have received less academic scrutiny (Brown 1999; Hope 2004a, 2004b, 2006c, 2007). Yet, as my exploration and analysis of dancehall culture progressed the radically and under-explored aspect of dancehall's masculinities continued to clamor for more attention. The various forms of maleness performed and discussed in dancehall culture[4] are symbiotically wedded to Jamaica's gendered structures of power that create a shortage of socially acceptable yardsticks of manhood. The persistent frustration of working class male effort in the face of a male-oriented society that purportedly underwrites the patriarchal guarantee of male privileging has been a persistent but often underlying theme in the dancehall since the early 1980s. This has been paralleled by growing academic and social concern about the 'crisis of masculinity' that is said to be affecting Caribbean and Jamaican men.[5] Accordingly, an examination of dancehall culture, and its representations of Jamaican masculinities is extremely valuable in the quest for a fuller understanding of the gendered structures of power and the play and interplay of hegemonic definitions of masculinity that operate in contemporary Jamaica. This examination within popular music culture can also suggest modes of intervention within the broader social sphere that could result in useful policy frameworks towards real gender and social equity. In this regard, some exploration of the work that has gone before is useful.

Sustained and critical academic work on Anglophone Caribbean and Jamaican masculinities is a fairly recent phenomenon and studies of Caribbean men and masculinities lag behind the highly developed arena of work on Caribbean women and femininities which crystallized with the 'advent of the regional Women in the Caribbean Project in 1979' (Barrow 1998, xviii). Since that time, a significant volume of largely empiricist work blossomed, which retrieved Caribbean women from the periphery of intellectual discourses. As a part of this historical framework, the binary and confrontational gender ideology that operated (and continues to operate) in the Caribbean served to condemn men as 'marginal', put women in their place, constrain the lives of both and confuse gender relationships. Consequently, while the focus in Caribbean gender studies has shifted from women only to woman and man, and correspondingly from women's studies to gender studies, a strong feminist lens remains in the studies of gender in the Caribbean.

This feminist focus in Caribbean gender research has, however, inevitably energized awareness about men and Caribbean masculinity because of the complementary nature of masculinity and femininity. Since the late 1970s, several researchers have produced works that speak to the multiple valences and social practices that underpin the lives of Caribbean men and their definitions of maleness and masculinity. These include the dismissal of men as marginal in early anthropological studies (Alexander 1977; Smith 1956; Wilson 1971), and their sensationalism as 'at risk' or 'in crisis' in later work (Miller 1987 & 1991). As Lewis, (2003a, 121) notes, studies of Caribbean masculinity 'is coming of age'. This is reflected in the contemporary development of works that historicize the ideological underpinnings of Caribbean masculinities (Beckles 1995, 1999, 2003, 2004a & 2004b; Barrow 1998; Brereton et al 1995; Linden 2003a; Mohammed 1998b; Reddock 1986 & 1998; and Shepherd 1993), sustained, critical ethnographic and anthropological attention on the multiple ways of attaining manhood and being masculine in the Caribbean context by Caribbean academics (Chevannes & Brown 1998; Chevannes 2001), as well as academic theorizing about the impact of changes in gender relations and access to power on the lives of men in the educational setting (Figueroa 2004; Miller 1987 & 1991; Parry 1996). As an important part of this documentation, edited collections (Barrow 1998; Lewis 2003b; Barriteau 2004b; and Reddock 2004) provide detailed and sustained explorations of masculinity as a gendered construct, its historical and ideological underpinnings, and its cultural manifestations in the Caribbean. The selected works in these edited collections give critical attention to the interaction of power and sexuality in the creation and maintenance of masculine identities in the Caribbean region.

And so, we get to this work on dancehall and Jamaican masculinity which extends my earlier and more recent explorations in dancehall culture. This book is built on my doctoral research, (conducted between 2002 and 2005) which aimed to marry popular culture debates with theories of gender/sexuality and thereby examine the process and progress of Jamaican masculinities in dancehall culture. The work herein, documents and analyses the relationship of specific variants of masculinity in the dancehall, with the particular elements of the overarching hegemonic definitions of Jamaican masculinity. Using dancehall's own emphases, I explore five prominent masculine debates that are highlighted in dancehall music and culture. These are promiscuous heterosexuality, (gun) violence, anti-male homosexuality (homophobia), conspicuous consumption and the noveau presentation of a fashioned and styled dancehall variant of maleness. In each instance, I examine and theorize on the relationship between dancehall music and culture and the masculine exemplars that these dominant discourses project upon and into the lives of Jamaican men, as well as the relationship between each of these masculine exemplars in dancehall culture, and the hegemonic standard of masculine being in Jamaica that is historically relevant. In the final analysis, since dancehall culture emanates predominantly from among the marginalized poor of the inner cities of Kingston, St Andrew and St Catherine, this is additionally a work on marginalized Black masculinities.

The following chapters set out my examination and analysis of performative discourses and representations of masculinities in dancehall culture. Chapter One delineates the theoretical framework that sets the foundation for the overall discussion and analysis in this work. Additionally, it examines the historical specificities of Caribbean masculinity, as well as the main elements of Jamaica's hegemonic masculinity. Chapters Two to Five examine the traditional masculine stereotypes that are inflated and explicitly debated and privileged in dancehall culture without making any claims that these masculine stereotypes are monolithic representations of masculinity.

Chapter Two examines dancehall culture's promotion of a discourse of promiscuous and polygamous male heterosexuality as a cultural space for the validation of masculine identity that is patently hegemonic. Chapter Three focuses on the discourse of (gun) violence that underwrites the masculine trope of 'Badman' in dancehall culture. It zeroes in on articulations of the Shotta and Don that are linked to the phallic celebration of the gun as male empowerment, particularly in the inner city and also argues that this variant of masculinity in dancehall is hegemonic. Chapter Four concentrates on the anti-feminine paranoia that seeks to police male heterosexuality which is exemplified in the rise in anti-(male) homosexual discourses in dancehall culture since the late 1990s and argues for its ambivalence and minor transgressive nature, even while it remains hegemonic. Chapter Five examines conspicuous consumption as a masculine fantasy that celebrates a feminized culture of 'bling bling', posing and feminized dance as an embodiment of male identity. This chapter utilizes a case study approach to examine the British Link-Up Crew, a popular dancehall and diasporan group of men, which uses sartorial excess and posing to present a fantasized image of masculinity and personhood that garners respect and status from among their peers in dancehall culture. This feminized use of narcissistic dress and posing is identified as incrementally more transgressive, even while being simultaneously brokered on the hegemonic imperative towards material wealth. In addition, this chapter speaks to the rise of explicit 'money' lyrics in dancehall culture as a component of this ethic of conspicuous consumption that drives male activity in modern-day dancehall.

Chapter Six examines a contemporary and highly transgressive form of dancehallized masculinity which I label as 'Fashion Ova Style' masculinity. I discuss the role of feminized aesthetics, fashion and styles of dress and analyse them as forms of masculine transgression in dancehall culture. I also highlight the role of popular Master Dancer, the late Gerald 'Bogle' Levy and his progeny, and analyse the role of male dancers as a site of masculine transgression in the dancehall. This highly feminized variant of Fashion Ova Style masculinity clashes with dancehall culture's historically extreme and hardcore masculinities.

The conclusion synthesizes the findings made discussions in the foregoing chapters and presents arguments that propose dancehall's representations as signifiers of the reconstitution of Jamaican hegemonic masculinity.

CHAPTER 1

THEORIZING MASCULINITIES
IN DANCEHALL CULTURE

'Jamaica is a man-focused society and dancehall is no different…'[1]

In locating dancehall culture in the context of popular culture, cultural expectations and wider societal structures which operate as mediators of power and social control, this work cannot posit that the dancehall is solely responsible for the production and reproduction of gender divisions as gendered interaction in the dancehall is informed by constraints of history, class, and socio-economic status, among others. Additionally, gender identities are not interpreted as the manifestation of inner essences but as socially constructed, as well as historically shifting (Kimmel 2001). Accordingly, this work explores the means by which dancehall culture provides an arena where male adherents debate, create and articulate exemplars of Jamaican masculinity. Dancehall culture's performances and lyrical debates publicly exhibit the gendered cues that are encoded in Jamaica's rigidly bound classed and gendered hierarchies which tacitly encourage and/or privilege particular ways of being masculine in Jamaica. Simultaneously, dancehall culture selectively appropriates particular elements of Jamaica's traditionally middle class variations of hegemonic masculinity and marries these with other elements from within Jamaica's inner cities and without Jamaica's mediated borders to problematize the gendered terrain by articulating masculine exemplars that generate dialectic of traditional and transgressive discourses of Jamaican manhood. Yet, the slippery nature of hegemonic constitutions means that these exemplars of masculinity that proliferate in the negated sociocultural spaces of dancehall culture are tightly bound to the cultural ideals that bestow hegemonic power on Jamaica's status quo.

Examining Hegemony and Masculinity

According to Carrigan, Connell and Lee (1987, 148–9), Patricia Sexton's early (1969) suggestion in her work *The Feminized Male* that 'male norms stress values such as courage, inner direction, certain forms of aggression, autonomy, mastery, technological skill, group solidarity, adventure and considerable amounts of toughness in mind and body'[2] reflected an 'appreciation of power that had a distinctly feminist flavor' (Carrigan, Connell and Lee 1987, 148). In later work, Donaldson (1993, 644) identifies Sexton's statement on male norms as an early insight into the link between hegemony and masculinity.

Masculinity is neither a fixed category nor a biological given. It is a social and cultural construction that accretes a variety of meanings and multiple ways of 'being' or 'becoming masculine' in different historical contexts. Carrigan, Connell, and Lee (1987) and Connell (1987 and 1995) argue that hegemonic masculinity should not be understood as the 'male role', but as one particular variety of masculinity to which women and other young, effeminate, or homosexual men are subordinated. Carrigan et al. (1987) argues that this hegemonic masculinity is as a question of 'how particular men inhabit positions of power and wealth and how they legitimate and reproduce social relationships that generate dominance' (p. 179). This ascendant, hegemonic masculinity uses the pivotal concept of hegemony from Antonio Gramsci's Marxist analysis of class relations, where hegemony refers to a cultural dynamic by which a group claims and sustains a leading position in social relationships. Donaldson (1987, 645) states that:

> ...hegemony is about the winning and holding of power and the formation (and destruction) of social groups in that process. It "involves persuasion of the greater part of the population, particularly through the media, and the organization of social institutions in ways that appear 'natural,' 'ordinary,' 'normal'."

Hegemony is also about the methods utilized by the ruling class to secure and maintain its dominant position in a society. Grossberg (1997a, 226) notes that, a 'hegemonic project...does not demand the production of consensus... nor a process of incorporation. It does operate through the production of a certain convergence of interests through which subordination and resistance are contained.' Hegemony, however natural in appearance, is arrived at via the social processes of competition, domination, subordination and resistance. From within this struggle hegemonic masculinity emerges as the configuration of gender practice which surreptitiously legitimates patriarchy and guarantees a dominant position for particular groups of men alongside the subordination of women and other groups of men. The hegemonic ideal of masculinity that dominates at different historical junctures in any society is a culturally idealized form that men in their respective patriarchal societies (are expected to) strive to attain. Donaldson (1993,645) identifies heterosexuality and homophobia as the 'bedrock of hegemonic masculinity' and states that 'a fundamental element of hegemonic masculinity is the understanding that women exist as potential sexual objects for men while men are negated as sexual objects for men.' Of critical importance is the fact that while hegemonic masculinity may be perceived as the ultimate, it is not the only form of masculinity that exists in any society. However, it is constructed as the highest point on a perceived continuum of masculine exemplars and is, therefore, that ideal which all other representations of masculinity (are expected to) subscribe to or strive towards. Additionally, though hegemonic masculinity has a central connection to the institutions of male dominance, not all men practice it, even though most men benefit from its existence. Theorists on hegemonic masculinity note that while it exists across different classes it generally excludes black and working-class men. Additionally, hegemonic masculinity is theorized as being dependent on social arrangements and is often a lived experience, an economic and cultural force which is constructed through difficult negotiations (Brod 1987; Carrigan, Connell and Lee 1987; Connell 1987, 1990 & 1995; Donaldson 1993; Messner 1987; Rutherford 1988).

Yet, while the constitution of hegemonic masculinity conceptually guarantees ruling class power, its most influential agents and creators do not always hail from this social class. Individual agents who weave the fabric of hegemony include groups with social and cultural dominance like priests, journalists, advertisers, politicians, psychiatrists, designers, playwrights, film makers, actors, novelists, musicians, activists, academics, coaches and sportsmen, among others. These individuals regulate and manage cultural ideals through the articulation of experiences, fantasies and perspectives and project their interpretations of and reflections on gender relations into the society (Connell 1983, 236, 255, 256; Donaldson 1993, 646).

In the context of capitalism, which provides a framework for this study of masculinities in Jamaican dancehall culture, Hanke (1990, 232) argues that 'the ascendancy of men as a ruling bloc within capitalist patriarchy is achieved not only through violence and threats of unemployment but also through a cultural process in which masculinism, the dominant ideology of patriarchy, is resisted and challenged.' Issues of power, domination and control over resources remain contestatory and are consistently mediated by the politics of race, class, sexual orientation, national origin, ethnicity or some particular combination of these factors (Lewis 2003a, 101). Yet, there is never any homogeneous domination of all men in patriarchal societies. Indeed, the normative and public face of hegemonic masculinity at any given historical juncture, does not necessarily reside in real-life incarnations of male being at any given time. The publicized exemplars of hegemonic masculinity do not need to accurately reflect what powerful men are, but more importantly must reflect the current ideal of masculinity that sustains the power of this dominant group. In this regard, Connell (1983, 185–6 and 249) notes that 'hegemonic masculinity is naturalised in the form of the hero and presented through forms that revolve around heroes: sagas, ballads, westerns, thrillers,' and in other forms of public media including television, films, sporting events and books.

Jamaican dancehall culture's prominent placement as a dominant popular culture and music force in Jamaica since the early 1980s identifies it as an ideal stage from which artistes, performers and others articulate fantasies, experiences and perspectives that tackle gender relations and reflect on notions of hegemonic masculinity in Jamaica. Since its cultural ascendancy from the early 1980s to the present, dancehall culture's most prominent incarnations of masculinity arguably feed into and off the traditionally accepted definitions of Jamaica's hegemonic masculinity. The currently legitimized form of Jamaica's hegemonic masculinity at any given historical juncture is raised upon the wider terrain of Afro-Caribbean variations of hegemonic masculinity that have dominated over the region's historical development.

Historicizing Caribbean Gender and Hegemonic Masculinity

Feminist and gender theorists in the Anglophone Caribbean give credence to specific factors that arise from the particular historical experiences of these societies, and which impact on the construction of gender roles and the operation of the system of patriarchy in the Caribbean. Two of the most important historical factors are identified as plantation slavery (Beckles 1995, 1999, 2003, 2004a & 2004b; Barrow 1998s; Brereton et al. 1995, Linden 2003a) and indentureship (Linden 2003a; Mohammed 1998b; Reddock 1986 & 1998; Shepherd 1993). The historical legacies of these systems affected the construction of Caribbean gender identities and the particular configuration of Caribbean masculinities in the colonial and postcolonial era, which arguably persist into contemporary times (Alexander 1994; Chevannes 1999 & 2001; Miller 1987 & 1991).

Beckles (2004a) examines the historical configuration of black Caribbean masculinities by locating them within the hegemonic, white, patriarchal institution of plantation slavery. He suggests that hegemonic white masculinity during Caribbean slavery was associated with the 'monopoly possession of power, profits, glory and pleasure which was specified as a core element in the social translation of white masculine ideologies in which enslaved black men were relegated to otherness' (Beckles 2004a, 229). White slave masters employed two key strategies in their quest for masculine supremacy which deprived black men of domestic authority either as husbands or as fathers – the denial of black men to the right of patriarchal status, and the sexual control and appropriation of black women. As a part of the ritualistic definition of black males as Other during this period of plantation slavery, Beckles notes that, in slave owner literature, infantilization was linked closely with feminization in the conceptualization of both Black slaves and white and Black women. By virtue of being denied masculine roles or access to institutionalized support systems on which to construct counter-concepts, the Black man was conceived to have degenerated into pre-consciousness, a condition which Beckles associates with nothingness, innocence and femininity (2004a, 232–33).

Lewis (2003a, 103) notes that this institutionalized system of gender inequality that was developed and perfected under African slavery and Indian indentureship remained in place even after the struggle for decolonization by Caribbean men, which engineered the decolonization process and the eventual independence of Caribbean states from European domination. The struggles for national liberation focused on issues of political empowerment, sovereignty, autonomy, self determination and independence. What was critically absent was any attempt to deconstruct the patriarchal structures that came pre-packaged with these new sovereign states. Consequently, the Euro-centric patriarchal system of gender inequality that existed under African slavery and Indian indentureship was 'essentially consolidated and reproduced,' and arguably expanded by these Caribbean nationalists (Lewis 2003a, 103–104).

In the framework of this work on Afro-Jamaican masculinity, the historical impact of the structures that supported and maintained the white hegemonic masculinity of slave owners has implications for the importance which Afro-Caribbean males attach to the exercise of power and control over women (Johnson 1996). Plantation slavery's denial of black humanity simultaneously obscured gender and women and men were treated as equals in terms of their capacity to labour on the plantations and in the fields. One positive effect of this ungendering was the generation of high levels of gender equality between African men and women which, along with African retentions, has been credited for female economic autonomy in the Caribbean. It is arguable, however, the trajectory of this obscuration of gender in slavery had other, negative repercussions, for example during and after amelioration when both reproduction and motherhood were encouraged and rewarded in women, and the construction of a Black female identity began. Black slave men, on the other hand, did not transcend their former portrayals either as rebels and runaways, or as emasculated and irresponsible husbands and parents. As a result, the legacies of slavery and colonialism are often blamed for contemporary male behaviour, whether this is valid or not.[3] Both slavery and colonialism collapsed identities into sexed bodies, sexualizing Caribbean populations in racial terms, and racializing them in sexual terms. The various 'native' sexualities held the common fact that 'colonised sexualities were essentially subordinated sexualities.'[4]

Early work on Caribbean masculinities characterized the Caribbean male as powerful, promiscuous, derelict in his parental duties, often absent from the household, and/or unwilling to share in domestic responsibilities (Dann 1987; Barrow 1986; Senior 1991). This often feminist-influenced literature also generally projected the Caribbean male as 'possessing a propensity for female battering, and a demonstrated valorization of alcohol consumption' (Lewis

2003a, 107). In a similar vein, Parry (1996) notes that earlier ethnographic research conducted by Brown (1995) in communities in Jamaica, Dominica and Guyana suggests 'that 'manhood' is attested by sexual prowess, usually measured in terms of numbers of serial or concurrent female sexual partners, while 'secondary proof of 'manhood' resides in numbers of offspring whether inside or outside of a steady relationship.' Other factors, including the women's liberation movement, the harsh economic realities, and the impact of foreign media are perceived as contributing to the erosion of male authority and power in the home as well as to the development of power struggles between men and women. According to Parry (1996), Brown's early ethnography identified a 'causal relationship between the growing independence of women and these power struggles, apparent in group discussions in all the communities researched, seemed related most often to the growing economic independence of women.' Caribbean feminist, Patricia Mohammed (2004) also proposes that the shift in occupational roles and the capacity of women to be providers and breadwinners have challenged notions of Caribbean masculinity while simultaneously allowing women to extend concepts of femininity, and theorizes that this growing challenge is perhaps at the root of male fear that they are losing ground and privilege, and represent a real threat to their manhood. It is arguable that this male fear is the source of Caribbean Black male marginalization described by Miller (1987 & 1992).

Miller's work on the marginalization of the Black male in the Anglophone Caribbean is based on his own work conducted in the educational sector and resonates with the emasculation thesis in which black men once again become victimized by the dominant colonial order. Miller's argument of male marginalization operates within a paradigm of male dominance which is assumed as a natural ideological underpinning of society. In terms of feminist analysis and critique of patriarchy, Miller's work also means that the universal equation between men and patriarchy is put into question, for not all men have the same relationship to discourses and institutions of power. In most English-speaking Caribbean islands, it is men of a particular racial or ethnic group who predominate the economic landscape and it is in the interest of this group that hegemonic variations of Caribbean masculinities are negotiated and maintained. For example, in Barbados it is whites, in Trinidad it is whites, Syrians, Lebanese and Indians, and in Jamaica it is Jews, whites, and Chinese.

The political domination of Black men within these societies has been, for the most part, brokered on the social mobility attained through educational advancement with very little economic capital, in the form of solid material wealth, acting as a real foundation for their power.

Here, Barrow (1998b, xvii) argues that the contemporary social-gender system that operates in the Caribbean was built on an 'insecure and ambivalent foundation.' This historical insecurity and ambivalence is exemplified in the work done herein on dancehall's variation of masculinities which simultaneously play with, against and into the very structures that dancehall purportedly challenges. The ideologies of masculinity and femininity that were imposed on Caribbean society, throughout the course of slavery and colonialism, legacies of which persists today, did not build the requisite socio-economic scaffolding that was required for its practical support. Consequently the acquisition, performance and maintenance of the ill-supported hegemonic gender ideals that represent the Afro-Caribbean legacy face a growing crisis of gendered identities. Men who hold real material wealth and consequently exercise real power and control in these societies are radically differentiated from marginalized men who have no resources and must barter their labour for starvation minimum wages; who are chronically unemployed or unemployable; who exist on the fringes of society; and men who are emplaced in oppressed racial, ethnic, religious or sexual groups (Lewis 2003a, 108).

Lewis underscores the point that 'Caribbean men define their masculinity in much the same way as men in any other part of the world.' However, 'cultural peculiarities may result in emphasis on different dimensions of masculinity' (2003a, 97). The Caribbean male definition of self utilizes different factors including 'biological difference and specificity, in behavioural terms and in terms that objectify their masculinity – that is cars, boats, houses, dogs, guns may become extensions of one's masculinity' (Lewis 2003a, 97). Yet, as in other societies, the central issues that underscore Caribbean masculinity remain issues of power and control and the historical shifts in Afro-Caribbean masculinities are informed by the concept of hegemony which underwrites the most exalted notion of masculinity at a particular historical juncture.

Exploring Hegemonic Masculinity in Jamaica

Since the post-independence era, Jamaica's hegemonic masculinity has traditionally been defined in middle-class terms. This definition of a masculine ideal incorporates key elements which simultaneously draw on Jamaica's historical experience under plantation slavery and colonialism, as well as its current circumstance as a postcolonial, capitalist society. Connell (1995, 77) describes hegemonic masculinity as 'the configuration of gender practice which embodies the currently accepted answer to the problem of the legitimacy of patriarchy which guarantees (or is taken to guarantee) the dominant position of men and the subordinate position of women.' Here, the popular construction of Jamaica's hegemonic masculinity that was manifested at the historical juncture of the 1980s in which dancehall emerged was defined in middle-class terms. This 1980s constitution of hegemonic masculinity was brokered on several ideological and material factors which included, but were not limited to, middle-class background/status, tertiary education, white collar career, economic wealth, ability to provide for/ control immediate family, (polygamous) heterosexuality, access to leisure, access to/ownership of expensive cars, and domination of women. I highlight the foregoing as the most prominent features identified as constitutive of Jamaica's hegemonic masculinity during that era, without making any claims that this 1980s construction represented an ideal character type, role identity, or metaphysical identity (Hanke 1998), as Connell (1995, 77) reminds us of the 'historical mobility' of hegemony. Indeed, according to Connell (2001, 38) 'hegemonic masculinity is not a fixed character type, always and everywhere the same' but…'is, rather the masculinity that occupies the hegemonic position in a given pattern of gender relations, a position always contestable.' The hegemonic exemplar of that era in Jamaica's history represented Connell's (1995, 77) notion of the 'currently accepted answer to the problem of the legitimacy of patriarchy.'

The results of my doctoral research conducted towards this work underscored the ideological strength of this hegemonic standard in Jamaica particularly among members of Jamaica's underclasses, in that, attainment of manhood was also defined in related terms among Jamaican male respondents from the lower classes and inner cities. During my research and discussions with individuals from the inner city, who form the hardcore adherents of the dancehall, heterosexual activity, financial capacity to support resulting offspring and the mother, and leadership of/dominance over women as the 'head of the house' and 'being in charge' predominate in the responses to my queries about the factors that identify a 'real Jamaican man'. This is highlighted in Chevannes' (2001) work about Caribbean masculinity, where the discussions of manhood and male sexuality hinge on definitions of the Jamaican male (particularly in the urban context) as being a good 'Provider' and a polygamous heterosexual.

Yet, while the hegemonic postcolonial and traditional versions of masculinities purportedly hold social and cultural prominence in Afro-Caribbean countries like Jamaica, alternative and competing versions of masculinities also exist in other sociocultural arenas. In this regard, the 'ebb and flow' of the picture of Jamaican masculinities, over the period of the early 1980s to the beginning of the twenty-first century, is an important part of the gendered meanings of personhood that have been consistently debated in dancehall culture through its highly sexual and sexualized lyrics and performances. Dancehall culture's masculine fantasies arguably tackle the hegemonic ideals that articulate the power and control of particular groups of powerful men over the bodies of subordinated men by projecting fantasized constructions of Jamaican lower-class, black masculinities onto and against the bodies of Black, innercity and lower-working class men who must exist within Jamaica's contemporary hegemonic structure. At the same time, in a truly ambivalent twist, these dancehall fantasies also uplift constitutive elements of the very model that it purportedly tackles – Jamaica's hegemonic masculinity. In this regard, these masculinities are at once contestatory and ambivalent. They simultaneously wage a battle for hegemonic dominance from below, while projecting masculine images that draw from the very hegemonic structures they contest.

Theorizing Dancehall's Masculine Duality

This work refers to the predominantly black members of Kingston and St Andrew's inner cities as inner city and/or lower-class interchangeably. Using Stone's (1980) work on class and status in Jamaica, this group is differentiated from the rural poor and rural working-class by attitudes to education and politics, economic activity, and lifestyle. One must note at this juncture that while particular attitudes are shared across the different classes in Jamaica, it is becoming increasingly clear that there is a strong correlation between adherence to particular attitudes, behaviours, practices and lifestyles and place of origin in or socio-ideological orientation, for example in the inner cities of Kingston, St Andrew and St Catherine. Jamaica's rapid urbanization over the past two decades has resulted in the spread of inner city attitudes, behaviours, practices and lifestyles that have long been negated and denounced by the traditional middle-class gatekeepers in the society. These attitudes, behaviours, practices and lifestyles, have increasingly spread outwards from the Kingston Metropolitan Area towards the rapidly urbanizing rural areas via the media, person-to-person contact with family members, peers and others, and also by the examples presented in popularized lifestyles of many inner city icons, which are usually narrated, discussed, and performed in dancehall music and culture. This phenomenon is theorized by Meeks (1996, 124–43) as a breakdown of traditional hegemony, and he argues for an emergence of 'a moment of hegemonic dissolution' in Jamaica since the mid-1980s where the 'social bloc in charge of Jamaican society (i.e. the traditional middle classes) is no longer ruling over a people convinced of its social superiority and its inherent right to 'run things' (1996, 131). This period of hegemonic dissolution is characterized by sharp contestation over a wide sphere of social and economic issues. For Meeks, dancehall culture holds tremendous significance in this era of hegemonic dissolution as an alternative space, removed from the restraining confines of (high) society. This is exemplified, in one instance, by dancehall culture's prominent placement in the battle for language between British English and Jamaican Creole where, according to Meeks, the 'dancehall form has largely abandoned the tradition of resorting to the occasional refrain in Standard English' (1996, 132). In another instance, it is exemplified by the growing disparity in normative trends of fashion and dress with dancehall's propensity for unconventional modes and patterns of dress that suggest the refraction and reinvention of North American and traditional middle cues of dress and fashion 'through the lens of the urban ghetto experience into something not only peculiar to that experience, but in an adversarial position to traditional fashion' (Meeks 1996, 132).

To this end, Stone (1980, 51–68) identified a propensity for ambivalence towards and romanticizing of lower-class lifestyles, values, and culture that has resulted from the then relatively recent formation of the lower-middle and middle status groups.[5] Based on my earlier work in dancehall culture, individuals from the inner cities and lower-working class who have gained significant economic mobility from their informal activities in dancehall continue to perceive themselves as members of the inner city and/or lower working classes, even while their economic activities place them in the same economic strata as the affluent professionals and technocrats in the middle and lower-middle classes. Sustained middle strata ambivalence and lack of consolidation has weakened and diminished the traditional role of the middle classes as the guardians of the values and attitudes that provided the supportive belief system which had supplied the foundation and hegemonic underpinnings of development of the society in the postcolonial era. The unrelenting penetration of lower class language and inner city slang, styles of dress and music into the mainstream continues to heighten the ambivalence around status, class and gender. This has also, simultaneously, continued to raise lower-class and inner city confidence, awareness and self images and to encourage the proliferation of public display of the alternative masculine images emanating from dancehall culture.

Meeks's theory of dancehall culture's role in this period of hegemonic dissolution underscores my own earlier discussions where I argue that dancehall is a cultural dis/place[6] of ongoing dialogue, confrontation and contestation with the rigid socio-political, gendered, and class hierarchies of Jamaica. Its multiple discourse include the negotiations of gendered structures of power, heavy emphasis on sexuality and sex-play, and deep linkages with political violence, garrisons, 'donmanship'[7], illegal drug culture, gun culture and (gun) violence in Jamaica. These are exemplified in the movies *Dancehall Queen* (1997) and *Third World Cop* (1999) and are continuously played out across the stage of many popular dancehall events like the weekly street dance, *Passa Passa* held every Wednesday night through to Thursday morning in downtown Kingston, since February 2003.[8]

While it may seemingly operate beyond this structure, dancehall remains contained within Jamaica's patriarchal gender hierarchies. It actively challenges existing structures, while covertly re-creating and reinforcing these structures and its actors are, therefore, simultaneously demeaned and empowered (Gray 1994, 2004). I argue elsewhere that while the dancehall exists within a space that encourages the widening or loosening of the traditional patriarchal boundaries and facilitates male/female re-negotiation of traditional socio-political and socio-economic roles as defined by traditional Jamaican society, nevertheless the dancehall is rigidly patriarchal and heavily male-dominated. This is clearly evidenced at the most physical and visible levels of power and access to resources in the dancehall by the proliferation of male in comparison to female deejays/singers and the number of male in comparison to female promoters/managers/producers, among others. It is also evidenced in the proliferation of male-focused discourses of sexuality that seek to bestow power on marginalized men in Jamaica. Although popular women like Dancehall Queen Carlene, female artistes like Lady Saw and Dancers like Stacey and Keiva have gained prominence and economic and social power within its boundaries; the dancehall evolved as and remains a predominantly masculine space under masculine power and control. It creates a stage where men use lyrical narratives, performances and embodied representations to articulate the plural masculinities that are brokered on Jamaica's hegemonic imperatives and are radically intertwined with other social and political factors. Images of Jamaican masculinities flit ambivalently across the dancehall stage when dancehall lyrics encode narratives that celebrate practices and behaviours considered highly masculine, and dancehall narratives and performance embody fantasized versions of dancehall masculinities infused with themes from inner city and Jamaican culture. These dancehall versions of masculinities are brokered on the social, political, economic, historical and gendered legacies of postcolonial Jamaica.

The power of naming and the ability to control and use word/sound/power is perceived as masculine. Thus, while other dancehall actors enjoy significant visibility, the most prominent and visible remain the predominantly male artistes. Therefore, the term dancehall deejay/artiste signifies a young, dark-skinned, Afro-Jamaican male with strong ideological, social and/or physical linkages to the inner cities of Kingston, St Andrew and St Catherine. These men are usually conspicuously dressed in expensive, brand name clothing, jewellery and shoes and drive expensive, late-model brand name vehicles (e.g. Mercedes Benze, BMW, Escalade, Hummer, Lexus, Range

Rover).[9] Since its evolution in the 1980s, these predominantly male artistes continue to negate the politically correct, culturally 'appropriate' linguistic bias for British English and disseminate their lyrics in the Jamaican Creole (patois) that is heavily laced with the slang of Kingston's inner cities and cross-fertilized with the hip hop slang of North America.

This masculine incarnation of dancehall artistes is positioned on the lower levels of the race/class/colour and gender hierarchies that operate in traditional Jamaican society to rank individual status and personhood. Despite being labelled as of low socio-political and cultural status by the traditional middle-class gatekeepers, dancehall artistes have been successful in amassing economic wealth and using this wealth to appropriate social mobility and status in Jamaica. Here, the space of the dancehall provides its actors with ideological and economic tools for their attack on and revolution against the confining superstructure of their localized framework, traditional Jamaican society. The fact that many of these individuals have been bypassed by the preferred and prescribed routes to mobility (e.g. education, white collar career, marriage) has simultaneously interrupted and ruptured the socio-political, economic, cultural, and gendered hierarchies at work in Jamaica. As a result, while dancehall culture continues to maintain its interdependency with global capitalism in its quest for economic resources, it simultaneously utilizes the space of the dancehall to lyrically and symbolically disseminate cultural and moral imperatives that struggle against the traditional hegemony of social, political and gendered structures that constrain the lives of its actors who are the predominantly black members of the Jamaican underclass.

As a part of this socio-political and cultural contestation, dancehall culture articulates the notion that many Jamaican men who are placed lower down on the rigid class structure that dictates access to resources and power often articulate their masculine ethos by inflating and/or ritualistically performing particular heterosexual masculine characteristics that may potentially tighten their slippery grasp of masculine status. These ritualized and legitimated characteristics are often highly sexual however, they all draw their sustenance from the social, political and cultural landscape of Jamaica and, as a result, simultaneously play with and into the very hegemonic tropes that dancehall purportedly challenges. Thus, in its very moment of revolution, dancehall's masculine fantasies have historically projected variations of masculinity that hinge on the most popular and prominent themes of traditional hegemonic masculinity, for example, heterosexuality and homophobia (Connell 1987, 1995 and Donaldson 1993). In dancehall culture the impact of these traditional themes has resulted in masculine fantasies that are brokered on the domination or suppression of the feminine through promiscuous/polygamous sexuality and misogynistic discourse, the use of aggression and violence, conspicuous consumption and masculine posing, as well as overt or covert subscription to an anti-male homosexual ethos or homophobia. At the same time, dancehall culture's masculine fantasies are projected as extreme and often threatening variations of these hegemonic roles and therefore breach the traditionally accepted modes of 'decent' behaviour in 'polite', middle-class Jamaica, for example with dancehall's persistent 'outing' and rendering visible of the male homosexual who has historically been cast as invisible and powerless in traditional, hegemonic engagement with male homosexuality in Jamaica. As a result, even while they are brokered on hegemonic cues, dancehall culture's exemplars of masculinities have continued to feed the deepening hegemonic dissolution in their continued clash with the socially accepted models of masculine being in Jamaica.

CHAPTER 2

'OLE DAWG WITH NUFF GYAL'[1] PROMISCUOUS/POLYGAMOUS MASCULINITY IN DANCEHALL CULTURE

Introduction

This chapter evaluates the strands that coalesce in dancehall culture's explicit promotion of a promiscuous and polygamous male heterosexuality, and its notion that the sexual conquest and control of the feminine 'Other' is an important patriarchal and hegemonic site that validates masculine identity for marginalized men in Jamaica. This variant of dancehallized masculinity gained prominence in the initial stages of dancehall's development in the 1980s, which was exemplified in the early lyrical work of dancehall artiste King Yellowman, and was subsequently immortalized in the output of other prominent artistes who followed in his stead. This stereotypical and monolithic rendering of one variant of dancehallized masculinity aims to isolate, and thus capture, one form of masculinity that occupied the dominant position in dancehall's configuration of masculinity in one era, in order to flesh out its constituent elements and its relation to the process of hegemonic masculinity in Jamaica.

Dancehall's conversations and debates with heterosexuality as one power-making facet of an accepted version of hegemonic Jamaican masculinity, is examined herein through its selective constitution of what is labelled Ole Dawg with Nuff Gyal masculinity. Dancehall culture's extreme lyrical and behavioural invocations simultaneously create a lyrical and symbolic variation of hegemonic heterosexual masculinity that is excessively polygamous and promiscuously reproductive. The following sections examine the constituent elements of this excessively polygamous and promiscuously reproductive variant of dancehallized masculinity.

Additionally, research indicated the need to incorporate a related discussion on the conception and performance of biological Fatherhood in dancehall culture because dancehall's notions of Fatherhood are an intertwined and related discourse that works symbiotically with the hegemonic narratives of promiscuous/polygamous heterosexuality to grant masculine status and rank the attainment of manhood.

(Hetero) Sex and Jamaican Masculinity

(Hetero)Sexual activity is at the core of masculinity and, 'as often as it is mentioned that males are permitted and expected to be sexually active it is also mentioned that men must be virile, and that their virility is especially manifested by their sexual activities and their fathering of children' (Wilson 1969, 71). Since Afro-Caribbean manhood is achieved by doing and not by being, there is no ritualized status change that marks the transition from a boy to a man. Thus, to become and remain a man requires certain kinds of relationships with women, of which sexual intercourse and sexual initiative is primary, and a man is not a real man unless he is sexually active and free to engage in multiple, casual and promiscuous sexual relationships. This remains an important facet of Afro-Caribbean masculinity in a situation where women may not agree with or acquiesce to other kinds of interactive relationships that may be important to the attainment of manhood in other cultures, including moral and material control, defined roles in the household, and full control over personal movement. Early works on Caribbean masculinity discuss the lifelong concern with male sexual prowess that is usually accompanied by an overwhelming fear of impotence. In this regard, Smith (1956, 141) writing on Caribbean masculinity noted that: 'their interest in sexual intercourse continues...This cannot be regarded merely as a "biological drive", but must be seen as a means of expression of the desire to assert masculinity. From puberty to death, men are preoccupied with proving their potency.'

With regard to intimate and sexual relationships on the terrain of Caribbean masculinities, Chevannes (2002, 216–17) notes that

> ...in the context of the Caribbean, it is important to recognize the existence of multiple partnerships, including the dual marriage

system which spans different social classes. Attaining manhood as an African-Caribbean male activates the male privilege to engage in all forms of these sexual relationships – from the promiscuous and casual to multiple partnerships (unrecognized polygamy).

This emphasis on polygamous heterosexuality begins at an early age and the socialization of some Jamaican males includes their early introduction as young boys to highly sexual conversations and pornographic material by their adult parents or guardians. This cueing towards a hegemonic masculine imperative is particularly overt in communities from which dancehall culture draws its creative energies and in which its narratives and debates have significant ideological impact. During my doctoral research one adult male interviewee noted that his young sons (8 and 10 years old) had his permission to watch 'blue movies' (i.e. pornographic or adult movies) on the triple x-rated cable channel, *Ecstasy*, broadcast in Jamaica because he wanted them to understand the 'right way' to be a man. Other male and female interviewees from inner city or working class communities concurred with this approach, explaining very carefully that it was their responsibility as parents, guardians or older siblings to ensure that young men were made fully aware of how to have 'good sex' in the 'right way'. On the contrary, none of my middle-class, tertiary educated interviewees overtly concurred with this practice, though two university students in their early 20s expressed similar sentiments and justified same by their insistence that young men must be 'made aware of the correct behaviours that men must display,' especially with the prevalence of transgendered and homosexual identities in the media. These men and women emphasize and sanction this practice of providing young boys and teenagers with what they deem 'correct' and 'right' representations of male heterosexual practice because of the pervasive and prevalent perception that once they attain manhood, men will have to consistently display skill and prowess in sexual activity to continuously confirm their manhood. Open access to adult discussions about sex and the sex act, and permissive exposure to pornographic material act as normative behaviours in socializing many young men (particularly from inner city and lower-working class backgrounds) into an understanding of what is perceived to be a radically important facet of their masculinity. This is a starkly gendered activity where, as Chevannes notes, this 'normality about sexual socialization…applies only to the boy child' (2001, 193). In his ethnography on Caribbean masculinities, it was observed that young boys in one Jamaican community were exposed to highly sexual interactions and conversations as a normative part of their early socialization and also as necessary preparation adult roles as men in control of their women. One single mother informed me that she had 'bought' a prostitute for her young, teenaged son because he was acting too 'fenky fenky'[2] around women. She wanted to make sure that he knew the 'right way' to 'deal' with a woman and did not go into the 'batty business'.[3] Here, the impetus to learn "correct" male, heterosexual behaviour and practice is an explicit part of this sexual discourse.[4]

This socially and culturally sanctioned emphasis on promiscuous/ polygamous heterosexuality as one fundamental route to masculine status is explicitly produced and re-presented in dancehall music and culture, in what I label the 'Ole Dawg wid Nuff Gyal' discourse. This patently hegemonic facet of male heterosexuality is one of the most socially accepted discourses of traditional masculinity that exists across all classes in Jamaica, where, in the wider social context, for example among the middle- and upper-classes, public moralizing usually gives way to hidden dalliances with multiple partners. Several male interviewees from one inner city community in Western Kingston explained in great detail the particularistic status-generating meanings that multiple sexual partners encoded for masculine status in their own and other similar communities thus:

> When a man can have more dan one ooman, him ratings go way up. Is like him is a King. Even if him don't have no gun or no money, him hold plenty points inna di community. Is a Kingly ting. Worse if him can get di whole of di babymodda dem fi live good togedda and just acknowledge say is him rule. Is him run tings. Man nuh stop boom off him fist[5] an big him up.

> [If/When a man can be involved with several women he is highly rated. It is as if he is a King. Even if he does not have a gun or any money, he holds a great deal of status in the community. It is a form of Kingship. It is even more so if he can get all of his children's mothers to live in harmony and acknowledge that he rules. Then, other men (his peers) will salute him and speak highly of him.][6]

Dancehall discourse and worldview re-produce and extrapolate this hegemonic, patriarchal tenet that gives men power over (their) women and encourages promiscuity and the use and near abuse of women as objects of sexual gratification and masculine empowerment. This emphasis is encoded in the lyrical output and performed and parodied in an almost grotesque aberration that denotes high levels of masculinity to men, particularly men from Jamaica's lower-classes and inner cities. For these Jamaican men, the use of sex and sexual symbols to create a highly sexual(ized) masculinity is foremost as a site of empowerment that asserts manhood and symbolizes one form of masculinity, and forms an important core of dancehall culture's explicit discourse of male identity formation and maintenance.

Subjugating the Feminine, Elevating the Masculine[7]

In the male-dominated dancehall in Jamaica, this 'Ole Dawg' discourse is translated into the courting, conquering and/or dominance of female sexuality, femininity and women. Arguably, this is an instance of patriarchy's operation at its elemental, basest and most sexual level, oftentimes labelled misogyny and is, as Connell notes: 'A thin, contemptuous misogyny, in which women are treated basically as disposable receptacles for semen, coexists with a much more respectful, even admiring view of women's strength. Sometimes these views coexist in the same head (1995, 108).' I have argued elsewhere[8] that the apparent ambivalence about the role of women in the lives of men in the dancehall is reflective of the tensions and ambivalence that characterize their own personal negotiations of highly qualified and status-generating masculinities and, thus, cannot be classified exclusively as misogyny.

In the dancehall, the role of women as sexual objects used in the masculine trade-offs and discussions are most clearly illustrated in the performances and lyrics that speak overtly about the sex act. In its earliest manifestation, dancehall's profusion of lyrical emanations sought to either court and/or conquer the *Punaany* – a colloquial term for the female sex organ, the vagina that is very popular in dancehall culture. The heavy emphasis on the feminine essence in the mythologized narrations of the sex act in dancehall culture has, engendered many 'dancehallized' synonyms for the famed *Punaany*. These dancehall/creole slang terms include: Buffulus, Buff Bay, Bombo, Bombohole, Cratches, Fat till i' buff, Front, Glamity, Good Hole, Gum, Hole, Muss come back, Needle Eye, Okubit/Ukubit (Little bit/small), Panty-meat, Peepie-meat, and Property.[9] The greater proportion of these synonyms encode symbolic references to the purported muscular agility, tightness, fatness, flexibility, elasticity, glutinousness, suppleness or other essentialized and highly sexual feature of the female sex organ. These features are perceived as positive and make the *Punaany* desirably and ultimately worthy of conquest, courtship or praise by men in their quest for elevated levels of masculine status at the expense of the feminine Other.

The dancehall discourse of men who can claim to be an Ole Dawg with 'nuff gyal inna bungle' (an Old Dog with many women) is related to the foregoing discourses of courtship and conquest. In an update of this conquest impetus, ace dancehall deejay and Grammy winner, Beenie Man, exhorts 'ghetto youts' to engage in a set of sexual practices that will guarantee their status as Ole Dawgs in his song *Nuff Gal*:

> *Man fi have nuff gyal an gyal inna bungle,*
> [A man should have many women, and women in a bundle]
>
> *Gyal from Rema, gyal from Jungle[10]*
> [Girls from Rema and girls from Jungle]
>
> *Man fi have nuff gyal an none ah dem nuffi grumble,*
> [A man should have many women and none of them should grumble]
>
> *All ghetto youts oonu fi tek mi example*
> [All ghetto youths, you must take (follow) my example]
>
> *Di one burna business nah work agen, caw one man fi have all fifty gyal fren*
> [The one-burner business isn't working anymore, because one man should have up to fifty girlfriends]
>
> *If yuh stop drink roots start drink it agen, we haffi have di stamina fi service dem*
> [If you have stopped drinking roots then start drinking it again, (because) we have to have the stamina to service them (i.e. the women)]

Beenie Man continues his exhortations in his song, *Ole Dawg* to encourage men to give in to their urges and engage in multiple sexual liaisons, thus legitimizing their status as 'Ole Dawgs':

Ole Dawg like we, wi haffi have dem inna twos an trees
[Old Dogs like us, we have to have them (women) in twos and threes]
An everybody know wi wile aready,
[And everyone already knows that we are promiscuous]

Believe you me, wi navel string cut unda (pum pum) vagina tree
[Believe me, *our umbilical cords were cut underneath the vagina tree*]

From mi see ah gyal weh look good mi haffi fool har an get weh mi want
[Once I see a woman who looks good, I have to trick her and get what I want]

Caw mi nuh live outa Shortwood so mi haffi bunks har mek she drop inna mi paw
[Because I do not live *out by Shortwood*, so I have to bounce her to ensure that she drops into my paw (i.e. my clutches)]

Ah nuff gyal wi ah go pass trough like Patra an di one Lady Saw
[We have passed through (i.e. been with/used up) many women *like Patra and the one Lady Saw*]

An mi deh hear bout di Ouch Crew wheh have them gyal x-rated an raw
[And I (now) hear about the *Ouch Crew* that has some x-rated and raw girls]

Dat mean mi ah go want dem an mi haffi get dem an nu tell mi say mi cyaaan...
[That means I am going to desire them, and I have to get them, and don't tell me that I can't]...

(Beenie Man, *Old Dawg*)

Textual analysis of some central phrases that have been highlighted in this song unearths some of the prominent sexual themes that are geared towards upliftment of this variant of masculinity in dancehall culture.

First, in *Nuff Gal*, the artiste makes it clear that he is delivering this treatise for and on behalf of 'ghetto youts' whom he encourages to 'take his example' and see him as a role model in selecting the gendered cues that they emulate and practice. This cueing involves their engagement in what are narrated as natural and manly practices of having women in what Beenie Man refers to as 'twos and threes,' i.e. engagement in multiple sexual liaisons. While many dancehall treatises of sex and sexuality do not explicitly encourage 'ghetto youts' to take their example, Beenie Man makes explicitly signals to his primary audience, 'ghetto youts', which also implies the large majority of other 'youts' who derive ideological or social rewards from this hardcore label.

Second, in *Old Dawg* he insists that his 'navel string cut unda vagina/ pum pum tree.' In Jamaica, one traditional practice, particularly in the rural areas, is to bury a baby's umbilical cord or 'navel string' at the root of a fruit tree. The tree that is chosen is usually a young seedling or plant whose growth should parallel/represent that of the child. The belief is that as long as the tree is healthy and prosperous, the individual will also enjoy a similar pattern of growth and development.[11] Additionally, the belief is that the individual will have a marked fondness for the fruit of that particular tree under which his/ her navel string was 'cut'. Beenie Man's reference to the vagina tree is used to explain his 'wildness', i.e. his promiscuity, or rather his love for pum pum (vagina) He cannot help being promiscuous/ 'wild' because his navel string was buried beneath a symbolic vagina tree. Consequently, sexual promiscuity is 'natural' and ingrained. In his position as a dancehall icon and creator of word-images, Beenie Man's entreaties further normalize this practice and belief, and position it as an important expression of masculinity and a legitimate route to attain masculine status.

Third, the term Shortwood in *Old Dawg* encodes a deliberate double entendre. In Jamaica, Shortwood is an upscale, middle class community in St Andrew. Jamaica's class hierarchy places middle class men, particularly those from St Andrew, way above the greater mass of Afro-Jamaican men from the working and lower classes. In a sexually driven ideological backlash against this classist hierarchy, middle class men are generally reputed to have less sexual prowess than their counterparts who are placed lower on the socio-economic ladder. Many times during my countless hours in the barbershop or during research on the street corners with men from inner city and lower working class communities, I would be regaled with stories of how many 'uptown' (i.e. middle or upper class) women had to turn to a virile 'ghetto youth' with 'stamina' for sexual satisfaction, because her husband could not satisfy her, or was impotent. This classist myth of the sexually powerful and virile 'ghetto youth' or lower working class man, parallels the racist myth of the 'well hung' sexually insatiable Black man that often creates a panic and frenzy about Black male sexuality in predominantly white societies. In classist Jamaica, this myth is re-scripted and deconstructed by marginalized men at the base of the classist hierarchy to grant a ritualistic form of sexual power over the image of the purportedly sexually incompetent/impotent middle-class/uptown man. Within this sexual and gendered paradigm, a poor, ghetto youth is infused with a sexualized cache of power that is brokered on an accepted, legitimate hegemonic imperative, but which, in this rendering, bestows symbolic and not real power in an imagined setting. His sexual prowess grants him the power to challenge his middle class/uptown counterpart exclusively on the terrain of sex, and assert his marginalized masculinity, for example by what one of my inner city interviewees stated was, 'taking away his woman.'

(c) 1994 The Gleaner Co. Ltd.

Queen Patra

In addition, the term Shortwood can be related to the Jamaican colloquialism for the penis, 'hood', often rendered as 'wood'. The addition of the prefix short- to 'wood' (Shortwood) denotes a small penis which connotes less sexual potency and prowess and Beenie Man proudly declares that he does not 'live outa Shortwood'. Thus his masculinity cannot be related to Shortwood, however rendered, whether as a middle class enclave or as a haven for men with short (small) penises.

The role of the feminine remains critical to the upliftment of heterosexual masculinity. In this regard, female dancehall artistes Patra and Lady Saw are referred to in *Old Dawg*. These women are aggressive, daring female dancehall deejays who are noted for their use of explicit, raunchy and sexual lyrics that draw on the male propensity to use 'vulgar' sex talk as part of their performance. Both women also dress in sexy, tight and revealing outfits which belied their aggressive, masculinized posturing in the dancehall. Patra and Lady Saw's aggressively sexual lyrical and performative interventions in dancehall alter the relationships between deejays and the audience on two fronts. First, dancehall deejays are generally male and second, dalliance in vulgar, sex talk is perceived as masculine (word) play. Thus, their purported sexual conquest or 'cutting down' bestows high ratings to the male artiste as these women are highly ranked as aggressive, daring, and independent. Patra earned international fame as the first international queen of dancehall music after her debut with Epic Records in the early 1990s and the success of her first Epic album, *Queen of the Pack*. Her career subsequently went into remission with a later attempt at revival in late 2008, including a performance on Sting 2008. Lady Saw, on the other hand has maintained her position as the Queen of Slackness and, to date, continues to enjoy significant notoriety and publicity in dancehall culture and beyond as the real *Mumma*[12] of the dancehall.

The Ouch Crew is also identified as a desirable representation of femininity in Beenie Man's *Old Dawg*. This Crew was a group of young women whose daring, colourful and erotic dress styles and energetic, erotic dance styles garnered them intense popularity within the dancehall fraternity during the late 1990s. During their reign they were perceived as symbols of the daring, sexy, voluptuousness that guarantee many female dancehall models and dancers significant publicity and fame within and beyond the dancehall. Ouch Crew Members were identified as sexually desirable by many men, who claimed that they often had lustful fantasies about these women. Indeed, their exhibitionism and popularity in the dancehall earned them an appearance in the Island Films movie, *Dancehall Queen* (1997). Beenie Man's reference to the Ouch Crew in *Old Dawg* underscores the magnitude of their eroticism and perceived desirability as prominent and highly sexual women on the forefront of the dancehall stage at that time. Consequently, their sexual conquest would generate high levels of masculine status to any man.[13] This is related to the symbolic rewards that he intimates may be achieved from his conquest of the aggressive and raunchy Lady Saw and the similarly perceived Patra. Beenie Man's foregoing exhortations for and encouragement towards the promiscuous/polygamous heterosexual lifestyle of the Old Dawg are, of necessity, underwritten by hegemonic masculine codes that depend on feminine sexual conquest for the projection and promotion of the heterosexual male.

Unveiling that Buddy, the Anaconda – Discoursing Male Sex as Sexuality

A related discourse of sex and its primacy in defining male sexuality exists in dancehall culture and, as a result, the male sex organ is placed at the forefront of lyrical discussions about sex, and the penis is consistently re-defined, reconstructed and repositioned. Yet, the patriarchal focus of journalistic and academic debates on the extremes of sexual discourse in dancehall culture has historically prioritized and highlighted discussions around the representations of feminine sexuality and the female body and elided dancehall's discussions about masculine sexuality and the male body. In particular, these discussions orient around the abuse and maltreatment of the vagina and the sexual objectification of women and obscure the similarities and symbiotic relationships between the overtly sexual discussions about the vagina and the necessary and corresponding discussions about the penis.

The multiplicity of colloquial and slang synonyms for the penis, which are replete in dancehall music and culture, incorporate shades of meaning that are ideologically geared towards the re-casting of the male sex organ as powerful, monstrously gigantic, pleasurable and/or desired by women. These synonyms include the term Anaconda, associated with the lyrics of popular dancehall artiste Elephant Man and which refers to a large, powerful, and poisonous snake that is unleashed in all its monstrously frightening proportions to a cowering (female) audience. This term is also aligned to Shabba Ranks' use of the reptilian term, 'Rattler' in the 1980s to connote his sexual potency and virility in his lyrical treatises in the dancehall. Both terms – Anaconda and Rattler – exemplify dancehall's propensity to construct the male sex organ, the penis as an organic, monstrous, powerful, lethal and sexually violent weapon. The term Anaconda or Rattler has positive meaning for many Jamaican men when lyrically wielded in this context of virility, sexual prowess, and conquest of women. Indeed, the public crotch-grabbing and hip-thrusting that is a regular and important feature of the on-stage performance of many of dancehall's male artistes, like Elephant Man signify, project and purportedly highlight the power, strength and size of the penis to the admiring gaze of women, and the envious gaze of men.[14]

Another dancehall synonym for the penis is Dicky(ie). The use of the diminutive 'Dick' is further infantilized with the addition of 'y' or 'ie' and these linguistic devices symbolize a smaller, non-threatening entity. Consequently, this term signifies a pleasurable, lovable, desirable and humanized penis. In dancehall's discourses, the Dicky(ie) is constructed as far less monstrous and, therefore, encodes less sexual aggression and violence and more pleasure. While the particular construction of this may be said to connote less virility than say, the Anaconda, it is narrated as in high demand by admiring women, many of whom allegedly engage in hand over hand battles because of their desire to 'get it'. This female-female competition ultimately translates into high levels of desirability for the cuddly and lovable Dicky/ie as narrated in Buju Banton's pre-Rastafari conversion treatise about the Dicky(ie):

> Over the Dicky(ie) the girls ah gwaan bad;
> Anyhow them nuh get it then them will act mad.
> [The girls are behaving very badly over/about the Dicky/ie]
> [If they do not get it, then they will act as if they are mad]

> Over the Dicky/ie, Jackie get stab, and get bun up wid acid bad bad bad
> [Jackie got stabbed and badly burnt with acid because of (fighting over) the Dicky/ie]

Other synonyms for the penis that are very popular in the dancehall include Buddy, cock, cocky, (Donkey) cod, dick, long steel (+magnet), plane (+airport), private, womb-shifter, womb-turner, hard and stiff, peg, rod, hood, Jack, John, grizzle, long ting, Tree trunk, and Length an' strength. Some of these synonyms like *long steel* and *plane*, are used with the implicit or explicitly stated intent of mirroring them against a receptive feminine counterpart to emphasize and provide a connote the awe-inspiring strength and power of the penis. In his song, *Coulda Deal*, Spragga Benz informed women that regardless of her own feelings in the matter her "magnet haffi sample di long steel" (magnet will have to sample/get a taste of the long steel). Additionally, Spragga Benz threateningly informed women in this same song that regardless of her actions to the contrary "inna yuh airport mi muss fly mi plane" (I must fly my plane into/inside of your airport).

A noteworthy component of these fantasized erections of the penis in dancehall culture is their linkage to sex as violent. This is connected to the conquest impetus, where, for example, Red Dragon and Spragga Benz disseminated their own early versions of *Agony* and *Jack it Up,* respectively. Sexual violence is a continuing theme in dancehall culture, and is explicitly (and often simultaneously) linked to sexual pleasure and control. Vybz Kartel's 2003 *Tek Buddy* explicitly renders sexual violence as a means of controlling and/or punishing an errant and, in this instance, a greedy, materialistic woman:

> *Tek buddy gyal, yuh tink it easy,*
> *Who yuh a ramp wid, yuh waan live easy?*
> *Tek mi tings and yuh tek mi money too*
> *So tek buddy too, tek buddy too!*

> [Take buddy girl, you think it's easy]
> [Who (do you think you) are you playing around with? You want to live (the) easy (life?]
> [You have taken my things and my money too]
> [So, take buddy too, take buddy too]

The phrase 'tek buddy' was rendered in harsh, staccato vocals that evoked the stabbing motions of the sex act. The preferred dance style for this song parodied the classical 'doggy style' or 'back shot' position that is most favoured in dancehall and inner city discussions about hardcore sex. Women would assume a bent over position with head down, outstretched arms and palms held flat down against their feet. This meant that their posterior was elevated and the male partner would assume a position behind holding her tightly in position by placing both arms around her waist.

During the renditions of *Tek/Tek Buddy* of the song in particular the sections where Vybz Kartel stabs out his murderous 'tek buddy gyal', the male partner would make forward stabbing movements with his hips in a simulation of the sex act. The female partner's passive position means that the male exerts almost total control over her body however some flexible women do vibrate their waistlines and posteriors, creating an even more erotic image. The entire lyrical and corresponding physical exchange, however, is associated with the 'murderous' sexual impetus that the male is encouraged to use to remind women of his power and control over the sex act, and therefore, his (perceived/preferred) control over her sexually and socially.

Dancehall myths and fantasies project the doggy style or back shot as the most physically demanding and painful sexual position *for women.* Dances like

'Tek' and 'Daggering' are extreme manifestations of the male desire to exert power and control over a woman coupled with the woman's willful acceptance of this act. Women who willingly acquiesce to this sexualized dance activity also reap accolades on the dance floor. In the broader terrain of sexual myth and fantasy women who can 'tek backshot', (i.e. seemingly enjoy and display great sexual prowess and agility during this purportedly painful sex act) are revered and lauded for their sexual prowess by men. In effect such sexually prolific women are purportedly placed higher on a mythologized and/or lyrical hierarchy that is created and maintained by men.[15] For example, in his contribution to the dancehall medley *Dreamland*, dancehall artiste, Frisco Kid praises a woman who can display this type of prowess/agility and confirms that this will ensure that she 'keeps' her male partner:

> *Doggystyle, no gyal can do like you;*
> *Headtop a nuh nutten caw yuh do dat to*
> *Chue a gal neva see di style dem yuh ah do*
> *Mek she tink she can tek yuh man from you*
>
> [Doggystyle, no girl can do that like you]
> [Dancing on the top of your head is not difficult because
> you do that too]
> [It is because a girl has never seen the styles that you do/can do]
> [Why she thinks/believes that she can take your man away from you]

Dancehall's 'daggering' craze of 2008 to 2009 extended this male-female discursive practice where the explicit and erotic lyrics of 'daggering' songs, accompanied by a dance style similar to that used in *Tek,* earned the ire of agenda setters and resulted in a targeted directive from the Broadcasting Commission in Jamaica that banned the public dissemination of daggering songs and music videos on radio, television and cable television stations. According to the directive issued by the Broadcasting Commission on February 6, 2009:

> Daggering" is a colloquial term or phrase used in dancehall culture
> as a reference to hardcore sex or what is popularly referred to as "dry"
> sex, or the activities of persons engaged in the public simulation
> of various sexual acts and positions. The Commission has found
> these recordings to be explicitly sexual and violent, contrary to the
> provisions of Regulation 30(d) and Regulation 30(l) of the Television

and Sound Broadcasting Regulations which state: 30. No licensee shall permit to be transmitted – (d) any indecent or profane matter, so, however, that any broadcast to which regulation 26 relates shall be deemed not to be indecent; Reg. 30(d) (l) any portrayal of violence which offends against good taste, decency or public morality. Reg. 30(l) This content also offends against the tenets of the Children's Code for Programming.

In this 'daggering' craze, the erotic doggy style/back shot dance favoured in *Tek* and earlier versions of dancehall erotica was upgraded to include not just the simulation of sex with a kind of 'dry hump' but wild and freaky body slams, gymnastic body launches from elevated positions (rooftops, trees, fences) and multiple male dancers targeting single female dancers. Dancehall's soundtrack for this phase included a range of songs indentified as 'daggering' songs including Busy Signal's *Dah Style Deh She Want/Up Inna Har Belly*, Hector Frass' *Daggering Time*, RDX's *Bend Ova, Dagga Train* and *Daggering*, and Baby Chris' *Dagga Train.* Vybz Kartel and Spice's very popular *Ramping Shop* was also erroneously identified as a 'daggering' song when this song was actually a manifestation of dancehall's focus on male to female sexual relationships and used explicit and erotic male-female lyrics to discuss the sex act.

The intense weeks of discussion gave way to an update from the Broadcasting Commission, with a non-genre specific directive for removal of all songs with bleeps from the public airwaves which significantly cut into and across the playlists of media houses as almost all genres of music were affected. The 'daggering' craze reflected the continued edgy manifestation of dancehall's journey through the musical landscape which is complemented by the rise of artistes like Vybz Kartel, whose musical exploits find significant favour among the youth generation[16] even while earning the ire of the agenda setters in the media and the wider society. As with Peter Tosh, Ninja Man and Bounty Killer in their respective eras, the rebellious anti-systemic stance of an artiste like Vybz Kartel, finds favour with the youth of that moment as they rage against the strictures of well-meaning parents, teachers and other authority figures.

However, where the issue of sex is concerned in Jamaica, while the hegemonic cues of heterosexuality proliferate in the media and other sites of socialization, there is a critical dearth of relevant and accurate information about sex and sexuality emanating from the prescribed authority sources. Consequently, the overwhelming volume of information about sex, sexuality, and the sex act that spew forth from the print and electronic media and which circulate among youth and adult peer groups is often the main source of information on which many rely. The fantasies and myths that emanate from the dancehall are part and parcel of this popular pool of misinformation. This general outflow of misinformation is often supported by the generally untrue boasts and self-praise that form the major portion of discussions about sex in many male only enclaves (for e.g. at street corner gatherings, bars, domino tables and barbershops) and may lead to a warped understanding of 'pleasurable' sex if men are encouraged to believe that all women 'enjoy' violent sex. The propensity to expose young boys (who grow up to become boasting men) to pornographic material also contributes to this distorted view of sexual expression because the media is considered an important source of information by many individuals. Media images like those in pornographic films that show women 'enjoying' violence during sex can have very powerful influences on the development of male sexuality, especially in the context where accurate information about human sexuality is not easily available. Dancehall music and culture provides powerful and ongoing discourses and images about the relevance of sex and sexual practices, particularly in the lives of young and adult men who perceive its output as authoritative and informative and, therefore, accept its ideological and gendered cues as ways of being male and powerful in their marginalized spaces. This propensity of dancehall to transmit information about ways of being to fill the vacuum left by the social institutions was confirmed by several interviewees who noted that 'dancehall tell plenty truths bout ooman and man and bout life. Look how dem diss up di politician and battyman dem regular.'[17] The role of oral sex in the lives of dancehall adherents in general and Jamaican men in particular, is another related discourse of sex and sexuality in dancehall culture.

'Dem Bow' – Negating Oral Sex in Dancehall Culture

The ritualistic denunciation of oral sex is one other sexualized discourse that is used to underscore the primacy of male sexuality and notions of manhood in the dancehall as status-generating. In the context of this work, it also exposes the Janus-faced debates that feature in dancehall's projections of masculinities where what is often preached is not necessarily practiced.

In the dancehall, the performance of fellatio or cunnilingus is referred to as 'bowing' and men or women who perform these acts are referred to as 'bow cats' or 'bow seed'. The word 'bow' as disseminated in the dancehall, signifies the low status assigned to the act where one must stoop 'down low' to show deference or respect for a higher authority figure, in effect willfully accepting and participating in one's own subservience and subjugation. During on-stage performances at multiple dancehall events including Reggae Sunsplash, Reggae Sumfest, Sting, Spectrum and Dancehall Daze, over more than two decades, I witnessed a myriad of male dancehall artistes ritualistically engage in lyrical and symbolic denunciation of the 'bow cat'. During these performances, men and women who bow were usually lumped in concert with other incarnations of deviance, including politicians and male homosexuals, and lyrically or symbolically denounced and disposed of by tortuous and/or fatal means.

Shabba Ranks' 1980s hit song, *Dem Bow*, highlighted the varying methods by which one identified the 'bow cat' and simultaneously negated male and female engagement in this sexual practice. Dancehall artiste, Mr Vegas' own *Heads High* of the later 1990s discouraged young women from engaging in oral sex and encouraged them to keep their 'heads high' and 'mek a bwoy know dem nah bow' (inform a man that they will not bow). Babycham's *Boom* however, intimated a growing acceptance of fellatio which places women in a subject, 'bowing' position while men remain erect and dominant. Related treatises that continue to be produced and disseminated in the dancehall include Cobra's *Not this Face* which cleverly, defiantly, and humorously reminds men that they should not perform cunnilingus, thereby giving women power over them. He uses the retained African mechanism of call and response that is so popular in the dancehall to involve an unseen audience of men into confirming that they have not crossed these boundaries thus:

> *From nuh gyal can't call you furniture face (say) not this mouth, not this face,*
> [As long as no woman can call you furniture face (say) not this mouth not this face]
> *From nuh gyal nuh have no secret fi yuh mouth, want fi see di rude bwoy hands ah push out.*

[As long as no women are keeping secrets for your mouth, I want to
see the Rude Bwoy hands pushed out/up].

For Cobra, the term 'furniture face' refers specifically to the use of the
'face' as a 'chair' where, as Beenie Man notes in his song, *Crazy Notion*, 'no
gyal neva sit inna yuh face like chair.' The act of sitting in a chair is related to
a woman's sitting on a man's face during oral sex and, as a result, subjugating
the man by placing her 'bottom' in his face. Additionally, Elephant Man
reinforces this by insisting in his song *Never Bow*, that members of the audience,
signify that they 'never bow' by raising their hands in the air. He makes it clear
that this while this treatise speaks about the 'bow cat,' it is directed specifically
at men and is in negation of cunnilingus. This is done by his overt references
to the fact that men who cannot raise their hands are unable to do this because
'inna dem face gyal ah dive' (women are diving in their faces) and his repeated
references to men who have 'bowed' by 'nyamming off' or 'eating off/out'[18]
women. In this regard Ce'Cile's 2003 *Do it to me,* faced resistance and received
very little airplay because of her breathless exhortation 'do it to me baby' that
encouraged her man to perform cunnilingus and subject himself to female
dominance.

The foregoing lyrical and performative exhortations and myths that
explicitly privilege promiscuous/polygamous heterosexuality as masculinity
in the dancehall are linked closely to the selective performance of fatherhood
as a uniformly biological activity which enhances masculine status. Notions
of fatherhood (and not parenting) are closely intertwined with the symbolic
use of promiscuous/polygamous heterosexuality as a marker of manhood
and, therefore, an extension or definer of masculinity. Public claims for true
male virility can most significantly be confirmed by the most relevant evidence
– children.

Ambivalent Readings of Biological Paternity as Traditional Male Empowerment

Mi ah di bes babyfaada inna Jamaica
Come fi all ah di ooman dem who nuh have nuh babyfaada
[I am the best babyfather in Jamaica]
[I have come to be here for all the women who have no babyfathers]
Shabba Ranks, *Bes' Babyfather*

Paternity is never announced by any physiological changes which can be even remotely compared to pregnancy, and, therefore, has to be manipulated and publicized within social settings to ensure that the biological is related to the social, where, the terrain of fatherhood is invested with its own social significance as a marker of manhood and status for men, especially during male-male interaction among groups of men. This demonstration of masculinity, or what Smith (1988, 147) refers to as the 'having of children all about' is validated in public, social settings where male exploits are recounted and his sexual conquest of many girlfriends and 'ownership' of many babymothers are important scoring points. This symbolic use of fatherhood to rank masculine status impacts on the notions of parenting that abound and are reflected in the heterogeneous practice of fatherhood, particularly in the communities from which dancehall culture gains its creative impetus.

In his work on Caribbean masculinity, Chevannes outlined five snapshots of fatherhood in one Jamaica inner city ('Joetown') (2001, 183–92) which belie any homogenous conception of this role as merely engaged in empty, ritualistic posing. These snapshots include 'a young man marching into a dreaded garrison community to get back his son; a father seizing custody of his daughter; a stepfather who was a true father, whose untimely murder changed the personality of his stepson; and a young man struggling with the plaiting of his daughter's hair.' In this context, the term 'Faada' is invested with honor 'and reserved for any mature adult male deserving of respect' (2001, 192). Correspondingly, the term 'Dads' or 'Big Dads' occupies a similar space. Additionally, the term 'Faada' is also clearly linked with notions of Fatherhood where a man (willingly) exercises his social responsibility and provides for his family, and his children. Sometimes, these men are bestowed with the title Faada, even when they have no biological ties to the children that they support economically i.e. 'provide for'. This focus on Faada as an ultimate provider predominates in much of the discussions about parenting and the role of fathers.

At the other end of the spectrum is the 'Babyfaada' or 'Babyfather' which literally means the man who fathers a child. The corresponding Babymodda or Babymother literally means the woman who mothers a child. These two terms predominate in dancehall's discussions of parenting and Fatherhood and the underlying meaning for both male and female terms is that these children are born out of wedlock in a variety of relationships – visiting, semi-visiting or common law. In Jamaica, particularly in the inner cities, the terms Babymother and Babyfather are additionally invested with symbolic power, where a man who gets a woman pregnant is perceived to have a lifelong connection to her that parallels that of marriage and, correspondingly, the woman who bears a child for a man can claim a special, lifelong linkage to him, akin to marriage. Consequently, many women in these situations have high expectations about the material and economic rewards that should come with pregnancy and/or childbearing, and many men correspondingly have a high degree of apprehension (and sometimes outright fear) about the mainly economic demands that will be made on them. However, it should be noted that for many men, the fear of economic, physical and social commitment that Fatherhood brings is often balanced by the desire to 'get' a child, particularly if the child is male. One male interviewee who was raised in an inner city community in St Andrew reminisced on the subtle and overt pressures that older, mature men in his community of origin placed on younger men and/or men who had not yet fathered any children:

> When we playing football on the field in the evenings or on Sundays, we would sometimes be split us into two teams, one called Geldings and the other Babyfathers. Geldings were those of us who had not yet gotten any children and babyfathers were those who had already done so. It was funny then and we didn't think much about it. But now I look back and realize that the "babyfathers" would jeer the geldings and use every opportunity to remind them that the reason why they missed a ball or a goal was because they had no children. I can still remember the laughter and shouts of 'is a gelding man, him can't do no better'. At that time I was still a gelding but it did not stay that way for too long.

Arguably, the interlinkages between dancehall music culture and inner city culture accounts for the specific manifestations of the discourse of fatherhood in the dancehall. Within its staged confines, dancehall culture deflates social fatherhood and inflates the biological in the ranking of masculine status. The real anxieties about the demands of fatherhood as a solely economic activity is married to the terrain of promiscuous/polygamous heterosexuality, exemplified by the discourse of the Ole Dawg with Nuff Gyal examined earlier in this chapter. This marriage blossoms into a field of 'best babyfathers' where fatherhood, defined as a purely biological activity, provides a cultural stage from which to project another sexualized trait of masculinity on the supportive terrain of Jamaican patriarchy and hegemonic masculinity. This discourse of masculinity is one where men often father several children, usually with several women, because the man who can produce evidence of his sexual prowess is praised by his peers in all-male discussions, and rewarded with higher levels of masculine status as a potent and virile man. These men are revered and mythologized in dancehall culture's narratives. The pride in this monumental achievement reflects the patriarchal impetus to have ultimate control and unlimited sway over the feminine body. It is also underpinned by a driving productive ethos – the masculine urge to produce – which is forced into regression by high rates of unemployment, diminishing marketability, and economic poverty in Jamaica. In the context of economic poverty and social deprivation, fatherhood can, and often does, increase a man's sense of failure and vulnerability, particularly when he is aware that he cannot adequately protect or provide for his child(ren) and their mother(s). Consequently, while many men are often truly concerned about the economic and emotional welfare and upbringing of the children who spring from their multiple unisons, these concerns are often suppressed in the face of daunting economic and employment odds and, consequently symbolic and ritualistic fulfillment predominates. As a result, the overarching concern is transmuted to become one that uses empty ritualism to focus on the higher levels of masculine status that other men bestow on them during public discussions about their 'youts' and 'babymothers' in all-male gatherings at the street corners, in bars, on the factory floor, at the domino tables, and so on. This drive to consistently symbolize and produce evidence of his sexual and masculine prowess encourages the often economically-deprived 'babyfather' to engage in multiple sex acts with different women, which grant him greater yields of masculine status and guarantees him a legitimate position on the field of dancehall's and Jamaica's masculine play.

The urge to 'breed' and, therefore, earn significant allocations of masculine status, in the form of children is secondary only to the urge to publicly discuss and display his engagement is multiple sex acts with various women, i.e. to signify his firm grip on heterosexuality. It is also noteworthy, that philosophical and existential meanings are added to fatherhood where, in my discussions with fathers and/or aspiring fathers, a man's ability to 'give life' or 'bring life' is seen as a significant and powerful capacity. He is the author of another being's existence, even though he may lack any real social and/or economic power. In a true corruption of the productive ethos that is often denied him in other spheres of life, he plants and fertilizes the seed, and often abandons the seedling to grow and mature on its own, to weather the perils of childhood, adolescence, adulthood and maturity without the necessary paternal support (financial, emotional, physical etc.). This cycle of ritualistic fathering results in many fatherless children, some of whom become young men who, like their own fathers, become 'grilled up'[19] in a legacy of poverty, promiscuity and posturing masculinity. The significance of this legacy is often articulated in dancehall narratives as one component of a promiscuous/polygamous masculinity as Merciless discourses in his song *Ole Gallis*:

> *Mi puppa was a gyallis, same way mi come*
> *All ah mi bredda dem get fifteen son.*
> *Couldn afford fi let di ole man dung.*

> [My father had many women, and I am just like him]
> [All/Each of my brothers had fifteen sons]
> [(We) Could not afford to let the Old Man down]

In this regard dancehall narratives of masculinity play with the notion of virility through promiscuous/polygamous heterosexuality and multiple children as lyrical and visual fulfillment of the productive ethos. Dancehall's lyrical and discursive representations highlight the biological over the social functions of fatherhood and bestow high levels of status to men who accede to this definition of Jamaican masculinity. Nonetheless, this work does not deny the existence of Jamaican men whose roles as social fathers predominate. Indeed, in her work on Caribbean masculinity and the family Barrow (1998, 356) notes a generational change in the imaging and defining of fatherhood in the lives of men in one ethnography, stating that 'the social fathering of a few emerges at least as importantly as the biological fathering of many.' I have encountered a growing percentage of Jamaican fathers from the inner cities and lower working classes, whose fervent desire is to provide economically, emotionally and socially for their children. However, in its quest for masculine status and power generation, dancehall narratives deliberately elide the sacrifices and actions of men from inner cities and other communities, many of whom perform and prize the social roles of fatherhood as important components in their own definitions of masculinity. It foregrounds the impressive cache of status and personhood that public confirmation of the practice of 'fathering children all about' can engender.

Additionally, dancehall culture's popular representations of fatherhood are the affect of a sociological structure where mothers are particularly close to their sons and sons are particularly close to their mothers, especially where these sons are the product of a single-parent household, headed by the mother. In her early sociological study of Jamaican families first published in 1957, Clarke (1999, 123) outlined the reasons for this mother-son closeness as the result of 'the failure of the paternal relationship' which results in 'excessive reliance on the mother.' Clarke further notes the lasting impressions that mothers create in their sons minds of their lifelong reciprocal obligation to their mothers for the 'hardships she endured as the sole or principal support of her children.' As a result of this type of socialization when the boy becomes a man, he will feel bound by this lifelong obligation to contribute to his mother's support, even when his own earnings are at best, mere subsistence. According to Clarke (1999, 123) 'a son who knew his mother to be in want, and was unable to help her, felt both guilt and failure.'

Many male respondents in the dancehall expressed a deep, abiding love and regard for their mothers and scant regard or outright hatred for their absentee or abandoning fathers. Even when the father had been present, his contribution was often negligibly compared to that of Mama, who as one interviewee noted 'work hard and try keep me out of trouble.' In his song, *Idiot ting Dat*, Dancehall artiste Assassin throws negative slurs against a 'successful' man who leaves his mother to suffer while he enjoys a materially successful life:

> *Man a buy gyal Lexus; Mama a walk an a tek bus*
> *Idiot ting dat!*
> [Man/He has bought a Lexus (car) for a girl/woman; (while) Mama
> has to walk and take the bus]
> [That is pure idiocy!]

Vybz Kartel's *Mama* of 2009 highlights a similar sentiment and crowns his mother as queen thus:

> *Me nah go mek she broke*
> *Me put food inna di house*
> *Me everything fi maintain you*
> *Hail the queen so mi name you*
> *Some bwoy gi dem gal everything and dem madda ah suffa*
> *Me everything fi mantain you*
> *Hail the queen mummy you are my queen*
>
> [I will not allow her to be out of money
> I ensure that there is food in the house
> Everything I have is to maintain you
> Hail to the queen, that is how I name you
> Some boys/men give everything to their women and their mothers
> are suffering
> Everything I have is to maintain you
> Hail the queen, Mummy you are my queen]

Thus, the latter are child molesters and the mothers are child protectors.

In the dancehall, the greater majority of hardcore, male dancehall artistes (particularly those from the inner cities) claim to be 'fatherless' and often outline how they suffered the pains of paternal abandonment or absenteeism during their formative years. For example, of the four male dancehall artistes interviewed in for a *Sunday Observer* article for Fathers Day, three had been raised by a single mother[20] and, most male dancehall artistes like Elephant Man and Mr Lex reputedly have several children with different mothers. With regard to this practice one male interviewee noted, 'is ah artiste ting man, dem have nuff ooman and babymother bout di place.' [It's a part of being an artiste. They have many woman and babymothers all over.] The male artistes, as the most visible segment of the male dancehall body who project this gendered practice of multiple fathering, accentuate the perception that this practice is status-generating. Fathering is coded as a temporal and temporary activity in the dancehall. Indeed, where it is explicitly discussed, Father is usually coded as deviant or negative, as Elephant Man notes in his a line in his song '*2000 Began*':

> *2000 Faada molest dem dawta,*
> *2000 madda bun dem up wid hot wata*

[2000 Fathers molested their daughters
2000 mothers burn them(up) with hot water][21]

The dancehall selectively draws on the most visible and popularized models that are/have been present in their own surroundings (particularly the inner cities) and, hence, projects the primary image of father as either one of absenteeism or abandonment. Where he may be physically accessible, father is usually defined in terms of his ability (or inability) to provide economic sustenance, i.e. in the role of Provider. Parenting (read as caregiving) is constructed as motherhood/feminine in dancehall narratives, with fatherhood/masculine its polar opposite, and father is often coded in dancehall narratives as worthless, lazy and incompetent. It is mother (as opposed to woman)[22] who bears the burdens of childbearing and childrearing and it is this manifestation of gender that is invested with the social roles of parenting – as a single parent who cares and provides for her children, oftentimes in extreme poverty. For example, this is emphasized in dancehall artiste, Bounty Killer's narrative on poverty and parenting:

Mama she's not in a good mood the basket inna mi kitchen running out of food
[Mama, she is not in a good mood because the basket in my/our kitchen is running out of food]
Papa can't find no excuse, him drink out wi money gamble and lose
[Papa cannot make any excuses because he spent our money on liquor/alcohol and also gambled and lost it all]

Mama can't find the next dime, she might can buy rice but not the meat kind
[Mama cannot find the next dime/cent, maybe she can buy some rice but not meat]

Through the wickedest struggle Mama nuh leave us,
[Throughout the harshest times, Mama did not leave us]

She stand by mi side, Mama - Daddy grieve us,
[She stood by my/our side, Mama – Daddy caused us pure grief]

Vybz Kartel's *Mama* and Nuclear's *Single Mother* of 2009 continue this trend of idolizing 'mother' as the nurturer and queen and eliding the presence or contribution of a father to the support and nurturing of his children. The role of man, as parent is deemed satisfied in the productive mode.

In her early work on kinship organizations in Jamaica, Clarke (1997, 66) noted that the man 'is satisfied by the proof of his virility and does not necessarily accept any of the obligations and duties of parenthood…which are generally accepted as the woman's responsibility and there is no public censure if he does not acknowledge or fulfill them.' In contemporary dancehall culture, abandonment of the social roles of fatherhood is narrated and is not met with lyrical sanctions and public censure. Furthermore, acceptance of the obligations and duties of parenthood is not met with loud and public accolades and praise in dancehall's discourses of parenting and fatherhood. The social ambivalence and lack of public denunciation or support that coalesces around fathering in practice results in the conceptual lack of any true models of fatherhood in dancehall culture where it is not modelled as either a typical or praiseworthy feature of masculinity. References to father and fatherhood are all but elided in dancehall discourses. Where notions of the father or notions of fatherhood are briefly mentioned, they are done so in the breach as negative or lacking.

Conclusion

In dancehall's traditional discourse of masculinity the authority/control and productive ethos is played out on the female body where the terrain of promiscuous/polygamous sexual relations and multiple offspring is also aligned to the ambivalence displayed about social and biological fathering in the discourses of fatherhood. Overt dialogues of masculinity in the dancehall highlight the promiscuous use of the sex act and sexual practice to underwrite the most prominent form of masculine role play that is revered in inner city and dancehall culture. Dancehall's cultural construction and maintenance of a polygamous heterosexuality is projected as an important, constituent feature of one type of masculinity that is brokered on a culturally accepted variation of hegemonic masculinity in Jamaica through concentrated sexual activity where marginalized men are encouraged to adopt these gendered signals as a route to empowerment and enhanced social status in their particular circumstances. Dancehall culture's stress on the negotiation of masculinity via this sexual route, particularly during the period of the 1980s, is contingent upon the hegemonic gendered cues and expressions that pervade the traditional, patriarchal spaces of Jamaican life and infuse the gendered expressions and articulations of the more extreme versions of 'dancehallized' masculinities. The incremental transition identified in the perception of oral sex points to a slight shift in how dancehall adherents relate to the sex act, while maintaining the erect and powerful position of the male heterosexual. This slight shift presages the future masculine transgressions that eventually manifest themselves clearly in dancehall. Ole Dawg with Nuff Gyal as dancehall masculinity reflects an important constituent element of hegemonic masculinity and thus, during and after its period of cultural dominance in the dancehall, is patently hegemonic.

This focus on an extreme and traditional form of masculinity in dancehall culture is connected to another popular discourse of manhood that predominated at a later period in the dancehall of the late 1980s, and which purportedly bestows high levels of masculine status on 'deserving' men who perform its rites with skill and dexterity. The following chapter discusses the importance of aggression, violence – and in particular gun violence – in underwriting another variant of dancehall masculinity that was brokered on the hegemonic impulses from the wider Jamaican society.

CHAPTER 3

'BADMAN NUH INNA DAT' – (GUN) VIOLENCE AS HARDCORE MASCULINITY IN DANCEHALL

Murda dem, murda dem, inna competition wi gwine murda dem.[1]
Ninja Man, *Murder Dem*

A guy a spy dat fi die, coppashot inna dem heart or inna dem eye.
Bounty Killer, *Spy fi Die*

Introduction

This chapter examines the constituent elements of another variant of dancehallized masculinity that is brokered on the notion that aggression and gun violence provide legitimate patriarchal and hegemonic spaces within which marginalized men in Jamaica can negotiate higher status and more powerful masculine identities. This variant of dancehallized masculinity gained prominence in the early period of dancehall's dominance in the mid-1980s and was popularized in the lyrics and performance of dancehall artistes like Ninja Man, Supercat, Josey Wales and later in the work of other artistes like Bounty Killer and Vybz Kartel. As in the previous chapter, I wish to note that in this instance, this stereotypical and monolithic rendering of aggression and violence as a variant of dancehallized masculinity aims only to isolate, and thus capture, another form of masculinity that occupied a dominant position in dancehall's configuration of masculinity in one era, in order to flesh out its constituent elements and analyse its relation to the process of hegemonic masculinity in Jamaica.

In this regard, dancehall's narrative engagements and discussions with aggression and violence is examined through its selective constitution of what is alternatively labelled as the Badman, Don or Shotta as masculine incarnations of violence which symbolically bestow status and power on marginalized men who adopt these identities. Dancehall culture's contestatory stance and its propensity for extreme lyrical and behavioural incantations render the Badman, Don or Shotta as a lyrical and symbolic variation of hegemonic masculinity that is excessively and intensely violent. The following sections examine the constituent elements of this excessively and intensely violent dancehallized masculinity that, by using the hegemonic masculine cues towards aggression as its foundation, ultimately feeds into what have been identified in chapter 2 as the traditionally accepted hegemonic variant of masculinity in Jamaica in that same era.

Violence and Masculinity

Violence and aggression are important definers of masculine identity (Brod 1994; Clatterbaugh 1997; Connell 1995; Hatty 2000; Katz 1999; Lancaster 1992; Segal 1990). Connell (1990, 83) speaks to an 'ideology of supremacy' that underpins male use of violence against women on a continuum that ranges from wolf whistling to rape, domestic assault, and even murder. In a similar vein, he discusses the use of violence among men to draw boundaries, make exclusions, and to claim and/or assert masculinity. Connell argues that most men who participate in this sort of violence feel justified by the ideology of male supremacy where violence operates as part of a system of domination. Indeed, Segal (1990, 261–71) discusses the categorization of violence as entirely masculine in a context where women also use domestic, interpersonal and sexual violence as a means of exercising their power over others.

The propensity to engage in more confrontational and extreme acts of male-female and male-male violence are arguably exacerbated by other contributing factors and Segal (1990, 264–5) discusses the correlation between lower-class status and higher levels of male violence that is undifferentiated by race:

> Just as there is a Black underclass, so too a white underclass exists, in which the men are the most likely of all men to adopt aggressive masculine styles and values whereby status is imparted to males who display loyalty and bravery in confrontation with 'outsiders. (p. 265).

The caveat is lodged that this aggressive (and often violent) masculine style is not exclusive to lower working-class men but also exists in the fantasy life (if not the lived reality) of other men who are enthralled by the images of masculinity that equate it with power and violence (Segal 1990, 265). Some prime examples of these popular and idealized fantasy images include Clint Eastwood, the Lone Ranger and Shaft in film.[2] Other examples include the 'gangsta' rappers in hip hop culture, and the Bad Bwoy, Don, or Shotta in Jamaican dancehall and popular culture,[3] which all work towards what Connell (1983, 185–6 & 249) identifies as the naturalizing of 'hegemonic masculinity...in the form of the hero and presented through forms that revolve around heroes: sagas, ballads, westerns, thrillers,' and in other forms of public media including television, films, sporting events and books.

JAMAICAN MASCULINITY AND VIOLENCE

In her work on the development of Caribbean gender identity, Leo Rhynie (1998, 247) states that 'the "man as warrior" ideology is strongly promoted in many cultures where manhood and masculinity are associated with street fighting, battles with police, bearing pain without flinching, violence, swearing and other aggressive behaviour.' In the Jamaican context, Brown and Chevannes' (1995) research revealed that one of the lessons being taught to boys on the street is that conflict is to be settled through fighting, with a 'win-at-all' costs attitude prevailing. The softness/toughness gendered dichotomy that polarizes 'soft' feminine behaviours against 'tough' male guise is operationalized when the young Afro-Jamaican boy is socialized to take on a tough personality that incorporates necessary behaviours, which include avoiding a show of tears on every occasion of inward or outward hurt, and learning to suffer deprivation with a self-sacrificing nobility of spirit.

Young men in communities like those from which dancehall draws its energies, – for example the inner cities of Kingston, St Andrew and St Catherine – learn from their early male initiations and continuous male bonding in the streets, that men must practice necessary survival skills in a highly contested, dangerous and challenging environment. Within these oppressed and poverty-stricken spaces, masculine codes and gendered cues are intertwined with social and community codes of violence and aggression which become normalized. This extreme masculinized violence often holds primacy in the rituals that bestow manhood on young men from many of these strife-torn communities. Indeed, the intra- and inter-community rivalries and often fatal violence that predominate in many of Kingston's inner cities are prized and protected by the very citizens who are its chief instigators and arbiters, and simultaneously its primary targets.

One young man whose trajectory of social mobility included moving away from his inner city community recalled one instance when he tried to broker a peace of sorts between warring citizens who lived on the same avenue. The bottom and top of this avenue had erupted into gun warfare over a minor incident. He was threatened by one young man whom he had played with in the streets as a child thus: 'Mi ah go stab up any man who talk bout peace roun yah so.'⁴ Additionally he was chastised by the women from this section of the street who declared that 'Dem bwoy deh up di road fi dead!'⁵ Within this masculinized culture of violence a prison sentence is normalized and returning convicts are hailed as heroes. Conversely, policemen are seen as the enemy and, therefore, are always potential targets. They are often referred to as Babylon where Babylon is a derogatory reference to the individual policeman (e.g 'Babylon Bwoy') and also to the collective body of the security forces. This use of this term in Jamaican Creole, inner city slang and dancehall discourse, draws on the ideology of Rastafari where the Biblical reference to the symbolic whore of Babylon was taken and invested with further negatives that are used to impute collusion with, and also a representation of oppressors, which include the State and its agents, as well as market capitalism. Babylon is everything that is polarized against Rastafari worldview however, in dancehall culture the term is selectively appropriated when its adherents wish to express acrimony towards state entities or personal and community rivals.

Additionally, the code of silence that typifies life in many of Kingston's inner cities means that individuals live and fraternize with known criminals and are often fully aware of the location of hidden caches of illegal guns that these men use. However, the type of informer-phobia that has developed as an important part of this culture of violence means that citizens fear the label 'informer' which has negative connotations, both physical and psychological. An informer is perceived as a community or group traitor. He/she is an individual who betrays the tightly-knit social and political cohesiveness of a community to an outsider (often depicted as a member of the security forces or a policeman). To become an informer in the inner city context is akin to committing an act of treason against the state, and dancehall's treatises engage in various discussions about the ultimate and fatal fate of the informer included the dreaded mantra 'Informa fi ded!' (Informers must die!). One should note, however that the informer is one among several characters perceived as social deviants and thus sentenced to death in the lyrically exaggerated dancehall setting. Others identified in dancehall include paedophiles, rapists, petty thieves and male homosexuals.

The antecedents of this informerphobia debate in Jamaican music culture coalesced in the era before dancehall's dominance with the Trojan Records release *Peeping Tom* by Toots and the Maytals lamenting the ever-present 'peeper' thus:

> *Tom round the corner, Tom in the tree*
> *Tom round the lane, Tom up the hill*
> *Tom in the house, Tom down the street*
> *Everybody cry out for Peeping Tom.*

The *Peeping Tom* was an unwelcome invasion into the private sphere of lives and an obvious social deviant whose appropriation of information from the private sphere resulted in unwelcome and unwanted exposure in the public arena.

During dancehall culture's early development, the first lady of dancehall, Lady Ann, identified this informer in her treatise *Informer* in 1983, however this was in the context of interference with her intimate relationship:

> *Certain bwoy 'pon de corner, informer*
> *Certain bwoy 'pon de corner, informer*
> *Caw 'im a fight gains me an me lover*

[A certain boy/man on the corner is an informer (Rept.)
Because he is fighting against me and my lover]

Her chant of 'murderer' in the context of this song can be read as both an exclamation of dismay and a lyrical identification of the informer as a murderer, i.e. a very bad person:

> *Say informer inna de area – murderer!*
> *Him unda watchin' and a-peepin' murderer!*

Informa inna di area – murderer!
Him unda nuff chat chatting – Murderer!

[Informer is in the area – Murderer!
He is watching and peeping – Murderer!
Informer is in the area – Murderer!
He is chatting and chatting – Murderer]

Admiral Tibet's 1980s treatise is also in this vein where he generally admonishes individuals to 'leave people business alone/leave people business and mind your own.' However, by the early 1990s the more virulent strains of the anti-informer debate had gained ascendancy with major dancehall artistes ensuring that the negation of this activity and identity remained a dominant component of dancehall's discussions. The informer was positioned squarely in the lyrical cross hairs and many a deejay hit out against them. In this regard, Bounty Killer's *New Gun* delivered the judgment and death sentence to informers and also declared that consorting with the police was a deviant activity:

New gun with shot bad bway a burst
All informa, a dem a dead first...

To be a informer that is not a nice work
Yuh time no deh far yuh life it don't worth
A dead yu ago dead an go unda de eart'
Cause yu inform pon man a Park Lane an Dunkirk
Bout dem rob bank an butt up bank clerk.

[Bad boys/men are shooting new guns that are fully loaded
All informers will die first...

To be an informer is not a nice job
Your final hour is not far, your life has no value
You are going to die and be put under the earth (i.e. buried)
Because you gave information against men from Park Lane and Dunkirk
That they robbed a bank and gunbutted a bank clerk]

In addition, Bounty Killer, clearly defines the informer and negates the propensity to fraternize and consort with security officers:

Informer give information
To police personnel an soldier man
I no sey yu fe shot policeman
Dem a do dem work an policeman no wrong.

[Informers give information
To policemen and soldiers
I'm not saying that you must shoot policemen
As they are doing their jobs and policemen are doing no wrong]

In Wayne Wonder's *Informers*, the informer is also despised in different settings, including the workplace, as a person who provides information on another employee's 'hustling', i.e. pilfering or petty theft in the workplace setting. In this instance, the same final sanction is passed:

I'm in a factory working
Hustling on the side
See the informers lurking
Trying to break my stride
How you fi stop man hustling
Trying to swallow my pride
Mi gat pickney fi feed an a ooman a breed
An you nearly mek me lose my life
Informers

(Chorus)
Muss dead.
Pussyhole you know we?
Tempted - A pure shatta grow we
Hot lead - A fling out a street caw rudebwoy mek up dem mind.
(Rept.)

[I'm in a factory working, and hustling on the side
I see the informer lurking and trying to break my stride
How can you stop a man from hustling?
I'm trying to swallow my pride
But I have children to feed and a woman who is pregnant
And you almost caused me to lose my life
Informers

Chorus
Must die
Pussyhole do you know who I am/we are?]

(I am) Tempted – because we were raised by gunmen
Bullets are being fired in the streets because rudeboys (bad boys/
men) have made up their minds].

Tony Rebel's *Chatty Chatty* marries the ethos in Lady Ann's *Informer* with that in Bounty Killer's *New Gun* to discuss different situations in which an informer is intrusive. These include dealing in marijuana, holding an illegal gun and an assumed relationship with another woman. At the outset of this song, Rebel explicitly names the informer thus:

> *Well you see true me no have nothing to hide*
> *All informers step aside*
> *Original guerilla Tony Rebel a tell you man*
> *Watch this now nuh*

> [Well, I have nothing to hide
> All informers please step aside
> The original guerilla, Tony Rebel is telling you man
> Now watch this]

For Rebel, a female informer (yuh ah mi friend baby mother and mi know say you a breed) takes information the police about his activities in 'trying a little hussling ah sell some weed' while another person 'run gone a station gone labba dem tongue' because they saw him brandishing a magnum even though they know 'how di ghetto run'. The other instance in which an informer suggests to Rebel's lover that he is with another girl is nullified when his lover simply says 'ah Rebel sista dat man.'

The chorus of *Chatty Chatty*, however, focuses on the informer-police relationship which is the most chastised aspect of all informer debates:

> *A true you chatty chatty chatty*
> *Mi can't live in peace*
> *Every little thing you run gone fi police*

> [Because you chat so much (i.e. inform)
> I cannot live in peace
> Every time some little thing happens you run to the police]

Bounty Killer's hit *Spy fi Die* in the early 1990s, explicitly details the final and excruciating sanctions that must be levelled against informers or spies. In the chorus of *Spy fi Die* the Warlord states:

A guy a spy dat fi die
Coppa shot inna dem heart or inna dem eye

[A man who spies must die]
[Coppershot/gunshot in his heart or his eye]

Bloody and fatal sanctions against the informer are clearly outlined throughout *Spy fi Die* and Bounty Killer's lyrical affair with the gun and violence in dancehall is explicitly detailed in this anti-informer gun treatise. For example, in Verse 2, he states that:

Heartless murderer cold blooded and dry eye
Feel seh that yuh wicked don't talk well just try
Si mi wid mi gun and come style mi like guy
Nuff shot a go buss a pure shot multiply
People a go moan and wholeheap a bwoy die
Murder informa and all gay guy
From yuh love chat well yuh get yuh bone fry
Ask mi no question mi tell you no lie
Informa chat a gunshot mi reply
Fi murder some now wi gonna plea and a cry and seh: (Chorus follows)

[Heartless, coldblooded, dry-eyed murderer]
[You believe that you are wicked, well do not talk, just try (something)]
[(If)You see me with my gun and disrespect me]
[A lot of gunshots will be fired, multiples and multiples]
[We murder informers and all gay men]
[Once you love to talk (inform) your bones will be fried (you will be shot)]
[Ask me no question and I will tell you no lie]
[If informers speak I will reply with a gunshot]
[We are going to plea and cry to murder some informers now and say:]

In this verse, Bounty Killer states 'murder informa and all gay guy.' Here the dreaded informer is lumped in with the gay male as related deviants who deserve similar, final sanctions.

The anti-informer debates in dancehall culture have continued as one component of the negative sanctions placed on particular behaviours that are considered deviant or unmanly. During the intense rivalry between Mavado and Vybz Kartel that was characterized by an ongoing salvo of clash songs in 2008, Mavado released a song called *New Name fi Informa Mr. Palmer* that typified Vybz Kartel (whose real name is Adidja Palmer) as the dreaded informer. This is considered a serious 'diss' in dancehall culture, particularly when the informer is male, as this overuse of 'the mouth' in the practice of gossip is typified as female activity. Therefore, male informers are perceived as de-masculinized. According to Mavado:

> *New name fi informa, Mr. Palmer*
> *Grudge mi fi mi X5 so mi sing dah psalms yah*
> *Strap wid mi arma*
> *Clip longer dan banana*
> *Bwoy come pass di corna*
> *Gunshot ring inna yuh ears like llama*

> [The new name for an Informer is Mr. Palmer
> Who begrudges me for my BMW X5 and so I have sung this Psalms
> I am strapped with my armour
> My magazine clips are longer than a banana
> If any boy/man passes this corner
> Gunshots will ring in your ears like llama]

This continued relationship of the informer with retaliatory violence is related to the wider terrain of violence that is an integral part of dancehall culture's debates with aggression and masculine engagement. In addition, the outward spread of the normalized violence and related values that characterize inner city lifestyles in Kingston and St Andrew has been facilitated by the out-migration of people from the inner cities of the Kingston Metropolitan Area who migrated first to the newer housing projects in Portmore, St Catherine in the 1980s and continues their outward spread to other communities along the Old Harbour Road area in St Catherine and into the adjoining parish of Clarendon. Several of my respondents gave personal testimonies and insisted that the familial linkages between individuals who leave Kingston to escape the poverty of their origin is often re-energized by their sons who develop a great fondness for the status that having 'shotta' and 'gangsta' relatives in the heart of Kingston's inner cities generates in their peers in these communities. Linkages are revived and the culture of the gun continues to replicate itself in its articulations across the bodies of these new and awestruck gunmen, even when their parents or other immediate family members do not support it. These personal, local and national testimonials and/or beliefs creep into dancehall culture's social and gendered discussions about life, personhood and masculinity in Jamaica and arguably result in the promotion of an idealized form of aggressive and violent masculinity that is brokered on the traditional, hegemonic standards of masculinity in Jamaica.

For example, the development of the Portmore Empire by dancehall artiste Vybz Kartel and the intense rivalry between Kartel and Mavado evolved from this out-migration where Kartel's quest for dominance at the top of dancehall culture from his location in Portmore, St Catherine, was presaged by his introduction of real, on-stage violence at Sting 2003 and his renunciation of his musical mentor's, Bounty Killer, leadership. The development of the Gully (Mavado) and Gaza (Vybz Kartel) brands in dancehall is underwritten by these desires. The lyrical gully/side is synonymous with the physical spaces occupied by dancehall's key creators and adherents – variously labelled ghettoes, inner cities, grassroots, trenches, garrisons, gullies and gullysides and symbolically tied to marginalized masses across Jamaica but moreso those who exist on the fringes of real gullies such as Mavado's community of origin, Cassava Piece in St Andrew. This lyrical/physical space provides a social and cultural place from which artistes like Mavado claim their legitimacy in dancehall culture. The name Gaza, on the other hand originated from a desire to distance Kartel's community, Borderline from what had developed into sexually laden name based on movements in popular Jamaica roots theatre. The term 'mi deh pon di borderline' was popularized in the popular Bashment Granny 'roots play' in a particular conversation between a police officer and the 'gender bender' Keith, 'Shebada' Ramsay where the officer inquires about Shebada's gender and receives the reply 'mi deh pon di borderline' (I am on the borderline). The success of this roots play and the intense popularity of this 'borderline' statement resulted in the word becoming indentified with alternative sexualities to the extent that was made synonymous with male homosexuality, which remains taboo in dancehall culture. Vybz Kartel, as the self-styled Emperor of Portmore decided to remove his community's identity from within this suspect category and chose instead to rename his community in line with one geographical area that had been identified as most prone to violent activity over several decades – Gaza.[6] This branding of Gully/Gaza found fertile ground within Jamaica's working classes whose continuous search for identity-spaces is most visible in the propensity for orientation around divisive poles of identification. This is most clearly epitomized in the success with which Jamaica's formal political directorate had successfully brokered political partisanship and tribalism to staggering heights under the PNP vs. JLP brands with controversial and fatal consequences for many Jamaicans, particularly during the turbulent period of the 1980s and beyond.

This search for identity-spaces is also actively engaged with the competitive ethos that feeds the development of dancehall music emerged around the newest dancehall duo, Mavado/Kartel as one key dichotomy. The upgrade of these individual artistes to the broad-based branding as Gully (Mavado) and Gaza (Vybz Kartel) since late 2008 has found supporters of each artiste/ brand oriented around these brands and reports suggest that some supporters

Las May Gully Gaza Cartoon from the Gleaner

of these artistes/brands seemed only too willing to use violence, where necessary to defend their musical turf. This leakage of artiste/brand support into the arena of violence is consistent with the high levels of emotional energy that accompanies the identity groups that are formed in Jamaica.

Dancehall and (Gun) Violence

The symbiotic relationship between dancehall music and culture, and the social and economic conditions that exist in the inner cities that give dancehall its organic life and creativity, play an important role in creating and projecting crime and violence as an important characteristic of a dancehallized identity. Accordingly, dancehall music and culture's own contribution to the creation of fantastic and fantasized role models in the form of anti-heroes and gun-toting men is undeniable. The fantasized model of the violent, gun-toting 'badman,' who becomes elevated to near god-like status in dancehall's narrative myths as well as within the arena of dancehall's continuous desire for lyrical and symbolic clashes, is primarily important as a male version of the ultimate, power-laden male body that is engirded with the ever-erect and deadly phallus, the gun. Guns and their ammunition are a continuous point of reference in dancehall culture whether by type, size, brand or other means of identification. These include AK, Bazooka, Smith an' Wesson, Glock, Forty-five, Nine, Carbine, Chiney K, Magnum, Chrome, chrome-plate, rifle, shine an kriss, Matic, M-16, SLR, Sixteen, Tall up, Thompson (wid di pan ah knock). Bullets are identified by various means including magazine, shot, bullet, copper, gunshot, lead, hot lead. Guns are also identified by the act of firing including buss it, clip, full clip, rise it, pop it off, fire and so on.

This focus on gun violence is married to the thrust for male survival, mobility and empowerment through aggression and violence as a continuous theme within dancehall culture and the articulation and embodiment of aggression and violence in the dancehall feed into the masculine discourses that underwrite Jamaican patriarchy. In dancehall culture, the costuming, bodily movement and embodied presence of particular male artistes and their mirrored articulations in the wider dancehall audience encode and re-present violent imagery that is signified in lyrical narratives and articulated across the male body of the dancehall. The cadre of dancehall artistes who engage primarily in disseminating songs of violence include like Ninja Man, *The*

Original Gold Teeth, Front Teeth Gun Pon Teeth Don Gorgon, Supercat, *the Wild Apache/Don Dadda,* Josey Wales, *the Bad Bwoy Colonel,* and Bounty Killer, *The Warlord/Poor People Defender/ Ghetto Gladiator/Grung God,* Vybz Kartel/ *Addi di Teacha* and Mavado/*Gangsta for Life/Gully Gad.* However, dancehall artistes who are famed for their sexually explicit or humorous songs, like Shabba Ranks and Elephant Man, also disseminate their own versions of this important facet of dancehall's masculine discourses, for example, Shabba Rank's popular *Shine an Kris* and Elephant Man's *Replacement Killer.* These artistes, among others, engage in re-presenting an aggressive and violent form of masculinity as potent, powerful and empowering. The following treatise from Bounty Killer, *Down in the Ghetto,* can be analysed in this regard:

> *Who give di gun who give di crack? No man to take di blame*
> [Who provides the gun, who provides the crack? No man to take the blame]
>
> *An a who import di guns an cocaine?*
> [And who imports the guns and cocaine?]
>
> *An a who inoculate di ghetto youts brains?*
> [And who inoculates the ghetto youths brains?]
>
> *An mobilize dem inna di bloodsport game?*
> [And mobilizes them into the bloodsport game?]
>
> *Say if you want to rich you have to kill Shane?*
> [Saying if you want to rich you have to kill Shane?]
>
> *An wicked enuff to kill him modda Miss Jane*
> [And wicked enough to kill his mother Miss Jane]
>
> *Mek dem say yuh ah di wickedest man pon di lane*
> [So that they can say you are the wickedest man on the lane]
>
> *An if you want yuh respect fi long like a train*
> [And if you want your respect to be as long as a train]
>
> *Well you betta mek shot fall like ah rain.*
> [Well you had better make shots fall like rain]
> Bounty Killer, *Down in the Ghetto*

Down in the Ghetto is first a plaintive treatise on behalf of the residents of the inner city who 'nuh have a thing' (have nothing) and are mobilized into the 'bloodsport game' by nameless men. Yet, it simultaneously documents and narrates to an unnamed audience the perceived wealth-creating and status-generating potential of dalliance in the 'bloodsport game' where, if you want storehouses of riches you are reminded that murdering 'Shane' and engendering enough heartlessness ('wicked enuff') to kill his mother, Miss Jane, is a sure route to accessing this craved wealth and power. The title of 'wickedest man pon di lane' bestows supreme authority and power to the individual male who can wield this Machiavellian fear and ascend to his princely throne in his community. The conflation of the ultimate levels of respect ('long like a train') with the metaphorical raining down of shots in this dancehall narrative underscores and highlights the empowering potential of gun violence as a wealth and status-generating route to masculinity in inner city communities. This idealized incarnation of violent masculinity in Jamaican popular culture has developed over time to the contemporary Don and Shotta within dancehall culture.

Idolizing the Violent Male Body in Jamaican Popular Culture

The differences and the similarities in the hegemonic renderings of masculinity as violence in Jamaican popular culture are performed first in the image of the popularized, masculine anti-hero, Rhyghin, the Rude Bwoy of the 1970s in *The Harder They Come*. These images progress through the persona of Priest, the Shotta of the 1990s, parodied in the 1997 release of the movie *Dancehall Queen,* and related manifestations of Badman (Badman Police and Shotta) in the 2000 movie, *Third World Cop*, and the illustration of Real Badman in the 2002 underground DVD release, *Shottas*. These filmic images encode the dynamics of this masculinized violence that operates simultaneously in Jamaican popular culture, inner city culture, and the wider sphere of Jamaican life[7] and are negotiated and mediated through factors including the use of gun violence, murder, extortion, drug trafficking, and betrayal where the violent male is perceived as simultaneously anti-systemic and heroic. Discourses of violent masculinity in dancehall music culture are organically linked to life in the inner cities or poor communities of Kingston, St Andrew and Portmore, Clarendon, St Catherine, St James, among others and, accordingly, focus its lenses on urban poverty, political tribalism, narco-culture and the culture of the gun, as well as other relevant factors. These discourses are connected to the high levels of social power that is encapsulated in the glamourized personas of the Don, Area Leader or Shotta in many of these inner city communities. The Don and Shotta are praised in dancehall music culture, revered in inner city and garrison culture and often act as role models for some young men from within and beyond these communities where aggression, violence and 'badmanism' are deemed as positive norms of socialization (among others) for young men in Jamaican inner cities.[8] This phenomenon includes the lyrical, symbolic and physical (facial contortions, body posture, style of dress and way of speaking) parody of violence in which select male artistes and their supporters in the dancehall engage. Many young men don this gendered costume of violence and go to great lengths to establish their 'realness' as truly violent men through recognizable gestures, behaviours and codes many of which are narrated and reified in dancehall culture and given full range of expression within the spaces of dancehall culture, for example, at dancehall events. Indeed, it is common to see young men at dancehall stage shows struggling to maintain the 'screw face' and slouching posture and to speak in the rough and coarse tone of voice that is purportedly associated with a 'real bad man' even while they obviously do not fit this profile and would more adequately be described as a 'sweet boy' or someone without any of the real qualities of a true bad man. It is in this setting, the performative spaces of dancehall, that the clash of dancehall culture and masculine status is played out ad extremis even while it makes the rounds of the *habitus* of dancehall adherents and within the wider Jamaican society. The more extreme projections of a violent, dancehallized masculinity often occurs in the on-stage lyrical clash between two or more male dancehall artistes who are considered lyrical Dons, for example during the highly anticipated lyrical clash between arch-rivals Mavado and Vybz Kartel at Sting 2008 hosted at Jamworld in Portmore St Catherine.

Competitive confrontations (aka clashes) that are edged with violence continue to be an integral component of dancehall music and culture. For example, the tensions between dancehall and the state as expressed through the Noise Abatement Act of 1997 and the Broadcasting Commission's directive against 'Daggering' in February 2009 continue to be parodied in

Kartel and Mavado at Sting Clash 2008

lyrical confrontations between dancehall artistes or selectors policemen. This lyrical/symbolic confrontation is illustrated in Babycham's song, *Babylon Bwoy* where an offending policeman, acting as an agent of the state, is taken to task for attempting to 'diss' (disrespect) the artiste:

> *You Missa Babylon[9] bwoy, mind how yuh a touch mi Versace cause it dearer dan yuh pay*
> [You Mr. Babylon boy, take care how you touch/hold my Versace (clothes) because it cost a lot more than your salary]
>
> *Lissen mi nuh Babylon bwoy ah walk an ah shove up yuh finga inna mi face like you gay*
> [Why won't you listen to me, Babylon boy, walking and shoving your fingers in my face as if you were a homosexual]
>
> *Hear mi nuh Babylon bwoy, same way Ratty[10] dem did end up yuh will end up same way*
> [Listen to me, Babylon boy, you will end up in a similar fashion like Ratty]

In the foregoing extract, Babycham fires four lyrical salvos at the offending policeman by first infantilizing him with the term 'boy'. Second, he reduces the policeman's status by reference to his paltry salary in comparison with the inflated disposable income of the dancehall artiste, exemplified by his brand name Versace clothing which would cost the policeman more than one entire month's salary. Third, he sexually demonizes the officer by comparing his actions to that of a homosexual and finally, he threatens the policeman with fatal violence in his reference to the murder of the character Ratty in the movie *Third World Cop*.

Aspirants, rising, and newly risen stars like Vybz Kartel are fully aware of the value that is placed on these publicly staged performances of violence in dancehall culture and are aware of the rewards to be reaped from the consistent performing of an important masculine trait that is often translated into a masculine role. A dancehall artiste who earns the title of 'Don' or real 'Badman' is afforded a primary position on the hierarchy of dancehall and inner city masculinities. This artiste is a lyrical Don, a lyrical 'Badman' who has earned his stripes and gained his moniker by publicly performing and enacting this gendered identity. As Ninja Man has exemplified since his entry into dancehall in the 1980s, a real Don or 'Badman' in dancehall must not only be lyrically dextrous but also must consistently and continuously recreate and construct this gendered identity in highly stylized and very public performances if he wishes to maintain this status-generating masculinity and continuously reap its rewards. This desire was epitomized in the choice of costuming for both Vybz Kartel and Mavado at their highly anticipated and well-publicized dancehall lyrical clash at Sting 2008 that drew thousands of ardent fans to revel in this staged violence where Kartel was dressed in full army fatigues and Mavado donned police riot gear. Unlike other popular dancehall clashes over the years (Ninja Man/Shabba Ranks, Merciless/ Ninja and Merciless/Bounty Killer) however, the Kartel/Mavado clash of 2008 remains unresolved, with many individuals claiming a draw and others selectively crowning Kartel or Mavado, depending on their personal biases. This lack of resolution continues to fuel the debates and posturing as supporters of rival camps argue for the supremacy of the Gaza or Gully overlord as the real, lyrical Badman.

DEFINING A REAL BADMAN

Elephant Man's song *Bad Man* is one dancehall treatise that systematically delineates the characteristics that define the Shotta, the contemporary rendering of the bad man in dancehall culture. In the chorus of this lyrical treatise Elephant Man distances a (real) Badman from 'lesser' representations of masculinity thus:

> *Bad man don't bathe wid him babymother rag;*
> [A (real) Badman does not bathe with his babymother's washcloth]
>
> *Bad man dweet hard, mek she go road go brag;*
> [A (real) Badman skillfully performs hardcore, violent sex, so that his woman can go on the streets and brag about it]
>
> *Shotta clothes don't wash wid gyal underwear;*
> [Shotta's clothing cannot be washed with female underwear]
>
> *Shotta yout don't play certain games round here*
> [Shotta youths do not/will not allow certain offensive behaviours here].[11]

A real man is a *Badman*, synonymous with the gun-toting 'Shotta'. On the continuum of masculine status, the role of badman as an ultimate signifier of masculine status is only paralleled by the operation of male heterosexuality in the adoption of the promiscuous/polygamous masculine role. In the inner cities, both roles operate in concert with each other and this symbiotic operation is underscored in dancehall discourses. In conjunction with the discussion of Ole Dawg in chapter 2, a vital convergence exists between (the perception of) sexual control over several women and the maintenance Don or Shotta status. Several male and female adult interviewees from different inner city communities insisted that a Shotta or Don loses respect if he is a 'one-burner', i.e. a man who is faithful and committed to a single partner or monogamous. The 'one-burner business' is a nail in the coffin of any Don or Shotta. Other male aspirants, including their supporters, who value and revere the supreme position of Don or Shotta, generally view monogamy in these 'powerful' men as a sign of weakness, reflecting an inability (as opposed to unwillingness) to control their women. This perceived weakness in the private sphere, is translated into weakness in the public sphere of the streets and the wider community and, correspondingly, the Don or Shotta's power is perceptually weakened or erased. Accordingly, Badmen usually claim relationships with multiple partners, and evidence this in the many children they have with several babymothers. This simultaneous operation of both the traditional Ole Dawg and Badman masculine roles to garner heightened status plays a critical role dancehall's promotion of extreme and traditional narratives and performance of dancehallized masculinities, as well as in the existential realities of men in many of Kingston's inner cities.

Elephant Man's treatise highlights other important characteristics of the *real Badman*. In line 1 Elephant Man states that 'badman don't bathe with his babymother's rag.' Here he articulates the masculine fear of feminine contamination, particularly in the persona of his intimate, sexual partner and Mother of his children, the Babymother who holds the feared Punaany. This is a reflection of the Delilah complex (Douglas 1966: 154) where female taboos are used to 'protect' the male from loss of power that can be occasioned by the betrayal of or weakening by women. This is directly polarized against the nurturing and more positive/supportive manifestation of Woman as Mother.

Additionally, in line 2 Elephant Man outlines the critical fact that a real, Badman must also display sexual skill and prowess in heterosexual relationships. The point is carefully made that 'Shotta yout dweet hard' to underscore the perceived value of violence during sex. As discussed in the previous, many Jamaican men are socialized to believe that all women actually 'enjoy' violence during sex and receive very little information to the contrary. His sexual skill and prowess must be publicly ratified by his woman ('go road go brag') who disseminates confirmation of his skill and prowess to other women and men. The centrality of sex and heterosexual prowess as an important component of male sexuality has been extensively discussed in Chapter 2.

The third line of the chorus is directly related to the exhortation made in line 1. It highlights very clearly the taboo that exists about female excrement that is related to the Delilah Complex, i.e. the power of women to weaken and/ or betray men. Female underwear, as a shield for and containment of female excrement, is considered very contaminating to the male. Most Jamaican men refuse to have their own clothing, including their own underwear, washed with female underwear. While they have no qualms about removing female underwear as a precursor to sex, the average Jamaican man will refuse to have any other contact with female underwear whether it is new or clean. A man who transgresses these taboos by touching, or heaven forbid, handwashing female underwear (Mother's, wife's, babymother's, sister's, daughter's) can be labelled a 'Maama Man,' a sissy or even perceived as homosexual if his transgressions are made public.[12] During my research several men indicated that they would remove, touch or even wash their spouse's underwear only under extraordinary circumstances, for example, where the woman was very sick and/or bedridden and no other female relative or friend was available to undertake what is perceived as a female-only task.

The final line of the chorus incorporates all the other anti-Badman behaviours that have not been overtly discussed in the text. 'Certain games' is a catch-all phrase that slyly includes all but says nothing. These 'games' that are not 'played round here' include the involvement in homosexual activities, oral sex and other practices considered anti-real Badman status (i.e. anti-male) and, therefore, deviant in this context.

Throughout this song, Elephant Man lyrically points a derisive finger at professed badmen, Shottas and/or Gangstas who are unable to cement their true status by controlling the feminine impetus, particularly among their female partners, spouses and/or babymothers. For example, in one of the verses of this song, he jeeringly taunts:

> *Dem ah say dem ah shotta dem nuff ah dem nuh have nuh balls*
> [They say that they are Shottas but a lot of them have no balls]
>
> *Whole heap ah dem ah violate gangsta laws...*
> [A great deal of them are violating gangster laws because...]
>
> *Cause gyal have him towel a wash wid har draws*
> [Because women are washing his towel/washcloth with her panties]
>
> *Is might as well him wear panty and bra*
> [He might as well be wearing panties and bras]

This marriage of heterosexual imperatives with definitions of masculinity as aggressive in and violent in dancehall culture play directly into the hegemonic imperatives of the wider society that define masculinity as simultaneously heterosexual and aggressive.

Conclusion

While violence cannot be viewed as an entirely masculine purview, aggression, force and violence are often defined as masculine traits (Brod 1994; Clatterbaugh 1997; Connell 1995; Hatty 2000; Katz 1999; Lancaster 1992; Segal 1990). In dancehall culture, the Don/Shotta or Badman is a lyrical, symbolic embodiment of an extreme form of aggression and violence as masculine identity that is socially and lyrically constructed, consistently performed, and continuously reinforced as a valid expression of masculine identity on the dancehall stage and in the lyrics and performance of dancehall artistes. Based on the positive responses and imitative gesture from the dancehall audience and adherents, this model of masculinity receives critical assent and support from within the dancehall. The accolades accorded to the Don/Shotta or Badman in contemporary dancehall music and culture, and his predecessor the Rude Bwoy in Jamaican popular culture, re-present contestations of power and identity within the lived realities (the 'livity') of actors in Jamaica's cultural, social and political spaces. The negatives and high levels of deviance with which traditional Jamaica qualifies this extreme form of masculinity are reflective of the tensions and contestations that are underway in the wider society, particularly during what Meeks (1996:124–43) identifies as an era of hegemonic dissolution in Jamaica.

In concert with this reification and enactment of violence, veteran dancehall artistes' use of the dancehall's public stage to promote and reinforce an extreme, ritualized, aggressive and violent masculinity reflects and maintains the gendered status quo as these gendered performances 'simultaneously sustain, reproduce, and render legitimate the institutional arrangements that are based on sex category' (West and Zimmerman 1987:146) which are encoded within the hegemonic structures in Jamaican society. The ritualized postures and lyrical/symbolic displays of (gun) violence in dancehall are underwritten and mirrored by the lived experiences of many who hail from the lower socio-economic levels of Jamaica. The overt aggressiveness publicized preening and lyrical/symbolic/real dalliances with the gun and violence that many of these artistes employ position them as signifiers of this extreme variant of masculinity that is articulated across the gendered structures of power in dancehall culture. Dancehall culture's dalliance with gun-talk, gunplay and violent lyrics and the succession of artistes who continue to embody and performing these lyrics re-presents an extreme form of aggressive/violent masculinity that plays into the typologies of violent masculinities that are idealized in inner city and lower-/working class culture. Even more importantly, it highlights the symbolically empowering potential of these hypermasculine spaces that are maintained within the gendered structures of power in Jamaica. Consequently, even while the Don/Shotta or Badman's extremely violent fantasies of masculinity purportedly depart from the traditionally accepted codes of good conduct and decent behaviour in polite Jamaican society, its contestatory mode plays directly into and within the accepted notion of aggression and violence as constituent components of hegemonic masculinity in Jamaica.

This focus on aggression and violence as one extreme and contestatory form of masculinity in dancehall culture, which remains closely linked to hegemonic masculinity in Jamaica, is related to anti-male homosexual debates as another popularised discourse of masculine empowerment in dancehall culture that draws it strength from the hegemonic imperatives in the society. The following chapter examines the overt discussions of what I refer to as the anti-male homosexual discourse in Jamaican dancehall culture, and assesses the relationship between dancehall culture's prominent anti-male homosexual exemplar and the hegemonic standard that is privileged in Jamaican society.

CHAPTER 4

'CHI-CHI MAN FI GET SLADI'[1]: ANTI-MALE HOMOSEXUAL DISCOURSES AS DANCEHALL MASCULINITY

We nuh like gay, we nuh like gay
[We do not like gays, we do not like gays]

Well ah just soh Jamaican stay
[Well, that is just the way Jamaicans are]

From yuh nuh like battyman[2] well mi waan fi see yuh gun right away
[Once you do not like male homosexuals, well I want to see your gun right away (now)]

Caw wi bun dem and wi run dem badman an battyman cyaan be friend
[Because we burn them and we chase them away; Badmen and male homosexuals cannot be friends]

(Scare Dem Crew, 1999)[3]

Introduction

This chapter examines the constituent elements of another variant of masculinity in the dancehall that is brokered on the hegemonic notion that homophobia, or the propensity to deny homosexual or feminized men social and patriarchal power, and the overt negation of male homosexuality, provide legitimate patriarchal and hegemonic spaces within which marginalised men in Jamaica can negotiate higher status and more powerful masculine identities. This variant of dancehallized masculinity gained prominence in the early period of dancehall's dominance in the early 1990s and the debates that it generates is marked at the outset by Buju Banton's clash with the gay rights group, Gay and Lesbian Alliance Against Defamation (GLADD) in 1992 and extended to the post-millennial, incendiary debates between artistes like Vybz

Kartel, Elephant Man, Beenie Man, Sizzla and the British-based, gay rights group, Outrage! and beyond. Amnesty International's Human Rights Watch report for 2004 also discussed the issue as a contributor to the HIV/AIDS epidemic.[4] For the purposes of this chapter, any stereotypical and monolithic rendering of homophobia, or more particularly, anti-male homosexuality as a variant of masculinity in dancehall culture aims only to isolate, and thus capture, another form of masculinity that occupied a dominant position in dancehall's configuration of masculinity in one era, in order to flesh out its constituent elements and analyse its relation to the process of hegemonic masculinity in Jamaica.

Dancehall culture's contestatory stance and its propensity for extreme lyrical and behavioural incantations utilize excessively violent and fatal imagery to render the homosexual male redundant and powerless. The following sections examine the constituent elements of this excessively and often lyrical/symbolic and violent variant of dancehallized masculinity that ultimately feeds into what have been identified herein as the traditionally accepted hegemonic variant of masculinity in Jamaica. In addition, this chapter examines the convergence with class in Jamaica that, in this instance, creates a contestatory dialogue of personhood, which is founded on dancehall's reaction to male homosexuality that renders the male homosexual as visible in a social and gendered setting where he has been cast as invisible.

Defining Homophobia

Connell (1995, 40) notes that the 'term "homophobia" was coined in the early 1970s to describe the long experience of rejection and abuse of homosexual men by heterosexual men.' He further notes that 'A central insight of Gay Liberation is the depth and pervasiveness of homophobia and how closely it is connected with dominant forms of masculinity' (1995, 40). Homophobic ideology provides a negative pole for the reinforcement of masculinity in a space where the boundaries between masculine and feminine are blurred (Atluri 2001; Connell 1995; Gutzmore 2004; Hopkins 1992; Kimmel 2001; Lancaster 1992; Segal 1990; Weeks 1977). Like misogyny, homophobic ideology is irrevocably bound up with notions of aggression and violence where the boundaries of masculinity are rigidly policed against perceived gender traitors. Indeed, Segal notes that there is generally a close cultural link between homophobia and misogyny. Homophobia is the repression of the 'feminine' in men and is a powerful tool for regulating the entire spectrum of male relations (Segal 1990, 16–17). Connell argues that homosexual men are perceived as feminized men while lesbian women are viewed as masculinized men (1990, 41). The texture of homophobia in the wider Caribbean region, and in Jamaica relate specifically to this focus on masculinity. In this regard, Atluri (2001) proposes that sexism, heterosexism and homophobia combine to make Jamaica, and other societies of the Caribbean region, into what she images as a 'closet' for lesbian and gay citizens. In the context of the overt policing of the male sexual body that is the colonial legacy of many Anglo- and Caribbean contexts like Jamaica,[5] any behaviour or activity defined on a continuum from overtly effeminate to outright homosexual are used to label and define men as a homosexual. This argument cannot be applied as a theoretical blanket across different societies in the region. For example, in his work on Nicaraguan *machismo*, Lancaster (1992, 238) notes that the *cochon* (*el cochon, la cochon/a*) is markedly different from its Anglo-American counterparts – the homosexual, faggot, gay or queer. In Nicaragua it is only the passive role in anal intercourse that defines the *cochon*. Additionally, oral or manual practices receive little or no social attention or stigmatization. This is in stark contrast to the discourse in a postcolonial, Anglophone Caribbean society like Jamaica where any form of sexual contact between two men is deemed homosexual and deviant and where, for example, oral sex of any sort is generally hidden and routinely condemned in dancehall culture as 'bowing.'[6]

Thus, a man is not a real man unless he is sexually active but his activism must be heterosexual, not homosexual. This distinction is of great importance to the definition and maintenance of Caribbean masculine status. In Jamaica, anxieties about homosexuality are particularly extreme and these anxieties are aired and discussed in dancehall culture. Here, a homosexual is generally conceptualized as male, and lesbianism, or female homosexuality, does not attract the same negative and paranoid attention as male homosexuality. In line with this propensity, lesbianism in dancehall culture is generally infantilized and usually treated with a humorous tolerance, with dancehall's stereotyping and stigmatizing of homosexuals and homosexuality placed squarely in the context of the masculine. The feminine 'Other' is utilized as a pole around which masculinity can be oriented, or, alternatively as a stage on which it can be elevated.

Anti-Feminizing/Anti-Male Homosexual Discourse in Dancehall Culture

The Delilah complex, where the female/feminine is treated as dangerous, with the power to weaken or betray men/male, is rife in Jamaican gender and folk culture (Chevannes 1994). This ambivalence about gendered identities is also related to dancehall's discussions about masculinity, where what is labelled as homophobia becomes critically intertwined with anti-feminine and anti-feminizing discourses against phenomena or behaviours that threaten 'true' male identity in the dancehall.

In my early work on dancehall culture (Hope 2001a, 64–83) I documented the existence of this complex in dancehall culture where the '*Punaany*' as female sex organ and female essence is simultaneously feared and revered in dancehall culture. Additionally, I argued that this dichotomous fear/ revere response to particular manifestations of symbolic femininity and the female in dancehall culture results in a generalized ambivalence to femininity in dancehall music and culture. This ambivalence about gendered identities is highlighted in dancehall's discussions about masculinity, where what is labelled as homophobia is critically intertwined with anti-feminine and anti-feminizing discourses against phenomena or behaviours that threaten 'true' male identity in the dancehall. Female taboos, or more critically anti-feminine discourses, are strategies aimed at protecting male power from decimation and erasure. Dancehall's anti-male homosexual discourse operates along this continuum as an important strategy for the protection, reification and solidification of heterosexual masculinity.

Consequently, this anti-male homosexual ethos in dancehall culture is predominantly a male-male discourse that highlights the male paranoia and unease about male homosexuality that, as a general rule, underpins Jamaican masculinity. This Jamaican homophobia, as debated in dancehall culture, is arguably a radical and extreme variant of Jamaican masculine paranoia of the feminine where in many instances, male homosexuals are deemed gender traitors who violate the accepted rules of gender identity and/or gender performance. Hopkins (1992, 114) notes that the most obvious forms of gender treachery 'occurs as homosexuality, bisexuality, cross-dressing and feminist activism.' Accordingly the heterosexist notions and practices that support anti-male homosexual paranoia is interrelated with behaviours, practices and discourses that are labelled misogynistic. The behaviours, practices and sexual preference of homosexual (and effeminate) men in Jamaica splinter the accepted notions of Jamaican masculine identity as heterosexual. Homosexuality is, therefore, viewed as a…'threat to manhood' (masculinity) and correspondingly…'a threat to personhood (personal identity)' (Hopkins 1992, 114).

Dancehall culture, as a discourse of personhood and the negotiation of sexual, social and political identities, uses its stage to articulate, re-present and perform these anti-male homosexual discourses that negate effeminate and male homosexual practices and underwrite the fantasized and extreme versions of heterosexual masculinity of the type that is idealized in black popular cultures like hip hop and dancehall culture (Gutzmore 2004; Hope 2001; Rose 1994). As Gutzmore (2004) argues, dancehall culture is underwritten by legislative codes, religious foundations, historical legacies, and social and popular culture, that create a field of play in which dancehall artistes are given ample sway to disseminate these discourses in the wider social and popular cultural arena of Jamaica.

Legislative Underpinnings for Anti-Homosexual Discourses

The Jamaican Constitution accords wide latitudes of freedom to citizens to express their disagreement with issues, practices or lifestyles. The generalized understanding of this provision underwrites the explicit lyrical treatises that emanate from within the dancehall as an outlet for heterosexual men to vocalize their fears and tensions about male homosexuality. These vocal and often vociferous outpourings are underwritten by the wider sphere of Caribbean/Jamaican dis/ease with homosexuality that is encoded in the legislative structures of these societies. For example, Trinidad and Tobago's Sexual Offences Act of 1986 makes sex between men punishable by up to ten years imprisonment, and that between women by five. The Bahamas' Sexual Offences and Domestic Violence Act of 1989 makes male and female homosexuality punishable by up to 20 years imprisonment. Under an order from the Privy Council, Britain scrapped anti-homosexual laws in its five Caribbean territories, Anguilla, the Cayman Islands, the British Virgin Islands, Montserrat and the Turks and Caicos after their legislatures refused to decriminalize homosexual activities between adults in private.[7]

Jamaica's Offences Against the Persons Act 1864 derives from the English parent Act of 1861. Section 76 of this Act states:

> Whosoever shall be convicted of the abominable crime of buggery, committed either with mankind or any animal, shall be liable to be imprisoned and kept to hard labour for a term not exceeding ten years.

Section 79 of this Act prohibits any public or private 'acts of gross indecency' between male persons. The act defines buggery as anal intercourse between a human being and an animal, which may also be committed between a man and a woman, or between two men. There is no age of consent.[8] Section 76 of the law does not specifically define buggery as anal intercourse between men, but the underlying assumption that it was specifically created for and against male homosexuality continues to be reinforced and disseminated by various methods of oral transmission in a society where oral culture predominates over the written word. The catch-all phrase 'acts of gross indecency' in conjunction with the term 'male' has also been defined and identified as legislative sanctioning against male homosexual engagement of any form. Alexander (1994) argues that, based on their inscriptions of citizenship, Caribbean states are represented as heterosexual. Non-procreative sex is prohibited by law and debarred from full moral citizenship. Thus the conflation of buggery, bestiality and criminality in the law entrenches the notion that gay sex is unnatural, while simultaneously promoting heterosexuality as the only viable and self-sustaining option. Indeed, the colonial legacy of many Caribbean societies resulted in homophobic legislation that had a clear link to the political economy of slavery in its insistence on anal sex as counterproductive to heterosexual relationships. In Jamaica, the maintenance of laws like the Buggery Act into the contemporary era reflects the continued conflation of notions of (hetero) sexuality with ideas of citizenship.

This means that the majority of dancehall artistes and supporters of the anti-male homosexual ethos operate in a framework where there is a perception of strong legislative support for their dissemination of condemnatory, inflammatory and phobic lyrics and symbols. The knowledge or perception of the underlying support of the country's legislation is secondary only to the more powerful ideological encouragement that Jamaica's religious sector provides for anti-male homosexual treatises in dancehall culture.

Religious Underpinnings

Jamaica is predominantly a Christian and fundamentalist society steeped in the Protestant principles of hellfire and brimstone. Popular myth states that Jamaica has the most churches per square mile than any other country in the Western hemisphere. As a part of their early and continuing socialization Jamaican dancehall artistes and key dancehall adherents claim the same religious directives against homosexuality that guide Christian clergymen, and most artistes use these biblical directives in their lyrical treatises against male homosexuality. These directives include Old Testament scriptures like the story of Sodom and Gomorrah at Genesis 19; and verses that condemn homosexuality like those at Leviticus 18:22 and 20:13. In the New Testament emphasis is placed on Romans 1:26–27. The productive and procreative directive given to man and woman by God in the creation story at Genesis 1:28 is also very important in dancehall culture's discourse against male homosexuality and is clearly related to the hegemonic heterosexual impulses discussed in Chapter 3. It is common fare for dancehall artistes to state that man and woman are to 'Be fruitful and multiply...' and this is why God created Adam and Eve, not 'Adam and Steve'. Arguments for the archaic and backward nature of biblical scriptures ignore the strict religious conservatism that continues to guide Jamaica in its movement through the twenty-first century. Like Christian fundamentalist clergymen in Jamaica and other countries, dancehall artistes and adherents also rely on these and other scriptures in their damnation of homosexuality as an abomination that will be punished by hellfire. As a result, the profound persistence of Jamaica's oral continuum that is manifested in popular culture generally and dancehall culture in particular is conflated with the strong emphasis on male heterosexuality to encourage and support anti-male homosexual discourses of identity and personhood in Jamaica's class and status-driven social setting.

Convergence with Class and Status

The pervasive and rigid class and status hierarchy in Jamaica is also intertwined with the gendered structures of power to grant or deny personhood to the various sexualities that exist in Jamaica. Julius Powell of Jamaica Forum for Lesbians, All-Sexuals and Gays (JFLAG) underscored this notion in a radio interview thus:

> If you are gay and uptown (meaning you have money) you are immune to the discrimination and abuse to an extent. And depending on how high in the social stratum you are, then you are pretty much immune to abuse because of your sexual orientation.[9]

In this regard, the ambivalence that underscores Jamaican responses to gender identity means that gay men from the lower classes and inner cities are usually tolerated in their communities and this was consistently reinforced during my doctoral research when interviewees in inner city and lower working class communities identified at least one individual who might be or was suspected of being homosexual based on a combination of factors.[10] However, this man was an accepted part of the community and his sexual preference was tolerated as long as he maintained the accepted Victorian silence and kept his sexual liaisons and partnerships closely guarded and outside the community reinforcing the hegemonic imperatives that govern Jamaican society which translate into differential responses to male homosexuality that is fragmented along class lines.

During the research for this work, discussions and interactions with gay men bear out this convergence of Jamaica's class bias with gender in the manifestation of anti-homosexual sentiments. None of my middle class gay interviewees reported being stoned, kicked, beaten or physically persecuted on the basis of their sexuality, and none have reported an overwhelming perception of threats to their personal security during their day-to-day activities. One gay male colleague reported that in his own lower-middle class community of origin in St Catherine, he is highly respected for his educational achievements. This supersedes any inclination that the men who gather at street corners may have to be discriminatory or abusive towards him. Though he now lives in a different middle class community in Kingston, he is treated with great respect and as a special person of high status whenever he visits his former community. Yet, another middle-class homosexual man from St Andrew ('uptown') stated that he rented an apartment with a lesbian friend so that they could 'cover' their sexual preferences, noting that: 'When men visit, people assume they come to her and when women visit people assume they come to me.'[11] His main concern was the closeting of his sexual preferences in a situation where male homosexuality is tolerated but not openly approved.

The ambivalence that characterizes real gender relationships means that gay men who come from the lower classes and inner cities are also tolerated in their communities, where dancehall music and culture's creative and condemnatory ethos emanates. When asked if this man displayed any positive traits, all respondents were quick to stress particular social and economic factors, including the fact that this man was usually well-educated, self-sufficient, and held a steady job. At the same time, they highlighted the fact that he paid unusual attention to his personal aesthetics including the wearing of 'good' clothing that was well coordinated. Interviewees noted that this man usually had very good relationships with 'the women.' Many were careful to note that yes, he was an accepted part of the community because him 'come from here' or him always live here. However, he did face the usual verbal accusation/condemnation and slurs. The open flaunting of male partners was not tolerated as one interviewee noted 'We don't play that game round here.' Unlike middle- and upper-class male homosexual interviewees, the lower-class and inner city homosexual male cannot speak about his 'partner' openly as this can trigger a beating or result in his being run out of his community by a violent mob.[12]

Class remains the most important definer of personhood in Jamaica, therefore, a homosexual man from the middle or upper-classes is allowed freer rein to breach the patriarchal norms of masculine behaviour and practice without having to face any real discrimination. A homosexual male in an inner city or lower working-class community is tolerated, particularly if he is educated and gainfully employed. However, he remains more at risk than his middle class counterpart and must conduct his personal activities in secret and outside of the confines of the community. This convergence with class and status predominates in ranking personhood and here, dancehall's anti-male homosexual discourses from below transgress the accepted modes of engagement. The general propensity is for marginalized individuals, like those from Kingston's inner cities who are dancehall culture's main creators and adherents, to utilize ideological and superficial means to level the socio-political playing field and thereby garner some social and political. Ranking a male homosexual as deviant and powerless in dancehall culture, particularly a man from Jamaica's middle classes, is highly contestatory as it challenges the hegemony of the middle classes at the nexus of its power which is first and foremost based on social class positioning. The self-motivating phrase 'dem nuh more dan me/we'[13] which is a phrase commonly used in inner city slang and dancehall culture reflects this propensity to consistently and continuously seek out and identify a lesser being to be labelled as deviant and thus utilized as an anti-mirror to reflect some modicum of personhood and status towards the identifier.

Popular Response to Male Homosexuality in Jamaica

Lewis (2003a:109) notes that tolerance levels for male homosexuality vary along a continuum in Anglophone Caribbean societies. Places like 'St Thomas in the Virgin Islands and Trinidad and Barbados operate at the higher end of this continuum of tolerance, while Jamaica, St Vincent and St. Lucia occupy the lower levels' (2003a:109). Since its evolution in the 1980s, Jamaican dancehall music and culture has been engaged in a routine denunciation of male homosexuality. This has fluctuated from passing comments in its early stages, to a topography of vociferous volleys, beginning in the early 1990s and exploding into the new millennium, all aimed directly at the heart of male homosexuality in Jamaica. In analysing the underlying rationale for the increasing cultural attention to male homosexuality, Gutzmore's (2004) discussion focuses particularly on Jamaican patriarchy and homophobia in his examination of the condemnatory and violent stance that is taken against male homosexuality. He identifies five ideological imperatives that contribute to homophobia in Jamaica including: 'the religious fundamentalist anti-homosexuality imperative, the imperative of the 'unnaturalness' of homosexuality, the imperative of the purity and authenticity of a primordially homosexuality-free global African culture, the imperative to protect vulnerable youth from homosexuality, as conflated with paedophilia, and the imperative of the illegality of homosexuality.'[14]

In Jamaica, the popular response to homosexuality is most clearly articulated in the use of language and popular slang. Terms like 'Number Two' are used to identify affiliation with the anus and thus homosexuality. Indeed, the 'Number Two' is so deeply entrenched as a marker of male homosexuality that many Jamaican men openly refuse to count from one through three in the normal fashion and resort to using 'one, twice, three' to avoid saying the word 'two'. Additionally, since the turn of the millennium, there is a displayed aversion to use of the prefix 'Man' and popular place names like Mandeville and 'Mantego Bay' are altered in popular slang to Gyaldeville' and Gyaltego Bay. The popularized Jamaican terms battyman and sadomite that are used to identify male and female homosexuals respectively are thus supported by a myriad of terms and slang that reject and chastise homosexuality, particularly male homosexuality. This is at its extreme in dancehall culture, as Jamaica's currently most popular music and cultural form.

It has become radically clear that the explosion and intensity in anti-homosexual dancehall lyrics is more particularly a direct result of the progressive unmasking of male homosexuality in Jamaica since the late 1990s and encodes the heightening paranoia of dancehall's male adherents to this revelation. The revelation of male homosexuality represents an inherent challenge to the hegemonic codes of Jamaican masculinity from which dancehall masculinity takes it cues. The sentiment among some dancehall adherents is that 'Di batty bwoy dem a get too bright up bright up;'[15] and 'Dem all a form group and come pon TV.'[16] This heightened visibility of the male homosexual body continues to be reflected in growing numbers of openly homosexual television programs broadcast during prime time on cable television stations that became increasingly accessible to a wide cross-section of Jamaicans with the legitimization of Jamaica's cable industry in the mid-1990s.[17] Many popular American and other foreign sitcoms also broadcast episodes that feature actors as homosexual men and women. In addition, the formation of the JFLAG in December, 1998[18] acted as an important sociocultural catalyst.

Male homosexuality in Jamaica has been tolerated for many decades, cloaked under a hypocritical form of 'respectable' and 'polite' silence as long as gays 'do their thing' in private. This 'respectable' and 'polite' silence maintained the hegemony of the status quo as heterosexual, in a context where the 'open secret' of male homosexuality remained simultaneously very open and very secret and the silenced and invisible male homosexual was effectively rendered as powerless. The middle-class response to the open panorama of homosexuality in Jamaica since the early 1990s has generally been cloaked in this same 'respectable' and 'polite' silence that had historically worked to effectively erase the persona of the male homosexual from the ideological power structures of Jamaican society. However, dancehall culture's extreme response to this uncloaking of male homosexuality has been a correspondingly vocal and inflammatory increase in anti-male homosexual lyrics where, as Gutzmore notes 'the earliest directly homophobic reggae song…is the 1978 King Sounds and the Israelites, "Spend One Night Inna Babylon"…which makes explicit mention of Sodom and Gomorrah and of the fact that these two ancient cities…are anathematized in the Bible' (2004, 126). During the 1980s dancehall lyrics mentioned gay men (or women) in a line or two of a song, however, from the early 1990s to the present, entire songs are devoted to condemning male homosexuality as an abomination that threatens to corrupt and overturn Jamaican society, like the Biblical example of Sodom and Gomorrah. These deeply patriarchal roots of fundamentalist Christian principles all corroborate with and underwrite the rigid codes of the dominant form of heterosexual masculinity which is privileged in dancehall culture. The anti-male homosexual variant of dancehall masculinity underwritten by these lyrical treatises is crafted as an anti-hero whose role is to guard the fortress of true heterosexual masculinity, as defined in dancehall culture, from breach by any means, whether violent or fatal. This extreme version of the anti-hero feeds on the hegemonic impulses in Jamaica's own traditional version of masculinity, as well as on the social and political cues that proliferate to negate male homosexuality.

Thus, dancehall culture's divergent and inflammatory response to male homosexuality is supported by the gendered cues, religious imperatives, legislative underpinnings, class and status debates and the overall dated, colonial and repressive Victorian responses that emanate from within the wider Jamaican society and linked to the composition of its main audience who hail from the inner cities of Kingston and St Andrew and the lower-working-classes of Jamaica.

Deconstructing Dancehall's Chi-Chi Man

In Jamaica, the aggressive, colourful slang of Jamaican Creole and dancehall slang translates many of these disagreements into verbal contestations and conflagrations, particularly relating to debates around sexuality and gender. In this very particularistic discourse of masculinity, Jamaican slang and dancehall lyrics variously label and negatively stereotype a homosexual man as pungai man, battyman, batty bwoy, funny man, chi-chi man, gay guy, Mr Faggoty, and Mr She. These labels imply either an involvement with anal sex or a willful renunciation of the accepted behaviours, aesthetics, and practices that denote 'true' masculinity. It is noteworthy that denigrating labels similar to those used in dancehall lyrics and slang are used in ordinary dialogue as verbal missiles against male homosexuals or men suspected of having homosexual leanings, particularly during arguments or other confrontations with other men or women. The most intense and sometimes violent confrontation may occur if a heterosexual man believes that he is being publicly undermined, challenged or sexually solicited by a gay man.

The more popularized term Chi-Chi is a Jamaican colloquialism for termites, i.e., insects that eat wood or wood-borers that create a corruption. The term gained prominence in dancehall culture at the turn of the millennium as a modern label for male homosexuals. In this culture, the term Chi-Chi man (as separate from a Chi-Chi woman) is coded as a male homosexual who is sexually involved with other men. This linguistic rendering represents a corrupted and socially unacceptable form of masculinity. The notion of Chi-Chi as 'wood-borers' in Jamaican Creole may underscore a linguistic parallel between wood and 'hood,' where hood is a colloquial term for the male penis. In addition, Cooper (2004, 163) 'wonders if the chi chi man slang extension of the meaning is intended to represent the homosexual as a diminutive man. Also, since "wood/hood" is a Jamaican Creole metaphor for penis, chi chi man could also suggest the vulnerability of the homosexual's manhood to chi chi of all kinds.' The flexibility of dancehall slang throws up female derivatives, namely 'di Chi-Chi ooman' or 'Chi-Chi gyal dem,' i.e., lesbians.

In the early 1990s, Buju Banton's *'Boom Bye Bye'* affirmed the primacy of this anti-male homosexual discourse in dancehall culture. Since then, a cadre of anti-male homosexual songs (often referred to as Chi-Chi man songs) has developed in dancehall culture and most dancehall artistes can claim at least one such song in their portfolio, as the male homosexual holds a prominent position in the hierarchy of social deviants whose naming raises a 'forward' from the dancehall audience. Other prominent social deviants of this nature include politicians, informers and paedophiles.

Dancehall culture's lyrical debates insist that, by their very definition, *real men* are expected to police the boundaries of heterosexual masculinity and, where necessary, expose another man's feminine traits or homosexual leanings. This naming, calling forth or 'outing' of compromised masculinity is exemplified in dancehall artiste, Alozade's, treatise *'Chi Chi Crew'*:

> From dem a par inna Chi-chi man crew
> Dem a Chi-chi man too Chi-chi man too
> From a gyal a par inna Chi-chi gyal crew
> Dem a Chi-chi gyal too Chi-chi gyal too.[19]

> [Once they are socializing with gay men,
> Then they are also gay men (rept.)
> Once they are socializing with lesbians
> Then they are also lesbians (rept.)]

Alozade documents the notion that the conscious fraternizing with known or reputedly gay men (and women) is taboo. In related vein, Rastafari dancehall artiste Capleton highlights the notion that individual responses to anti-male homosexual treatises can be used to identify those who are gay thus:

> Bun battyman, only battyman vex
> Bun Sadomite, only sadomite vex
> Bun informer, only informer vex

> [When you burn gay men, only gay men are vexed
> When you burn lesbians, only lesbians are vexed
> When you burn informers, only informers are vexed]

At this juncture, the deeply patriarchal focus of the Rastafari movement is expressed in hardcore dancehall treatises that are simultaneously tinged with the incendiary politics of Rastafari. The 'fire burn' or 'bun them' ethos that signifies Rastafari's religious fundamentalism and Victorian notions of sexual conservatism are conflated with the patriarchal impulses of dancehall/ Rastafari in complicit renderings of male homosexuality as an aberration of male heterosexuality that demands urgent attention. At the same time, Capleton highlights the propensity to lump deviants in the same space, thus naming the male homosexual and the correspondingly dreaded and negated informer in the same breath.

Dancehall quartet T.O.K.'s anti-homosexual treatise in 2000 is an extension of Alozade's and Capleton's lyrical discussions to denote the need for ritualistic purification and cleansing as well as sanctions against those (men) who fraternize with or are suspected of being homosexuals:

> From dem a 'par inna Chi-chi man cyar
> Wave di fiya mek wi bun dem
> From dem ah drink inna Chi-chi man bar
> Wave di fiya mek wi bun dem

> [Once they are (seen) sparring in a homosexual's car]
> [Wave the fire and let us burn them (up]
> [Once they are (seen) drinking in a homosexual's bar]
> [Wave the fire and let us burn them (up)]

For T.O.K., guilt by association is a valid and viable option that merits the same sanctions as those reserved for male homosexuals.

Indeed, in concert with TOK's lyrical entreaty to 'bun dem' many interviewees in the inner cities and dancehall context displayed that to publicly take a violent, anti-homosexual stance is to stand up for masculinity, male sexuality and male dominance. This is exemplified, for example, in Bounty Killer and Babycham's song *Another Level*:

> Bun a fiya pon a poop an Missa Faggoty!
> Cocky deh yah so fi wheel unda Dorothy
> Face ah bend up an a wrinch unda agony
> Poop man fi dead dat ah Yaad man philosophy

> [Fire on/for gay men!]
> [The penis is here to (be used to) have sex with Dorothy (women)]
> [(Her) face is twisted and wrenched with (sexual) agony]
> [Gay men should die, that is the philosophy of Yard (Jamaican) men]

The most extreme manifestation of this anti-male homosexual discourse is reflected in songs that suggest the outright elimination of this group from the face of the earth. Elephant Man and Ward 21's turn-of-the-millennium treatise *'Chi-Chi Man fi get Sladi'* suggested extreme and final sanctions for male homosexuals thus:

> *Chi-chi man fi get sladi*
> *Di whole a dem a fi go tell di whole world ba-bye*
> *Mi nuh wann nuh chi-chi frien man so nuh frien I*
> *Run pass Olive an gawn wine pon Popeye*
>
> [Male homosexuals should be slain
> All of them will have to tell the world goodbye
> I do not want any male homosexual friends so do not try to befriend me
> (You have) Run past Olive and are wining up on Popeye]

In this instance, the very idea or thought of male homosexuality is strongly denounced and fatal sanctions are proposed – all male homosexuals should be removed from the face of the earth. The final line of this verse proposes the underlying rationale for this extreme proposition: Men have run past Olive and are wining up on Popeye. The symbols Popeye and Olive from the fictionalized world of popular cartoon suggest the quintessential male/female couplet that is revered in dancehall culture. Consequently, those men who have 'run past' or ignored the 'natural heterosexual' couplet and have entered male-male relationships with Popeye deserve this fatal and final sanction as they have corrupted the 'natural' ordering of heterosexual relationships.

While a burgeoning cadre of dancehall songs debates the existence of the male homosexual, there is a blatant imbalance in any related cadre directed at female homosexuality. The underlying idea that is communicated and legitimized is that, by its very nature, female homosexuality fails to undermine the traditional tenets of Jamaican patriarchy that bestow varieties of Jamaican heterosexual masculinity on the bodies of its men. This also reflects the patriarchal tenet of male superiority vs. female inferiority that pervades all patriarchal societies.[20] The importance of the penis in biologically defining and signifying male identity is emphasized in dancehall treatises that explain its dominance and use in conquering and subduing the feminine Other. Dancehall's lyrical treatises consistently document this 'truth' of the fantasized and fantastic hyper-masculine and powerful penis. For example, Cutty Ranks' treatise of the 1980s, *'Grizzle,'* connotes an almost inhuman prowess that resides in this male sexual organ:

> *Pon mi Mi waan some girl hitch up pan mi Grizzle*
> *One press off a mi trigger a girl get cripple*
> *Who nuh get pregnant gwine end up down a Madden*
> *A ten thousand dolla weh dem use buy them coffin*
> *Down a May Pen Cemetry unda the gravel*

> [Upon my grizzle, I want some girls to come and be hitched upon my grizzle
> One press of my trigger and a girl becomes crippled/paralyzed
> Who does not become pregnant will end up down by Maddens (Morgue)
> Their coffins will cost ten thousand dollars
> Down by Maypen Cemetery under the gravel]

For Ranks and others, the mythologized and hyper-masculine penis (in this instance 'grizzle') conquers and dominates the feminine on the battlefield of sex and sexuality. The conflation of the grizzle/penis with the phallus/gun that is popularized in Jamaican dancehall is underscored in the verbal imagery of the phrase 'one press off a mi trigger' and fits neatly into the continued dalliance with gun lyrics and images of the gun/phallus as a tool that bestows supreme power (even over life and death) on its holder – the gun is a symbolic and perpetually erect penis.[21] The word grizzle falls into the range of dancehall's synonyms for the penis that position the male and masculinity at the centre of dancehall's sexual discourses and which are brokered on notions of superhuman size, strength and length (anaconda, rattler, long ting, tree trunk, length and strength) and on power and prowess (womb turner, hard and stiff, rifle, nozzle). The importance of this mythologized penis in the construction of male heterosexuality in dancehall culture suggests that a female homosexual is rendered invisible because of this biological lack and pins the male homosexual in the centre of this lyrical bull's eye.

Dancehall's progressive engagement with male homosexuality is highlighted in Wayne Marshall's song *'I Forgot Them'* reflects a transformation in the production and reproduction of the male homosexual in dancehall culture. Marshall states:

You remember dem guys from when (Ah fagot dem)
We an dem are no longer friend (Ah fagot dem)
Dem switch, I done wid dem (Ah fagot dem)
Dem can't come back pon we ends (Ah fagot dem)
No, wi nuh like dem trends (Ah fagot dem)

[Do you remember those guys from way back when? (I forgot them)
They are no longer our friends (I forgot them)
They have switched (roles) and I am through with them (I forgot them)
They can never visit our personal spaces (I forgot them)
No, we don't like their current trends] (I forgot them)

Marshall refers particularly to some 'guys' who have recently become homosexual (i.e., 'dem switch'). The term 'guys' encodes a subtle reference to men as homosexual where it is common practice to refer to gay men as 'gay guys.' To 'switch' is also often used to encode what is perceived as a transformation from heterosexuality to homosexuality, i.e., to switch gender codes. Marshall highlights the notion that these former acquaintances are now social outcasts and have been 'forgotten,' i.e., erased from his memory and socially negated. Marshall underscores the cessation of any form of social interaction, noting that 'dem can't come back pon wi ends.' The repetition of the term 'Ah fagot dem' in Jamaican Creole literally means 'I have forgotten them.' However, the complexities and linguistic intricacies of Jamaican Creole allow this repetitive phrase to encode a more pointed and different interpretation. 'Ah fagot dem' as it is rendered is also translatable as 'Ah faggot dem' or 'They are faggots' and can thereby be interpreted through its connotations with a Westernized version of another label for male homosexuals. The dual interpretation of this song-text reflects Wayne Marshall's propensity for word play and double entendre. Indeed, his most recent song, '*Mi Nuh Astronaut*,' also uses this lyrical strategy of innuendo and double entendre to engage the anti-male homosexual debate thus:

Nah fly no rocket through nuh black hole
Can't breathe inna space so mi sure nah go roll
Mi ah stay dung to earth with mi satellite pole
Mi nuh ass-tronaut so mi nah go Uranus
Man neva mek fi breach di ozone
From you can't breathe is a no fly zone

Mi nah go explore dem deh unknown
Mi nuh astronaut so mi nah go Uranus

[I am not flying my rocket through any black hole
I cannot breathe in space so I am sure not going to roll
I am staying on earth with my satellite pole
I am no astronaut so I am not going to Uranus
Man was not created to breach the ozone layer
Once you cannot breathe it is a no-fly zone
I am not going to explore that unknown
I am no astronaut so I am not going to Uranus]

Marshall's use of the term 'astronaut' encodes a reference to frontiers unknown to man. However, his pronunciation of the word as 'ass-tronaut' identifies the ass or posterior that is emphasized in anti-male homosexual debate and places this treatise squarely in the middle of the anti-male homosexual debate. He states that his rocket/penis will not be flown through any black hole that negates 'breathing.' Again, the particularities of Jamaican Creole suggest an alternative meaning – that this rocket/penis will not enter this black hole because he cannot breathe/breed in space. The barren black hole swallows all and eliminates the productive capacity that is highly prized as a signifier of true masculinity and there is no room for breeding. Therefore, he will stay grounded on the productive soil of earth (read female) with his satellite pole/penis. Throughout the song Marshall reinforces the point 'I am not an astronaut so I am not going to Uranus,' which is simultaneously read as 'I am not an ass-tronaut so I am not going to your-anus.' Of interest is the use of the word 'man, throughout, which in this instance specifically refers to the masculine gender and not to human beings as a generic group.

Nearly 20 years earlier, Lloyd Lovindeer's 1987 *'Mad Puss Tonic'* used a similar strategy of repetition (forgot, forgot, forgot) and double entendre (forgot/faggot) to poke fun at and negate male homosexuality:

Come! Some girls will have to wait in line
Bow! Cause a real man is so hard to find (like me)
Everyday I tell them don't bend down
But they don't listen to my sound
I sing and preach to them a lot
They don't remember, they forgot, forgot, forgot.

Lovindeer documents the lengthening cues of women that result from the dwindling numbers of 'real' men. The term 'don't bend down' suggests a sexual focus on the rear which is at once hetero and homo. Once the male homosexual is called into being, Lovindeer introduces the play on the word 'forgot,' which is repeated for emphasis forgot/faggot, forgot/faggot, forgot/faggot.

Almost two decades removed from Lovindeer's treatise, Wayne Marshall's contemporary dancehall discourse 'I Forgot Them' and 'Mi Nuh Astronaut' reflects a critical loop in the lyrical constructions and representations of male homosexuals in dancehall culture. This patent attempt at 'political correctness' suggests an enlightened awareness of the negative perceptions that abound globally in the debate on the inflammatory and violent dancehall lyrics aimed at male homosexual/ity in the local/national sphere. Thus, dancehall is caught between local/national perceptions of politically correct sexual behaviours and practices and the tensions between acceptable modes of public discussion in the local/national and international spheres. In this regard, dancehall's discursive paths uphold rigid patriarchal ideals while attempting to carve new modes of hegemonic engagement with localized visions of Jamaican masculinity.[22]

These transformations in popular dancehall culture are brokered within the social and political movements in the society. For example, the call for a removal of the Buggery Act from Jamaica's legislative framework by a few of Jamaica's politicians, including Delroy Chuck, then opposition spokesman on justice, who insisted that the law had no place in private morality[23] when the parliamentary committee on human resources and social development, chaired by then junior Education Minister Dr Donald Rhodd, proposed a debate on legalizing homosexuality and prostitution as a matter of public health in July 2005.[24] This progressive tone may be a reaction by Jamaica's legislature to global pressure precipitated by the clash between Jamaican dancehall artistes and gay and human rights activists and the publication of the controversial Human Rights Watch report on homophobia and HIV/AIDS in Jamaica (November 2004). Conversely, this progressive tone may articulate the 'currently accepted strategy' (Connell 1995, 77) of hegemonic masculinity in the face of changing conditions of local patriarchy in its conversations with the global terrain of sexualities and accepted sexual practices.

Related discussions about male homosexuality continue to appear in Jamaican print and electronic media, usually in reaction to a topical or controversial incident related to male homosexuality, as with the prison riots of 1997 and the clash between dancehall artistes and international gay rights and human rights groups in 2004 and 2005. These media discussions, including letters to the editor and opinion pieces in the print media, influence and inflect the dissemination of public anti-male homosexual discourses in Jamaica. For example, one Letter of the Day in the *Daily Gleaner*, entitled 'Gov't Right to reject blatant demands' (November 2004), highlighted the outright rejection of homosexuality that colours many Jamaican debates on this issue. In his response to the controversial parliamentary debate, noted journalist and religious leader Ian Boyne highlighted his stance on the matter in his *Sunday Gleaner* opinion piece en titled 'Boomerang – Dancehall's chickens come home to roost'; while weekly columnist, Melville Cooke denounced 'homofibia' (Cooke 2004). Other strands of debate in the newspaper addressed the hypocritical role of the private sector in supporting homophobic output in dancehall culture (Johnson 2004), while others attempted to unearth the sociocultural linkages between dancehall's homophobia and Jamaican life and gender (Hope 2004a and 2004b; Simms 2004; Taylor 2004).

The debates in the halls of power in Jamaica share the same space as Prime Minister Bruce Golding's controversial anti-gay statements on the BBC in May 2008 and the responses to same liberally documented in Jamaica's print and electronic media.[25] MP Ernie Smith's controversial statements in his contribution to the debate on the Sexual Offences Bill and the heated public response to his statements[26] underscored Prime Minister Golding's final stance against any changes to the Buggery Law during the closing of the debate on sexual offences in March 2009.[27] Nonetheless this debate on same-sex engagement in the Jamaican parliament suggests the need for continued public engagement with what is considered a highly controversial and very political issue deeply rooted in the varied social, political and cultural traditions of Jamaica that coalesce within and emanate from the dancehall. The clash of dancehall artistes with international pressure points that seek to reverse the trend of anti-male homosexual lyrics is a continuing trend which at the time of this work was highlighted by Elephant Man's challenges in Europe and the intense activity generated around Buju Banton's 2009 'Rasta Got Love' tour. Like Elephant Man and Buju Banton, many dancehall artistes face cancelled concerts and tour dates, picketing and lobbying by gay groups and intense negative publicity and smear campaigns orchestrated by groups supporting the gay lifestyle.

Conclusion

The contemporary topography of dancehall culture's explicit anti-male homosexual dialogue is a direct result of its historical, religious, legislative, social and gendered circumstances. Since the early 1990s, dancehall's anti-male homosexual discourses communicated an anti-feminizing ethos in response to the early movement of the homosexual male body from the hidden corners and cloaked spaces of Jamaican life and culture to the heterosexual public space of Jamaica. Public male homosexuality tampers with the definitions of masculine identity through sex, i.e. conquering of the female other – the vagina and erodes an important site of heterosexual male identity in Jamaica where marginalized men who are stifled by unemployment, lack of education and economic opportunities can fulfill their productive impulses by planting their 'seed' in the wombs of their women.

Yet, dancehall culture's vocal 'outing' and persistent invocations against male homosexuality transgress against the preferred hegemonic method of silent erasure that renders the male homosexual as an invisible and powerless figure in Jamaica. In dancehall culture, loud and vocal denunciations of male homosexuality perceptually drive male homosexuality into remission, and consistently projecting vociferous and extreme anti-male homosexual discourses across the male dancehall body re-positions the dancehall male as everything that his homosexual counterpart is not. Where the male homosexual is discoursed as effeminate, the dancehall male is discoursed as macho; where the male homosexual is discoursed as weak, the dancehall male is discoursed as strong; where the male homosexual is discoursed as in perpetual fear of the vagina, the dancehall male is discoursed as in eternal control of the vagina. As a result, where the male homosexual is emplaced as feminized and powerless, the dancehall male is called forth as masculine and powerful. Dancehall culture's vocal and extreme anti-homosexual lyrics are a part of the wider terrain of Jamaica's hegemonic, patriarchal structure as its consistent and extreme invocations vocally and ritualistically empower the

Jamaican male by any means. Consistent lyrical renunciation, denunciation and metaphorical assassination of the male homosexual provide a foundation upon which the incarnation of dancehall's masculine anti-hero, the anti-male homosexual man, is raised. Thus, the discursive representation of the powerful, masculinized dancehall body is incarnated and elevated on the cadaver of the powerless, feminized male homosexual body. Conversely, in traditional Jamaican culture, the male homosexual is cast as an invisible being and this empowers the hegemonic rendering of heterosexual masculinity. In dancehall culture's battle with the male homosexuality, it is the lyrical and symbolic visibility of the male homosexual that empowers the heterosexual dancehall male. The male homosexual is named, called forth and constantly revisioned. At the same time, this revisioning of the male homosexual in dancehall culture creates a tension with the hegemonic structures from which dancehall takes it cues.

Consequently, in a truly ambivalent twist, these extreme and traditional anti-male homosexual discourses in Jamaican dancehall culture simultaneously denounce male homosexuality while calling into being a form of heterosexual masculinity which is, of necessity, eternally bound to a visible incarnation of its once invisible nemesis. This anti-male homosexual discourse reflects dancehall's dialogue with initial reversions in its conceptualization of its hegemonic structures even while dancehall is labelled as rabidly homophobic by homosexual Jamaicans, foreigners and outsiders to Jamaican culture. In today's dancehall, fashioned, coiffed dancehall men with 'bleached out faces' dance and prance onstage in choreographed groups while wearing skintight pants and flamboyant costumes that reflect a creeping homosexual aesthetic. These dancehall men display playful camaraderie and high levels of homosocial bonding. These signals of the transitions underway in the contemporary construction of dancehall's masculine exemplars are examined at length in chapter 6. In the final analysis, dancehall's vocal response to male homosexuality upholds hegemonic masculinity from below by condemning the existence of male homosexuality, but simultaneously breaches the accepted modes of silent engagement preferred by the makers of hegemony from above and so dancehall's reactivity is at once hegemonic and transgressive.

The following chapter analyses the role of 'Bling Bling' or conspicuous consumption in dancehall culture as a site for the promotion of another form of masculinity that is brokered on the hegemonic element of wealth and status. I examine the overt presentation of fashioned and costumed men as one other element in the progressive development of the deepening tensions within the ambivalent variations of masculinities in dancehall culture and argue for the strengthening of dancehall's developing dialectic of masculinity.

CHAPTER 5

'HAFFI BLING AND CLEAN': CELEBRATING MASCULINE CONSUMPTION AND POSING

'Up inna di video yuh haff i bling and clean'.
Elephant Man, *Pon di River*, 2003.

'Right now di man dem a run dung di hypeness'.[1]
Jack Sowah, Dancehall Videographer.

Introduction

This chapter extends the discussion on dancehall's masculine exemplars and their relationship to the process of traditional hegemonic masculinity in Jamaica. In so doing, I examine the use of conspicuous consumption ('Bling Bling') and posing by men to refashion the male body as visible and powerful in dancehall culture. This is achieved in the first instance through the employment of spectacular, sartorial and conspicuous fashion and style, and related accessories, as status-generating by increasing groups of dancehall men. I wish to lodge the caveat that what may be perceived as a stereotypical and monolithic rendering of conspicuous consumption or posing as projecting a variant of dancehallized masculinity in this chapter is but a specific association that aims to isolate, and thus capture, another form of masculinity that occupied a dominant position in dancehall's configuration of masculinity. This particular application helps to deconstruct the constituent elements of this masculine exemplar and analyse its relation to the process of hegemonic masculinity in Jamaica.

Bling Bling and Dancehall Masculinity

Modes of dress play a central role in the social construction and maintenance of identity, particularly in contemporary societies that are progressively more dominated by images. Post-modern modes of dress and fashion, particularly among males, have significantly erased the long-standing modern paradigm of drably clothed and accessorized males in contrast to adorned females (Flügel 1930, 110–21). In this eclectic mix of postmodern styles of dress and fashion, the use of sartorial fashion and styles is an important method of claiming masculine status and personhood within the globalised swirl of images, ideals and identities that form the contemporary terrain on which raced and gendered identities are constructed and maintained.[2]

In line with this discussion, we note, Hebdige's analysis in *Subculture* which explored the use of style and fashion by various subcultural groups (teds, mods, skinheads, Rastas, punks) as a conjunctural historical moment in the 1960s and 1970s that was marked by the existence of a variety of English male subcultures. In the context of Black masculinities, Majors and Billson's (1992) work on African American masculinity in the USA, examines the notion of 'cool' or 'cool pose' as a Black man's cultural signature that often acts as his only source of pride, dignity and worth in a culture that measures and ranks success, status and personhood by the presence or absence of particular outward status symbols of materialism and title. The 'cool' persona is marked by particular noted mannerisms including physical posture, style of clothing, dialect, walking style, greeting behaviours, and overall demeanor. This cool pose exhibits a form of masculinity that struggles to compensate for a perceived lack in the markers of success and masculinity and many of these mediated images are today cleverly marketed to a sophisticated populace through the electronic and print media. This approach and attitude is distinctively replicated and projected in dancehall culture's images of masculinity. As a part of this imaged discussion, Wernick (1987) examines and demonstrates the flexibility of the dominant conceptions and portrayals of masculinity through his analysis of popular advertisements geared towards an ambivalent masculine audience. These advertisements encode images that simultaneously project a hard masculinity and a narcissistic/almost feminized version of male identity. This projection of a paradoxical hardened/softened or hardcore/feminized masculinity is discussed more at length in the following chapter. However, this paradoxical presentation of masculinity also flits briefly across the images that project an almost narcissistic engagement with conspicuous masculine posing and materialistic fashion. As a part of this discussion it is useful to define the term 'bling bling,' especially in its relationship to dancehall culture.

The MSN Encarta Online dictionary defines *bling bling* as an adjective that means – 'rich: having or displaying ostentatious material wealth (slang) [Probably an imitation of the sound of a cash register].' However, colloquially, Jamaicans identify the ringing up of the cash register as a *chi-ching* sound, and not as *bling bling*. Consequently, dancehall dancer/poser/artiste Chi-Ching-Ching draws his name from this idea of the 'money sound' where, since 2008 'money' is made visibly important in dancehall's explicit and multiple lyrical debates on money as material and social advancement.

A more useful definition of the term *bling bling* (which entered the Oxford English Dictionary in 2003) encapsulates the aura of the 'ghetto fabulous' in the USA where it is idealized in concert with the music and culture of hip hop. In linguistic terms, bling is an ideophone intended to evoke the 'sound' of light hitting silver, platinum, or diamonds. In this regard, it is not onomatopoeia, because the act of jewellery shining does not actually make a sound. The form bling-bling is a case of reduplication for emphasis. According to the Wikipedia Online Dictionary, the concept, of 'bling bling,' 'is often associated with either the working and lower middle classes, or the newly wealthy, implying that the concept of riches and shiny items is something new to them. Used in this sense, it can be derogatory, suggesting lack of good taste.' Where the term 'bling bling' or 'bling' is used in this chapter or elsewhere in this work, it is mainly adjectival and captures the essence of the ostentatious aesthetics and conspicuous consumption that works itself across the bodies of ordinary, often poor, working class individuals, in the form of expensive, brand name clothing, hairstyles, shoes, jewellery, cars and other methods of accessorizing and enhancing the body, including expensive cellular phones, and the public consumption of expensive liquors. The significant element of 'blinging,' 'to bling' or to be 'bling bling' is the public and conspicuous nature of this ostentatious consumptive aesthetic where it must be made visible and must be visualized by onlookers to generate and validate status for its bearer.

In Jamaica, the term 'bling bling' or 'bling' is intertwined with ideas of the flashy and pervasive urban, working class popular music culture of the day – dancehall – and consequently the terms bling bling, bling, and dancehall are often used synonymously in Jamaica. If it is 'bling,' it is dancehall and if it is dancehall it is 'bling bling.' As noted in the Wikepedia notation regarding 'bling bling' in Jamaica, this concept is also loaded with notions of impropriety and poor taste in the use of and response to newly acquired riches by the working or lower middle classes or those who have recently acquired wealth. In Jamaica's dancehall the use of 'bling bling' and cool pose to mediate status and masculinity has gained increasing popularity. Since the explosion of dancehall culture into the central spaces of Jamaican life and culture in the early 1980s, dancehall adherents have employed extreme representations of sartorial dress, fashion and style to forcefully demonstrate idealized and idolized representations of wealth and disposable income, and correspondingly to claim ascribed portions of personhood and identity which these materialistic displays purportedly generate. This ritualistic practice is a part of the wider Jamaican socio-political environment where class and status, often brokered on wealth and social visibility become primary determinants of one's gendered identity.

The notion of 'ritualism' is identified by Merton (1938 & 1957) in his work on anomie as one of the responses to a situation in which, because of structural constraints, like race and class, individuals are unable to achieve the goals and values held high in the society.[3] In this regard, men who are socialized to believe that they are expected to be breadwinners and leaders, but whose socio-economic status renders them unable to effectively perform their economic and social roles, often fall into the chasm between social status and economic prosperity that is often promoted by ruling groups as a strategy for dominance. Consequently, status which is often temporary or temporal is proffered and accepted in lieu of real social mobility and economic prosperity. The persistent tendency of the Black Caribbean male to pose and posture on the basis of little substance is a continuing legacy in the lives of Caribbean men from the lower and working classes. This legacy contributes to a ritualistic engagement in what one colleague identified as 'rituals of poverty.' In this framework, expensive, imported clothing has consistently played (and continues to play) a major role in defining high status and personhood in Jamaica[4] and, correspondingly, fashion, adornment, spectacle and sartorial excess play an important role in dancehall culture. Where dancehall culture is concerned, however, the application of feminist lenses has ensured that women's sartorial practices have been a site of vigorous debate on morality and sexuality. Dancehall Queens have been immortalized in discourses and academic debates on dancehall dress and female sexuality.[5] The role of masculine dress and posing has received far little attention, even while it demands a corresponding critical and analytical focus.

While the male artistes defined the lyrical and performative space, it was the female patron who reigned supreme in dancehall costuming and display with her flashy fashions and make-up, her hairstyles and colourful wigs, her jewellery and accessories, and her erotic display. This was particularly true during the earliest stages of the dancehall's evolution in the early 1980s. During this era, the greater percentage of male adherents in the dancehall replicated the traditional masculine norms of dress and fashion that guided male behaviour and practice in Jamaica, in concert with the hegemonic imperatives towards wealth from the traditional classes, by choosing an understated and less visible position from which to display their often fancy and well-decorated costumes (e.g. linen and lace) and heavy gold jewellery. This laid-back male display has been fairly constant with few interruptions by popular artistes like Pinchers and Shabba Ranks or icons like the late Gerald 'Bogle' Levy with their prominent display of male fashion and style in the 1980s and early 1990s.

(c) 1992 The Gleaner Co. Ltd.

Shabba Ranks in fancy dress

However, since the late 1990s there has been an erosion of the borders between dancehall's masculine and feminine aesthetics, particularly with regard to costuming and public display by dancehall adherents and audience members. Moving strategically towards dancehall central spaces, men in the dancehall strive to publicly display and signify their personhood by using available and accessible means. These include an emphasis on feminine aesthetic rituals, originally coded as feminine and, therefore, taboo for the real, hardcore men who dominate(d) the spaces of dancehall culture. While it may have been the norm in more cosmopolitan settings, in Jamaica and particularly within the dancehall, this convergence of narcissistic style with what have historically been coded as feminized aesthetic rituals is at once complementary and contestatory in the constitution of dancehall masculinities. Indeed, this transition is deemed most striking as hardcore dancehall men are touted as the most prominent guardians of heterosexual masculinity from feminine contamination in all its forms, including subtle signals such as a dalliance in feminine aesthetic practices or 'sensitive' feminine behaviours and practices. Despite these taboos, however, dancehall culture's hardcore, heterosexual image has undergone several transitions and its current manifestations challenge the traditional ideals of heterosexual masculinity in Jamaica. This transition includes a movement from the 1980s/1990s dalliance with multiple and heavy gold necklaces, pendants and rings[6] complemented by linen and lace costumes, to the platinum and 'ice' (diamond) craze of the late 1990s (a cross-fertilization with American hip-hop culture), to the current manifestation of dancehall male fashion is the male dancehall 'modeller' who complements his jewellery with expensive brand name clothing. Many of these men also favour skin-tight, feminized pants, pastel colours, and feminized hairstyles as components of their fashionable costumes. This appropriation of feminine aesthetics and the resultant blurring of gendered borders is discussed in more depth in chapter 6. However, as a component of this costume of bling and conspicuous consumption, the dancehall male body is adorned with myriad accessories that all together present an aura of luxury, wealth and suggest a corresponding social status. In dancehall culture, there are several material accessories that are important constituent components of the costume of 'bling bling.' The most prominent include brand name motor vehicles, cellular phones, expensive liquors and wines, and clothing, and these are now examined.

The adulation for particular brand name vehicles and late model SUV or sports car in dancehall and among Jamaica's underclasses has its own historical trajectory which may or may not often parallel the ideas of luxury automobiles in cosmopolitan metropoles. Dancehall culture's love affair with brand name motor vehicles was presaged in the 1980s by the high regard given to persons who could drive rental motor vehicles with the conspicuous white license plates displaying green license numbers beginning with the tell-tale 'RR.' Since then, the trajectory of vehicles identified as status-generating has moved from through the 1990s to vehicles like the 190E Mercedes Benz and the Nissan Maxima Sedan. Buju Banton's early 1990s hit *Massa God World a Run*/How the World a Run documented the perceived prestige of the 190E Mercedes Benz thus:

> *The rich man have the dallas an nuh want gi wih some*
> *Braggadocios and boasy talk him a fling dung*
> *A pear 190E Benz him bring dung,*
> *Sell the most crack the coke heroin and opium*
> *Dem nuh want see ghetto youth elevate out of the slum*

[The rich man has the dollars (money) and does not want to give us some of it]
[He is a braggadocio, speaking in loud and boasting terms]
[He imports only 190E Benz motor vehicles]
[He sells the most crack, cocaine, heroin and opium]
[They (i.e. rich men) do not wish to see ghetto youths elevated from the slums]

In the foregoing verse, Buju Banton identifies the 190E Benz as a vehicle which was perceived as one visible component of a 'rich man's' identity at that time in early 1990s Jamaica when owning a motor vehicle was an impossible dream for Jamaica's working classes and many ghetto youths.

However, the liberalization of the motor vehicle industry and the entry of a developing used-car import sector in the late 1990s provided a platform for the expansion of motor vehicle ownership and access for many Jamaicans. This expanded access and ownership resulted in a corresponding widening of dancehall's deliberations with and on brand name motor vehicles as an accessible component of an accessorized identity. Thus, this component of dancehall's 'bling bling' costume expanded and took on greater form. In the decade of the 2000s dancehall's brand name motor vehicle of choice has moved through the Mach II Sedan, the Escalade Truck, the Ford F150 Truck, the Lexus sedan and SUV, the Hummer, the BMW X5, the Range Rover SUV and the BMW X6. Macka Diamond's money-driven litany in *Lexus and Benz* documents several of these vehicles identified as lavish and status-generating in this era:

> *So tell Elephant gyal anaconda ah go share*
> *Cause mi want siddung inna di X5 chair*
> *Kartel di rims pon you truck look dear*
> *And mi well want feel when you fling in di gear*
> *Babycham Avalanche give mi nightmare*
> *Mi kin ketch ah fire any time it appear*
> *General B Surf nah go nowhere*
> *An mi feel like ah it a pop dung him career*
> *Marshall have a Lexus so mi nuh haffi tek bus*
> *Mi woulda radder con him off inna mi bed fuss*
> *Dis ya gal yah love car so much mi woulda drive from yah so to Texas*

[So tell Elephant Man's girlfriend that his anaconda (penis/sexual favours) will have to be shared]
[Because I would like to sit in the (his) X5 chair]
[(Vybz) Kartel, the rims on your truck look expensive]
[And I really would like to feel how/when you fling in the gears]
[Babycham's Avalanche is giving me nightmares]
[And my skin catches afire whenever it appears]
[General B's Surf is going nowhere]
[And I feel certain that it is the reason why his career has stagnated]
[(Wayne) Marshall has a Lexus so I do not have to ride the bus]
[As I would prefer to con him into having sex with me]
[This woman (I) loves cars so much, I would drive from here to Texas (i.e. drive very far distances)]

Macka Diamond's use of sexual innuendos and double entendre underlines the notion that these particular vehicles are also 'chick-magnets' which men can use to attract women, or to which women are attracted, thus offering to their male drivers the underlying promise of sexual favours. For example, the identification of Elephant Man's anaconda, a well-known dancehall pseudonym for a long and deadly penis with the notion that it will have to be shared is an outright promise of sexual favours, in concert with the notion of 'sitting in the X5 chair.' The fact that her 'skin catches afire' whenever Babycham's Avalance appears, suggests the sexual desire, i.e. heat, which overtakes her whenever Babycham and his vehicle are in sight. Of course, this sexual desire that generates such intense heat must be cooled.

In addition, Macka Diamond's suggestion that General B's Hilux Surf is 'going nowhere' encodes the negation of this vehicle as a status-generating brand. This is coupled with Macka's certainty that this out of time motor vehicle is main reason why the artiste's career 'pop dung' or has stagnated and underlies the negation of this vehicle as one that could generate status and mobility for dancehall superstars in particular or men in general. The chorus of the *Lexus and Benz* song, specifically highlights the Lexus and Benz as brands of choice for Macka Diamond and parallels Timberlee's 2007 dancehall hit, *Bubble Like Soup* which identified the BMW X5 as her vehicle of choice while negating the cheaper Nissan Sunny motor car, reserved for use as route taxis, or for those 'going nowhere' thus:

> *Hot gal ah hot gal, sweet like ah honey*
> *X to di 5 mi nuh drive inna Sunny*
>
> [Hot girls are hot girls (we are) as sweet as honey]
> [X to the 5 (i.e. BMW X5) we do not drive in Nissan Sunny motor cars]

The relationship between particular motor vehicles and the access to female bodies (which also denotes masculine status) is noted in Macka Diamond's and Timberlee's treatises, and Babycham's *Many Many* discusses the role that material objects and money play in attracting women to men. Babycham also highlights the false images that are sometimes projected by men on the backs of these conspicuous material assets, which end up entrapping women in their webs. One example is the omnipresent Mercedes Benz motor car:

> *Yuh see mi modeller friend name when name Danny*
> *Whe drive di criss Benz ah him bredda dem send it*
> *Beggy Beggy Jenny and har friend Shelly*
> *Get trick through them check say him have few penny*
>
> [Do you know my modeller friend Tommy?]
> [Who drives the shiny, new Mercedes Benz? His brothers sent it from abroad]
> [Well, Jenny, the one who likes to beg a lot, and her friend Shelly]
> [Got tricked because they thought that he was rich]

In essence, Babycham suggests that these women, Jenny and Shelly, were tricked into giving sexual favours to Danny because they believed that, since he drove a Mercedes Benz motor vehicle, he was indeed a rich man with status who could grant them financial favours in return for sex. Danny was really a 'modeller', i.e. a poser with little or no material wealth and corresponding status.

In another instance, Bounty Killer's *Benz and Bimmer* immortalizes the Mercedes Benz and BMW motor vehicles and metaphorically aligns these brand name motor vehicles to the most attractive female forms that he (and other men) find desirable. In the chorus of *Benz and Bimmer* he notes:

> *Gal dem have di face,*
> *Gal dem have the figure*
> *Remind me of the Benz, the Lexus and the Bimmer*
> *To have this girl would be my pleasure*
> *She is so precious like the gold inna mi treasure.. Again!*

> [The girls/women have the (prettiest) face]
> [The girls/women have the (sexiest) figure]
> [They remind me of the Benz, Lexus or BMW motor vehicles]
> [To possess this girl would be a great pleasure for me]
> [She is as precious as the gold that is in my treasures]

Thus, for Bounty Killer, a woman who is sexy and desirable is akin to a brand name motor vehicle and must be possessed as a rare treasure. This marriage of the female body to the most desired brand name motor vehicles underlines the masculine ethos that strives for status and 'respect' via approved heterosexual methods and is often replicated in many media advertising campaigns.

Additionally, the response of women to men who drive these vehicles as well as the high levels of adulation, social respect and status that are granted to these men by their peers, remains an integral component of the thrust to adopt these vehicles as one facet of the costume of conspicuous consumption that generates status in dancehall culture. One should note that dancehall culture's endorsement of particular motor vehicles as status-generating is often paralleled by a similar ethos amongst the icons of Jamaica's underworld and this drives the positive response that is generated from ownership of or simply being the driver of one of these vehicles. The majority of dancehall's superstars ensure that they are driving these brand name motor vehicles as a part of their flashy and conspicuous costumes and these vehicles make the rounds in the music videos of prominent dancehall artistes. Of course, dancehall artiste Mr Lex, formerly Lexxus, drew his name from this particular ethos. Another important component of this costume of 'bling bling' is the cellular phone.

While it remains for many Jamaicans a mode of communication, the cellular phone also functions as another conspicuous facet of dancehall's propensity to accessorize and costume. The democratization of cellular telephone service ensued with the introduction of the Irish company, Digicel, into Jamaica in 1999. This signalled the end of Cable and Wireless' (formerly Telecommunications of Jamaica and now LIME) monopoly over and stranglehold of access to telephone service in Jamaica. In their work, Horst and Miller (2006) skirt around the relationship between phone culture and status, yet the identification of telephone access with status in Jamaica has a long history that pre-dates the introduction of cellular telephony. The propensity to give selective access to particular resources based on a rigid social hierarchy in Jamaica was also evident in the type of telephone access granted to ordinary Jamaicans prior to the advent of cellular telephony.

Over a period of nearly four decades, the single, monopoly telephone provider in Jamaica[7] maintained a rigid cap on the amount of landlines that existed in each community and most landlines were found in homes of socially prominent individuals, mid-level professionals and established business and public sector entities. Limited access was provided for other members of the society via strategically placed call boxes, or at the few locations across the country where individuals could visit, book and pay for a telephone call. Indeed, there was a perception of a hierarchy of telephone access where those with some status, social or otherwise, were granted access to land lines in the comfort of their homes, while those without status, i.e. ordinary people, begged or paid for a call from their family members with land lines, used company phones to make personal calls at work, joined long lines at community call boxes, or made a trip to the Jamaica Telephone Company/Cable and Wireless/JAMINTEL Offices to access this service. Thus, for many Jamaicans, the correlation with social status and easy access to telephone service was clear and many took it for granted that selective access to telephone service was simply the replication of the rigid Jamaican social hierarchy at work. With the introduction of the Irish company, Digicel, into Jamaica in 1999, the explosion of cellular telephony at the turn of the millennium found fertile ground upon which to grant democratic access to telephone communication and to simultaneously market and sell ideas of high status and egalitarianism ('You too can be a part of this network'). The result of this historical marriage of status to telephone access has been an overwhelming boom in the rise of subscribers to Digicel's mainly pre-paid network and a dwindling interest in Cable and Wireless' (LIME's) cellular and other offerings.

Dancehall culture's conspicuous material costume gravitated particularly to this status/communicative network which immediately granted to members of the dancehall and working class community a dual mechanism for generating status and ensuring full communicative access in one fell swoop. Thus, within the confines of the status/communicative network brokered on access to cellular telephony, dancehall adherents and members of Jamaica's underclasses go to great lengths to sport what is identified at different points in time as the most popular and expensive, late model cellular phone. Aided by carefully crafted marketing campaigns that tap into the working class desire for status that is often brokered on displays of material wealth and posing, the hype of cell phone accessorizing as a component of dancehall and Jamaican identity has moved from the Motorola Star Tac®, the Motorola Razr® to the Blackberry Pearl®, Blackberry Curve®, Blackberry Bold® and the Blackberry Storm®. As at the date of this work, the IPhone has begun to gain incremental ground as another 'bling,' high priced telephone. One must note that the price of these telephone instruments range from a low of J$25,000.00 to a high of J$50,000.00[8] in a country where the minimum wage stood at J$3,700.00 as at the time of this work.

As a part of dancehall culture's insistence on documenting the variety of themes that coalesce within its borders, in 1999/2000 Dancehall Artiste Mr Lex (aka Lexxus) immortalized the rise of cell phone culture and documented the popularity of the Motorola Star Tac cell phone in his *Ring*

Mi Cellie:
Mi ketch a gyal inna di act, bout she want tief mi Star Tac
Den shi have di nerves fi waan come check mi back
Shi crack. Anytime mi tell a gal say pack

Skirt, blouse, shoes, wrap... brap
Suh mi have a gal a tic-tac
Grandma come in and come ketch wi shi shock
Shi can't believe a har grand pickney dat
Ha haha ha... hey better dan dat

Chorus
True di gal hear mi pon di radio si mi pon di tellie
(Ring ring, ring, ring) Ring off mi cellie
One bag a gal want come rub dung mi belly
Antoinette, Kelly, Suzy, Shelly

[I caught a girl in the act of trying to steal my Star Tac (cellular phone)]
[Then she had the nerve to wish to re-visit me]
[She is mad! Whenever I tell a girl to pack]
[Skirt, blouse, shoes, wrap, (i.e. all her clothing is wrapped)]
[So, anyway, I have a girl doing the tic tac (i.e. having sex)]
[Grandma came in and caught us...she was shocked]
[She couldn't believe that was her grandchild (in action)]
[Ha hahah, hey even better than that]

[Because the girl heard me on the radio and saw me on the television]
[Ring ring ring ring, She is ringing my cellular phone extensively]
[A lot of girls/women want to rub my stomach (get intimate with me)]
[(Including) Antoinette, Kelly, Suzy and Shelly]

The propensity of dancehall's masculine treatises to use the feminine body as a site of empowerment is reflected in Mr Lex's use of the female as first one who wants to steal his Star Tac phone and second in the chorus as intent on contacting him by cellular phone because of his superstar status (i.e. being heard on radio and seen on television).

Bounty Killer's *Cellular Phone* also highlights the utility and visibility of the cellular phone in the lives of ordinary individuals and its value as a tool for easy communication thus:

Excuse, pass mi cellular phone,
Mek mi call Antoinette and Simone
Tell them nuh move a muscle I'm coming home
To take a trip down inna the the love zone

[Excuse, pass my cellular phone]
[So that I may call Antoinette and Simone]
[Tell them not to move a single muscle as I am coming home]
[To take a trip down into the love zone (i.e. to make love]

As with his discussion in the song *Benz & Bimma*, Bounty Killer brings the female body into a relationship with the cellular phone, where, in this instance, the cellular phone plays an important role in ensuring that female bodies are made available for male pleasure. Thus, the cellular phone plays a critical role in male-female relationships and facilitation of what may be termed 'booty calls.' The fact that control over female bodies is another route to male empowerment is reiterated here.

In a more recent vein, the Blackberry fetish that has overtaken Jamaica and dancehall culture is debated in disc jockey Richie D and dancehall artistes Leftside and Raine Seville's *What's Your Pin*? Using sexual metaphors and double entendre, the song discusses a man who sports an IPhone rather than a BlackBerry® and who will, therefore, be unable to 'pick up' as many girls because he does not have a BlackBerry® with the requisite Pin. The Blackberry® Pin is a unique code made up of letters and numbers that belongs to each Blackberry® phone. Owners of Blackberry® phones can use these pins to extend their communication through the use of a feature called the Blackberry® Messenger that allows the digital transfer of text, photos and voicenotes. The Blackberry® Pin therefore functions as an extension of the Blackberry® community, broadening the scope beyond voice calling. The word Pin has therefore gained new meaning and the word 'ping' has joined the lexicon as a verb 'to ping.' Indeed, it has become the norm to see individuals in meetings, functions, sporting events and at parties busy texting and pinging, oblivious to the individuals or events around them. Many use this facility to converse with individuals in close proximity and thus camouflage their secret discussions in plain sight.

In the first verse of *What's Your Pin?*, Richie D explores the initial exchange with a woman named Cherry and the potential for transfer of information and intimate activity that presents itself upon the transfer of Blackberry® pins:

Dis girl Cherry
Dis girl a met from back in January
Never get di number but di pin to di berry

She a query, say she gonna ping me when she ready
Den she send mi pictures of di guineps and di cherry
Say she merry
But mi wonda wheh dis gal a study
A tell mi say she want me send her pictures of mi body
Gal no worry, baby just come over in a hurry
Cause you Curve inna different category

[This girl Cherry]
[This girl I met from back in January]
[I did not get her telephone number, only the pin number to her Blackberry phone]
[She was asking a lot of questions and said she would ping me when she was ready]
[Then she sent me pictures of the guineps and the cherry (i.e. her breasts and vagina)]
[Said she was merry (horny)]
[But I was wondering what exactly this girl/woman was up to]
[She said she wanted me to send her pictures of my body]
[Girl don't worry, baby just come over (to my place) hurriedly]

[Because your Curve (sexy body) is special]

The chorus of *What's Your Pin?* reinforces the importance of the Blackberry® Pin as a communicative stand-in for the prized telephone number. It identifies some of the more popular Blackberry® phones in use and some features of the Blackberry® such as Blackberry® Messaging and the ability to send voicenotes and Pictures, which the Pin provides:

Chorus
What's your pin?
It's just a BlackBerry ting,
The Storm, di Bold, di Pearl, di Javelin.
What's your pin?
BB messaging.
Voicenotes and picture sending

Leftside builds on Richie D's initial suggestions in the first verse and extends this through dancehall-specific metaphors that position the phone and the female body in a subject and intimate relationship that makes them available for male contact:

Mi step to her big and bold compliment her on her Curve,
And tell her sey inna fi har lane mi want fi merge,

She sey can I get your pin?
Specify which pin
The one fi di Berry or di one to mek yuh merry?
So she ping me and ah tell mi say she ready fi di Storm
Afta mi leff di club you know ah fi har yard mi gawn
I'm not Michael Jackson but I'm gonna rock her world
She get so wet when I'm touching up di Pearl

[I approach her boldly and compliment her on her Curve (phone/body)]
[And I tell her that I want to merge in her lane]
[She says, can I get your pin?]
[(I say) Be specific, which pin?]
[Is it the one for the Blackberry or is it the one to make you merry?]
[So she pinged me and told me that she was ready for the Storm (i.e. sex)]
[(So) After I left the club you know I went to her house]
[I am not Michael Jackson but I am going to rock her world]
[She got so wet when I am touching the Pearl (vagina)]

In this instance, Leftside uses the metaphor of the Curve to represent both the Blackberry® phone of that model and the female body, which is often identified as curvy and thus sexy. Additionally, the play on the word 'pin' suggests both a Blackberry® pin as a communicative facet and the pin as a sharp, pointed and phallic instrument that stands in for the penis, which is the one 'to make you merry.' The Storm, another Blackberry® phone becomes a metaphor for 'stormy' sex, and the Pearl as used translates into the vagina.

In the final verse of the song, Richie D underscores the notion that having a Blackberry® phone (regardless of its model) is a critical component of a 'hot' or fashionable identity:

Put up yuh Blackberry cause you know say dat you hot
If a IPhone you have den you whack

[Hold your Blackberry high because you know that you are in vogue and stylish]
[If you have an IPhone then you are not in vogue (dowdy)]

Thus, the status-generating Blackberry® is perceived as an important accessory that makes you fashionable and stylish, while owning an IPhone purportedly relegates its owners to the fringes of this stylish and 'bling' community. Most importantly, throughout *What's Your Pin?* the Blackberry® phone is discoursed as a critical resource in extending male sexuality and status by granting access to a wider community of female bodies with the promise of sex.

Additionally, as with the preceding discussion on brand name motor vehicles in dancehall culture, a critical component of this communicative/ consumptive fetish is the identification of one particular phone instrument as 'hot' or expensive, flamboyant and status-generating at different points in time, even while other instruments from the same or other brand may sport heftier price tags. As noted in the foregoing, this selective identification is often enhanced by carefully crafted marketing campaigns that imply a nexus between a fashionable, hip and in-vogue, high-status personality and the particular phone identified in the marketing campaign which has particular resonance in Jamaica's status-hungry society. Indeed, while communication is one facet of cellular telephony, there is usually little focus on the actual cost of making calls from one provider or another or the level of service provided by the telephone company. This is clearly evidenced by the emphasis on phone instruments as opposed to the type of phone service and/or phone package and the cost of making calls. Thus, it is commonplace in Jamaica to see individuals conspicuously displaying one or more expensive, brandname cellular phones in various social settings including at parties, dances and stage shows where phones are kept in hand or displayed at the waist to ensure that they are made visible, even with limited night-time lighting and visibility or while persons are dancing or drinking. The phone thus becomes one important extension of the overall costume and enhances the relationship between style and body for both women and men. In a related vein, the relationship between music and cellular phones cannot be underestimated where, for example, selective dancehall ring tones which add value to the expression of style, fashion and personal identity is particularly important to the dancehall adherent, as it is to many Jamaicans.[9] In the final analysis, dancehall culture's central positioning of cellular phones as one material accessory that enhances status is brokered on the democratic access to telephone service, via cellular telephony, which has provided an accessible mobile platform that purportedly levels the rigid social hierarchies which dancehall attempts to breach. The use of expensive brand name wines and liqueurs is another component of dancehall's costume of consumption and branding.

The use of expensive brand name champagnes, wines or liqueurs has gained ascendancy as an important accessory to the 'bling bling' costume of conspicuous consumption that pervades dancehall culture. This trend was set during the early days of dancehall culture in the 1980s, where a man's ability to purchase an entire crate (carton/box) of the most popular and masculine drink, the dark, Guinness Stout, at dancehall events would result in heightened levels of respect and adulation from the other participants. This respect and adulation would often transcend the event and move into the community, as stories of this individual's 'wealth,' made the rounds, often snowballing to mythical proportions. Thus, during this period of dancehall's heyday, it was, commonplace to see heroes of the underworld, popular dancehall icons or individuals who wished to display their wealth, standing in an almost regal pose behind a crate (carton/box) of Guinness Stout which was then identified as the drink of choice for strong hardcore men (other subsidiary beers included Heineken or Red Stripe). Inevitably, these men who could display this wealth and strength through their purchasing power and ability to swallow several bottles of the dark stout were surrounded by an entourage who partook of this libation and enjoyed the residual attention that this activity generated. A single bottle of Guinness Stout may not have been very expensive, but the purchase of an entire crate of 24 bottles at a time, at the inflated prices common to dancehall events, suggested that this individual had some amount of wealth at his disposal.

Dancehall's love affair with alcoholic beverages as an accessory to the flamboyant costuming choices of men has continued into the present era. During the late 1980s to the early 1990s, the cognac-based fruit drink Alizé (particularly the Gold, Gold Passion and Red Passion flavours) was considered to be the drink accessory of dancehall's flamboyant big-spenders. At the turn of the millennium, brand name champagnes like Cristal, Moet and Chandon were given dancehall's seal of approval. Since that time the trajectory has moved through Hypnotiq to Hennessey as the favoured beverages of superstars. While sporting different labels, levels and type of alcohol, these beverages all have particular characteristics that make them singularly important to dancehall's conspicuous costume of 'bling bling.' First, they are sold in bottles large enough to be plainly visible in any setting and with limited lighting. Second, most have a very conspicuous colour – example gold, red, blue – that makes them easily identifiable. And third, and most important, it is common knowledge that these are very expensive drink choices.[10] Yet, note the subtle transformation in the type of prestige that accompanies the conspicuous consumption of these beverages. Guinness Stout and its subsidiaries suggested a strong, hardcore, wealthy and therefore powerful male identity while Henessey and its related stand-ins suggest a flamboyant, wealthy and therefore powerful male identity. Flamboyance and magnificence has overtaken ideas of strength on which hardcore dancehall machismo was initially brokered. Dancehall artiste Alozade's name is brokered on this ethos where the ritualized use of alcoholic beverages bestows status and power. In this instance Alozade is a Jamaican Creole version of the word Alizé.

The relationship between champagne (expensive alcoholic beverages) and other forms of 'bling bling' is documented in Elephant Man and Delly Ranks' swaggering dancehall treatise *Headache*:

Delly Ranks: *Ah true wi ice ah nuh fake it ah give dem, headache!*
Tour state to state it ah give dem, headache!
Bentley parked ah wi gate it ah give dem headache!
Give dem headache! Give dem headache!

[They are getting headaches because our diamonds are not fake]
[Because we are touring from state to state (USA) they are getting headaches]
[Because a Bentley is parked at our gate they are getting headaches]

Elephant Man: *Champagne poppin up give dem, headache!*
Bank book fattin up, give dem headache!
Nuff gal slappin up, give dem headache!

[(We have) champagne bottles popping and giving them a headache]
[Our savings are increasing and giving them a headache]
[We have many women and that is giving them headache]

Here, Delly Ranks and Elephant Man clearly outline the materialistic relationship that exists across particular practices in dancehall culture including the display of diamond jewellery or 'ice,' ownership of expensive brand name vehicles (Bentley), frequent travel abroad, the regular "popping" of champagne, and increasing deposits of money at the bank. *Headache* also suggests that envious onlookers are traumatized by the visible signs of success that is conspicuously displayed, including increasing deposits of money in a bank account. The fact that one has to speak about these deposits in a public setting is one 'bling bling' facet that has paved the way for the excessive monetization of dancehall lyrics since 2008. This monetization has now become one other popular facet of dancehall's costume of bling which is performed and discoursed in dancehall culture.

For example, dancehall sensation Flippa Mafia, the Flossing King, generated intense attention at Sting 2008 and Reggae Sumfest 2009 with his signature 'flossing' on stage at these events. Flippa Mafia's 'flossing' includes the 'popping' and splashing of expensive bottles of Hennessey into the audience, along with the throwing of paper money (US and Jamaican dollars) into the crowd – a very popular move. Flippa Mafia is the organic incarnation of this money ethos in a similar fashion as Elephant Man is the incarnation of the male dancing ethos. The pure capitalist ethic that underscores the various 'money tunes' that coalesce in dancehall from late 2007 to 2009 has been matched by a similar ethos in the society where many ordinary Jamaicans lost billions of dollars in their quest for instant wealth via several unregulated financial schemes, including the ill-fated Cash Plus and Olint entities which many claim were pyramid schemes.

Since its development as a form of music culture, there have been routine discussions about money in explicit terms in dancehall, however, the ethos has been radically different from that which underscores the rise of monetization in dancehall since late 2007 through 2008 and into 2009. For example, General Trees' 1980s (circa 1984) dancehall hit, *50 Dollar Bill* was predicated on the obvious need for a note of that denomination at a point when the J$100 bill was the highest note in circulation. Supercat's *Trash and Ready* hit in the 1980s documented the value of his then 'bling bling' costume and itemized the dollar value of his clothing which he claimed cost a 'bag of money.' Of course, a hat that costs J$120.00 and a shirt costing J$250.00 has long been overtaken by inflation, with dancehall's modellers and posers sporting costumes that cost over a hundred times more than these figures. Elephant Man's focus in 2000 on what he called 'PNP Money' in his song *1000 Dollar Bill*, documented the introduction of the J$1,000.00 note in Jamaican currency. Elephant Man's naming of the J$1,000.00 bill as 'PNP Money' highlighted what he deemed a strategic move by the then People's National Party government to immortalize their former PNP party leader and Prime Minister, the late Michael Manley on what was then the highest banknote available in Jamaica.[11] The Jamaica Labour Party government's introduction and release of the J$5,000.00 note in October 2009 parallel's this move with former JLP party leader and Prime Minister, the late Hugh Shearer appearing on this note. As at the date of this work, no dancehall song has been penned to immortalize this move. What is more dominant and current is dancehall's insistence that money and more money is an important facet of dancehall's propensity to ritualize male (and dancehall) empowerment.

As the global recession expanded and took hold in Jamaica, dancehall has responded with a literal explosion of 'money tunes' that has far outstripped any similar engagement in any form of Jamaican music, and in any earlier era of dancehall culture. Dancehall culture's production of multiple variants of these 'money tunes' that hold out the promise of ritualized empowerment and high status to those who can claim this wealth via money include Assassin's *Money Machine,* Beenie Man's *Money Stock and Pile,* Black Rhyno's *Dolla Coin* and *Money Haffi Mek,* Busy Signal's *Money Tree* and *Me Love Money,* Charlie Black's *Rich dis Year,* Fire Link's *I Need Money,* Flippa Mafia's *Dem Yah, Unfinished House/My Money is Mine,* JahVinchi's *Dollar Sign,* Konshen's *Winna,* Lisa Hype featuring Vybz Kartel with *Hustle the Money,* Mavado's *Moneychanger, Money,* and *Dreaming,* Merital's *My Money,* Munga's *Money in My Pocket,* Serani's *Stinkin Rich,* Voise Mail's *Get the Money,* and Vybz Kartel's *Trailer Load ah Money, Dollars,* and *Million (Dollars) by a Mawning.*

These and similar dancehall songs project several explicit themes of which the most important is the idea of money as a tool to achieve social mobility and status, thus there is the underlying theme throughout all these songs that a very large sum of money guarantees status mobility, therefore an artiste or individual who comes from the poor 'below' can rise to the rich 'above' on a crest of money. Other popular themes include the fact that the local currency's value is paltry compared 'foreign dollars,' such as the highly prized United States dollar or the Pound sterling. In addition, they suggest that one can be empowered by using various means to achieve this money including 'hustling, working in the street' while avoiding certain taboo activities such as 'bowing for it.' Many of these songs explicitly discuss the determination to get rich by any means, whether legal or illegal, and the yearning desire to gain large sums of money (e.g. Kartel's *Trailer Load ah Money* and Merital's *My Money*). Mavado's *Money* documents several of these themes but twins them with the negative side where money can become the root of all evil. Yet, the idea that even if money does not bring you happiness it can bring material comfort to a life that may have other negative facets remains. Thus, the need and desire to gain large sums of money for personal advancement and also to aid family, friends and other loved ones locked in poverty in inner city communities is also common. One component of these ritualistic engagements that has moved into dancehall practice is the 'money pull-up' where dancehall participants throw money at or on the selector at a dancehall session or party. This is a signal for the selector to play a particular song once more, in effect, monetizing the desire for an encore.

Female debates with money have included the 'golddigger' ethic where women seek to gain money and other symbols of wealth from men, often through sexual exchange. This female golddigger ethic is reflected in several dancehall treatises including Lady Saw's *Beg Yu* and Macka Diamond's *Money-Oh* ethic (immortalized in her similarly titled album) along with Spice and Pamputae's desire to 'defend di money.' However, this current wave of monetization has moved these debates away from the often negated female discourses with the desire for money and is particularly centred around male identity and the desire for the corresponding wealth status mobility that large sums of money generate, which I refer to as masculinized monetization in dancehall culture. Gaza Kim and Lisa Hype's song, *Bill,* marries this male monetization with the golddigger ethic to remind 'all boasy man wheh out deh,' i.e. men who brag and boast about the content of their wallets, that they must be ready and prepared to take care of a woman's various expenses:

> *Mi want you pay da light bill deh, dah phone bill deh, dah wata bill deh*
> *Mi want put on dah hairstyle deh, dah shoes deh match with dah blouse deh*
> *Di rent fi pay by Friday and di nails haffi done by Saturday*
> *Yuh say yuh ah di realest man out deh…so put yuh money weh yuh mout deh*

[I would like you to pay that electricity bill, that phone bill and that water bill]

[I would like to put on that hairstyle and that pair of shoes which matches that blouse]
[The rent must be paid by this Friday and my nails must be done by this Saturday]
[You say that you are the man with the most status (and money) out there so put your money where your mouth is].

Riding high on this wave of masculinized monetization as power and status, Flippa Mafia's distinctive audience interaction of 'flossing' by dressing in designer brands, throwing money into the audience and splashing from his bottle of Hennessey, buys very particularly into a capitalist culture that responds to these conspicuous displays of wealth by granting higher status to the man who engages in these ritual displays at a time when many ordinary Jamaicans are faced with a daily erosion of their limited resources and a further downward slippage in their already marginalized standard of living. In this regard, the British Link-Up Crew is one important case study of a male group that used 'bling bling' as a strategy to harness masculine status and empowerment in dancehall culture.

The British Link-Up Crew

In the dancehall, groups, sects and crews (e.g. Black Roses Crew, Higglers Crew, Ouch Crew, Scare Dem Crew, Diplomat Crew, Fatherless Crew, and British Link-Up Crew) act as collective embodiments of overlapping and competing discourses.[12] The British Link-Up Crew is one such popularized dancehall group of men identified as promoters of street dances and parties in Jamaica, Britain and the USA who gained significant popularity and status in the dancehall because of their expensive, name brand costumes, flashy, expensive cars, and ostentatious lifestyles. For these men, the contemporary aestheticization of everyday life played an important role in their negotiation of cultural and gendered identity. They adopted a style of dress that projected a particular socio-economic situation and future, which translated into a group masculine identity that was legitimated under the hegemonic mores of traditional Jamaican masculinity as narrated and idealized in dancehall myths and inner city narratives. A rich man holds power and dominance and, consequently, this wealth must be consistently projected for it to be verifiable and empowering.

The trajectory of rural to urban to glocal movement that has become commonplace for many successful men in Jamaica and which is relevant to this group was epitomized in the persona of Owen 'Roy Fowl' Clarke, (a.k.a. Father Fowl or Sir Roy), the originator of the British Link-Up event who hails from the rural parish of St Mary, Jamaica and had his base of operations in the inner city community of the Waltham Park area of Kingston, Jamaica, and also in North West London, UK. Where the dancehall stage is concerned, Roy Fowl's early 1980s dancehall parties hosted in North-West London basements evolved into the modern, multi-faceted brand name British Link-Up product, the most conspicuous of which was first, the hyped persona of the body politic of the men who form the core membership of the British Link-Up Crew and second, the annual dancehall events/parties hosted by this group. This group was a male peer group that provides an avenue for socializing within their own community and status groupings which is one vital segment of Caribbean community life where, as Chevannes argues, in a structure that is devoid of clear formal and informal group structures...'a vast section of the male population, those separated from the education system, would be deprived of opportunities to participate in representative sports, the arts and culture' (2001:212).

The Crew was an informal grouping of the type that is characteristic of dancehall culture and its collectives, resulting in an amorphous membership. However, in a 2002 interview, Owen 'Roy Fowl' Clarke, noted that while many people identify as 'British,' (i.e. as members of the British Link-Up Crew) there are approximately 15 legitimate members in his group. However, this brandname label was appropriated by a cadre of young men from lower- and working-class backgrounds in urban inner cities of Kingston and the rural areas of Jamaica who were convinced that their economic and social activities fulfilled the criteria for membership in this group. Indeed, research conducted towards this work has shown that young men from some inner city communities, who migrate/wish to migrate in the quest for social and economic mobility, identify with the dancehall through membership in transnational crews like the British Link-Up. As part of their quest for visibility these marginalized men attempt to appropriate the high levels of masculine status that 'membership' in the elite grouping of the British Link-Up Crew generates among their peers and the wider dancehall audience. For these men, the perception was that the moniker of 'British Link-Up' identified them as a 'heavy man' or a 'big man,' i.e. a man with wealth, power and status.

Originally coined as the name of the dancehall event, the moniker British Link-Up encoded a specific diasporan masculine identity that was organically linked to the Jamaican underclass, and which was conspicuously wealthy and reputedly engaged in extra-legal/illegal activities. Within the ideological space of the inner cities and the dancehall, this underlying discourse of illegality and (gun) violence is of particular importance in solidifying and legitimizing the status and power of this incarnation of masculinity as one facet that is hegemonically inscribed.[13] Consequently, in the dancehall, the term 'British' signifies a truly diasporan re-orientation where an individual can lay claim to a trans-local identity that denotes a high level of personal status and economic power (symbolic or real) and is founded on the propensity for migration that characterizes Jamaican society. On the dancehallized/ghettoized hierarchy of personhood and status that mimics the traditional markings of hegemonic Jamaican masculinity, conspicuous consumption and expensive costuming is used to rank personhood. As a result, the label of 'British' transformed individual men from the Jamaican urban inner cities and/or lower or working-classes into a member of the migratory 'elite' who have attained (or will attain) significant economic wealth in a foreign country. For example, one narrative which outlines the ideological and social re-orientation that appropriation of this label signifies is that of a member of the British Link-Up Crew who was killed during his visit home to Jamaica in December 2002. The deceased's family (in Jamaica and England) made immediate arrangements to have his body shipped back to England for interment – an extremely expensive undertaking but a powerful example of the value placed on the status generated by one's identification with the former colonial motherland, as well as the importance of the public display of economic wealth that underpins this identification.

As a part of the focus on African retentions that is commonplace in discussions about Jamaican culture, it could be argued that this emphasis on elegant and expensive male costuming can be read as a sign of the re-emergence in the Diaspora of gendered African male dress in which male styles are often more elabourate than female ones. However, for the purposes of this work on dancehall masculinities I note that, like the Congolese *sapeurs* discussed by Friedman (1994), the overt fascination with this phenomenon in the Jamaican dancehall speaks more clearly to an appreciation of the multiple and converging historical processes that are at work in the colonial/postcolonial and capitalist-influenced spaces of the African diaspora. Costumes like those favoured by the men of the British Link-Up Crew and contemporary dancehall male modellers are intertwined with the colonial/postcolonial and capitalist mores of Great Britain and North America that are perceived as power-making and thus incarnated across the bodies of these men in the dancehall. Additionally, this re-costuming and recasting of the male body can be read as a constituent of the progressive refiguring of the once preferred mode of masculine being as costumed spectacle in a situation where hegemonic masculinity is in a state of flux or what Meeks (1996,124–43) identifies as hegemonic dissolution.

Conspicuous Consumption as Dancehallized Masculinity – British Link-Up

In his work on distinctive cultural practices, the social identity and habitus of Bourdieu's consumer is defined by the construction of a niche in the world of social goods, with consumption creating a definitive cultural space (Bourdieu 1984). In the dancehall consumption as a practice of social differentiation is linked to the appropriation of cultural power as well as to political, economic and gendered mobility. Here, appearances and identity are mapped onto one another as if they are accurate mirror reflections. Conspicuous consumption, as a means to a multifaceted end in a very distinctive space, is explored in dancehall artiste, Assassin's, treatise *How We Roll*:

> *How we roll? Inna Lexus, cruise control an' Benjies full wi billfold*
> *And how we roll? Inna platinum, ice and gold so wi neck and wi wrist well cold*
> *Say who we are - celebrity, superstar, wid all DSS inna wi cyar*
> *And who we are - some niggers who a buy out di bar and a blaze all a Cuban cigar*
>
> [How do we roll? In a Lexus motorcar with cruise control and our wallets are full of American dollars]
> [And how do we roll? Decked out in platinum, diamond and gold jewellery so that our necks and wrists are well cold (spectacular)]

115

[Say who are we? We are celebrities and superstars, with even Digital
Satellite Systems in our cars]
[And who are we? Some niggers who can afford to buy out the bar
and are smoking Cuban cigars]

Assassin's *How We Roll* exemplifies the 'dancehallized' ideological
discourse and practice where conspicuous symbols of wealth become a
strategy in the negotiation and promotion of mobility and status in the
tense socio-political, cultural and economic landscape of Jamaican society.
Assassin's Cartesian-like identification of self as 'celebrity, superstar' ties in
very clearly with the commodification of identity that is an important part of
the cult of celebrity associated with figures like Madonna, Michael Jackson,
Prince, Boy George that Kellner (1994,162–3) identifies in his work on fashion
and identity. Undeniably, Assassin's triumphant call and response heralds
and echoes his appreciation of the successful appropriation of elements that
are perceived as the most important signifiers of Jamaican upper class and
bourgeois respectability and which identify this commodified, dancehallized
variant of masculinity in the dancehall. As Assassin so triumphantly
articulates, the symbolic and cultural value of these materialistic elements
is not lost on dancehall actors and supporters, particularly on the men who
dominate and control the dancehall. Accordingly, these symbolic and cultural
elements are appropriated by dancehall culture's predominantly male actors,
like those in the British Link-Up Crew, in their selective refashioning and re-
imaging of the male dancehall body across the stage of the dancehall. British
Link-Up's re-casting of the traditional, hegemonic factor of wealth as male
power into the dancehallized promotion of Bling Bling and posing articulated
a masculine fantasy of conspicuous consumption across dancehall culture's
male body.

For example, the posers of British Link-Up used the British Link-Up
events as the most publicized stages from which to project their flamboyance
and extravagance. Consequently, the hosting of the annual British Link-
Up events/sessions in Jamaica around the Easter Holiday Weekend and
in December, close to Christmas, is of important as these periods hold
particular socio-political significance in Jamaican society and the Diaspora.
These two periods are traditionally marked with ritual celebrations linked
to the Christian celebrations of Jesus's sacrifice/resurrection and his birth,

respectively and, in Jamaica, these periods mark a strategic hiatus from the day-to-day rigours of life, with stage-shows, parties and other functions providing a cathartic stage for various actors[14] to release the toxic build-up of the stresses of everyday existence. The predominantly male actors who constitute the formalized British Link-Up Crew amass small fortunes which are expended in an explosive, highly ritualized and public trans-local historical moment of conspicuous consumption. This includes consumption of status-generating products including foreign travel (Jamaica/diaspora), diamond and platinum jewellery, Rolex watches,[15] Italian leather shoes, luxury cars (late model – Benzes, Volvos, stretch limousines, SUVs), brand name sunglasses, expensive cellular phones, expensive European and Parisian designs/clothing, shoes, hairstyles, cases of expensive champagne, and attachment to young, attractive girlfriends. Thus, British Link-Up's politics of dress and consumption was concurrently local and global and follows the staggering expanse of the network of contemporary consumer culture that is plugged into the micropolitics of identity negotiation in Jamaica. The 'cool pose' of these male icons in the dancehall re-presents a costumed reality and visual spectacle of celebrity and power that is mediated and policed within the (virtual) reality of the dancehall by a multiplicity of actors. For example, the elite status of particular members of the dancehall community, like British Link-Up Crew is protected, policed and mediated by the creators, disseminators and consumers of the dancehall – the artistes, photographers, videographers, cable television stations, and the gatekeepers in the print and electronic media, as well as by the members of the inner cities and the wider dancehall audience who identify with dancehall mores and values. The symbiotic relationship between the wider dancehall audience and the creators/disseminators of dancehall imagery results in the unfailing promotion of male 'modellers' like the British Link-Up Crew as individuals of high status whose every move and gesture within the dancehall are recorded by the videographers and photographers. In this symbiotic web of meanings, the dancehall/ghetto hierarchy of status is superimposed over the traditional race/class/colour and gendered hierarchy of status and power in Jamaica. Application of this dancehall/ghetto hierarchy transforms the men of British Link-Up into members of an ideologically exalted dancehall royalty that is revered by their peers, and garners the respect and adulation from their own group, that is comparable to that bestowed upon members of the traditional, moneyed upper- and bourgeois classes in Jamaican society. This manipulation of the politics of a style of dress, which is more traditionally identified with the middle and upper classes, advertises a complex and competing form of identity that simultaneously taps into and tampers with the superordinate position of the traditional hegemonic classes in Jamaica. This appropriation and/or imitation by men from the lower reaches of the socio-political hierarchy of the expensive styles and fashions that the upper classes would use to distinguish themselves from the lower orders also corrupts the politics of the body and fractures the hierarchies of personhood and gender that have been built on the cultural practice of reading individual worth off the superficial surface of dress, fashion and style. An expensively dressed dancehall male is repositioned on the dancehallized hierarchy as a man of worth and status, regardless of his socio-economic standing in the wider society. Indeed, several young male interviewees from inner city backgrounds insisted that they wanted to 'dress' and be like the men of British Link-Up because 'dem man deh have everything lock.'[16] Others insisted that 'man haffi bling out fi show say man large.'[17]

The women who operate within the confines of the British Link-Up space often act as symbolic canvasses upon which men display the signifiers of their wealth and status. The female consorts who are permitted access to the core of this space are young, beautiful, sexy and costumed in revealing and expensive ensembles often from some Parisian designer, complete with a king's ransom of jewellery, accessories and elaborate hairstyles. While this elaborate costuming and display of the female form predominates within the wider dancehall space (See Cooper 1993; Stolzoff 2001), the few women who occasionally occupy this masculine space are overtly presented and paraded by their British Link-Up male partners as an elaborate feminine extension of their masculine aura. Great pains are taken to ensure that these women remain within the immediate confines of the space occupied by the British Link-Up Crew at any dancehall event. Their every move, from the staged entrance of the group, through the elaborate posturing and contained self presentation, and final grand exit from the dancehall event (all videotaped) are carefully guided and guarded by the paternalistic attentions of the male partner and his peers. These women, while engaged in the wider space of the dancehall, are effectively confined and contained within the ambit of British Link-Up's all male identity crew. Their presence and symbolic containment is one other factor that panders to the hegemonic configuration of Jamaican masculinity via the control of women and thus confers status and power on these men in the dancehall. Here, this masculine identity articulates a dual discourse that acts as a counter to the opening up of masculinity and femininity that may be enacted in other guises in the dancehall. It simultaneously counters the hegemony of Jamaican 'high-culture,' and plays into a colonial rhetoric that supports these very hierarchies. Here, the use of 'bling bling' as masculinity reveals contradictions and inherent tensions.

Yet, in the midst of this ambivalence, the British Link-Up Crew's appropriation and conspicuous re-presentation of ritualized acts of consumption and public display as a strategy in their quest for selfhood, mobility and identity was overtly political, paralleling the activities of the Congolese *sapeurs* where strategies of clothing and the art of dress create a ritualized program that is used to transform ordinary youth and men into individuals of high status (Friedman 1994, 158). Friedman notes that for the Congolese, 'The art of dress...was and is the ultimate means of self-definition' (1994, 155) and 'fashion as a project was a self-evident solution to personal survival in a colonized population where selfhood was identical to the appropriation of otherness' (1994, 157). Like *la sape,* the consumptive practices of British Link-Up represent ways of fulfilling desires that are identified with highly valued and very traditional middle-class lifestyles in Jamaica and its Diaspora, and projects an attempted realization of the image of the 'good life' across the bodies of these men. For *la sape,* this transformation is bound up with the ritual pilgrimage to Paris, the colonial motherland. For British Link-Up, the localized impulse and convergence of competing socio-political discourses operating in Jamaica and the dancehall result in a multilayered costume that encode a tripartite ideological orientation. First, towards the hegemonic middle class mores of post-colonial Jamaica, second a dated colonial impetus for the former motherland, Britain, and third, the modern, postcolonial thrust for the contemporary global superpower, North America with its shiny, new, capitalist products. To this end, expensive, well-tailored, formal suits with matching jackets and pants are imported directly from Paris with fashions from Moschino and Versace complemented with 'ice' (diamond) and platinum jewellery and the omnipresent Rolex watch – a universal symbol of great personal wealth. One interviewee stated that his elabourate and clearly expensive formal suit was 'no regular brand' but 'straight outta Paris' and had been acquired by his girlfriend on one of her 'regular' trips to Paris. Another British Link-Up interviewee, who resided in England, noted that his clothes were purchased in New York because real 'bling and fashion' was difficult to come by in London and he had to 'look good and up to date' on his regular trips to Jamaica. As Kellner (1994, 176) notes in his discussion on Madonna 'in a postmodern image culture identity is constructed through image and fashion' where, for the men like the members of British Link-Up, a socio-political and gendered identity is modelled off the traditional, hegemonic ideal of masculinity as wealth and then continuously defined, redefined, encoded and decoded in the intricate process of social interaction and judgment.

Ultimately, this appropriation of one element of the hegemonic trope of traditional Jamaican masculinity results in the fantastic elabouration of the British Link-Up costume. Its attendant masquerade of elegance and overt consumption is the primary strategy that these men overtly wield in their attempts to wrest higher levels of personhood and masculine status from the dancehallized hierarchies of personhood and masculine identity and to simultaneously tap into what have been projected as the hegemonic standards of being in the society. The masquerade and fantasy that often underwrites this variant of dancehall masculinity was exposed when the June 12, 2004 *Guardian* newspaper headline announced 'Head of crack cocaine empire convicted' and reported the conviction of 'a flamboyant international drugs baron who ran a multi-million-pound crack cocaine empire spanning five countries and supplying every major city in the UK.' Owen 'Roy Fowl' Clarke reportedly lived in a modest, two bedroom bungalow in South London but led a fantastic lifestyle on the international stage of dancehall and narco-culture, throwing lavish parties and owning several luxurious homes in Jamaica. In July 2004, Owen Clarke was convicted on drug related charges in a U.K. and sentenced to 13 years in prison.

Mere posing, ritualized masculinity, dalliance in rituals of poverty or the appropriation of true wealth and status? Dancehall's masculine exemplars create fantastic images that often fuel more questions than they generate answers and ultimately leave its status-hungry audience in limbo. Even while it represents one installment in an ongoing lyrical duel, Flippa Mafia, the Flossing King's, recent release of *Foundation Ova Hype* is food for thought in this dialogue of 'bling bling,' as he states:

> *Some bwoy a run dung di hype and no have nutten yet*
> *A buy bag a champagne and no have nutten set*
> *When me splash champagne tell dem no fi fret*
> *Because mi foundation done set*

> [Some boys/men are chasing the hype and own nothing as yet]
> [They are buying a lot of champagne and do not have anything in place]
> [When I splash champagne, tell them not to worry]
> [Because my (financial/material foundation is already set]

Conclusion

In the contemporary context of globalization and market capitalism, the existence of collective identity groupings like the British Link-Up Crew within the space of the Jamaican dancehall and its Diaspora is fuelled by the dancehall's symbiotic relationship with global capitalism on the one hand and its engagement with hegemonic masculinity in Jamaica on the other. Dancehall's male modellers and collectives and groups like the British Link-Up Crew engage in an elabourate masquerade of consumptive masculinity that embody, perform and proffer an image and a masculine identity. Yet, the 'bling bling' that is made temporally and temporarily real paradoxically does not erase, but simultaneously undermines and reconstructs the traditional race/class/colour and gendered hierarchies of power and personhood in Jamaica.

Posing in, within or through the lenses of brand name motor vehicles, late model cellular phones, intense 'flossing' with expensive wines and liquors and using expensive, brand name clothing provides dancehall's male adherents with visions of high status that are often accessible but very rarely lasting. Thus, 'bling bling' as masculinity in dancehall culture re-scripts a variant of dancehallized masculinity that simultaneously cleaves to the very hegemonic imperatives of wealth as status that it claims to tackle on behalf of ordinary, poor Jamaicans. Consequently, while men like those of British Link-Up and the posers on dancehall's multiple states succeed in creating new and idealized power identities, they also succeed in simultaneously recreating the disparity between themselves and their fellow inner city and working-class brothers and becoming more Eurocentric and distanced from those untouched by this Midas wand. Accordingly, this complex form of stylized subversion plays with as well as against these classed hierarchies yet, in reality it offers only a limited form of liberation to its adherents who seek mobility via this route, many via illegal or extra-legal means. Nonetheless, the fact is, while many poor, ghetto youths may never inhabit this space authentically, the identities incarnated in crews like the British Link-Up, narrated in dancehall's materialistic treatises and performed on the dancehall stage by Flossing Kings like Flippa Mafia, are idealized and idolized in the dancehall and amongst Jamaica's underclasses. These images of consumption provide alternative models of social mobility and masculinity for some Afro-Jamaican men as luxurious fabrics, late model cellular phones, brand name motor vehicles and conspicuous displays of wealth become a currency of identity in the material desert that many must inhabit. The postmodern dancehall male eagerly slakes his thirst in riotous and celebratory moments of 'bling bling' and consumption that becomes an end in itself, in the absence of visible and accessible means of true social mobility.

At the same time, the overt focus on male costuming and accessorizing, sartorial excess and conspicuous consumption is a form of narcissism that is transgressive in the hardcore, heterosexual definition of dancehall's masculinity. Narcissistic behaviours and practices are encoded as feminine in dancehall culture, with the flamboyantly and extravagantly costumed female Dancehall Queens, models and dancers being conspicuously positioned. Thus, this move towards feminized aesthetics and practices by men in dancehall signifies a reversion in the traditional dancehall definitions of a real, hardcore man who purportedly displays a necessary disregard for his presentation and appearance in order to project a fully masculine and 'hard' aura. This incremental shift towards the feminization of male rituals of dress and appearance is examined in greater detail in the following chapter. The variant of dancehall masculinity examined is a direct outgrowth of 'bling bling' masculinity and represents the synthesis of the foregoing discussions by examining what is the most contemporary and popularized variant of

122

masculinity in Jamaican dancehall culture, which is most clearly energized through the appropriation of what have been historically coded as non-traditional, feminized and highly transgressive methods of masculine expression.

CHAPTER 6

'FASHION OVA STYLE': DANCEHALL'S MASCULINE DUALITY

Resistance is futile, you will be assimilated.
The Borg, *Star Trek TNG*

Introduction

This chapter examines one of the most contemporary and controversial expressions of masculinity in the Jamaican dancehall which I label 'Fashion Ova Style'. It is brokered on a range of feminized aesthetics, public presentation of the male body in dance performance and high levels of male homosociality in the public performance space. In this chapter, relevant examples are drawn from the costumes of men in the dancehall, dancehall performances, and the conspicuous attire and practices of male dancehall artistes like Elephant Man. The burgeoning appropriation and recasting of stylistic dancing by hardcore dancehall men is explored as a part of this re-fashioning and repositioning of dancehall masculinity as a newly constituted variant that incorporates facets of all four dancehall masculine exemplars examined in the foregoing chapters.

Men in Pink Dress (Styles) – Engendering Dancehall Fashion and Style

The Fashion Ova Style variant of dancehall masculinity is first highlighted in the transgressive aesthetic rituals and fashion choices of men in the dancehall, which marks a progressive move from the Bling Bling variant examined in the foregoing chapter. Here, Fashion Ova Style reflects the cross-fertilization with high fashion and style from the developed capitalist metropoles, American hip hop culture, and the historical imperatives for African flamboyance and ostentatious costumes. The result is a distinct preference for designer fashion as accepted high fashion and style for the hardcore dancehall male within the traditionally restrictive structures of Jamaican masculinity. At this juncture, external pressures heightened by the advent of globalisation, and its attendant economic, social and cultural facets, have converged with the dancehall community's agenda for self development and enhancement. Popular fashion magazines, mainstream cinema, electronic media and the internet project prescriptive (and often competing) images of the feminine and masculine ideal across the dancehall body. These and other factors feed into a creeping ideological acceptance and practice by hardcore dancehall men of feminized aesthetics and rituals that were once rigidly demarcated and branded as taboo. In Jamaica, practices and rituals of this variety include regular visits by even the most hardened ghetto youth to cosmetologists for facials, manicures and pedicures, and regular visits to salons for hair care. This is complemented by a corresponding explosion in the numbers of hardcore men sporting conspicuous and intricate hair styles (e.g. intricate cornrows), and plucked, trimmed and fashioned eyebrows. Men who cannot afford these costly rituals at formal establishments utilize the inexpensive route of over-the-counter skin care and skin bleaching (lightening) creams, visits to the community barbershop, and in-house hair care and maintenance by female family members or friends. This excessive and highly narcissistic focus on the body, its care and public presentation, is complemented with an emphasis on stylized coordination of expensive brand name clothes (Moschino, Versace, Dolce & Gabbana, etc.), jewellery (gold, diamond and platinum), shoes and other accessories. These aesthetic activities are accompanied by exaggerated public display and self presentation both within and beyond the performative space of the dancehall.

These practices and behaviours are linked to the sartorial excess and conspicuous consumptive ethos of men like those of the British Link-Up Crew examined in the foregoing chapter. However, a distinctive shift in the depth of narcissism displayed by these Fashion Ova Style men has simultaneously occurred, together with a radical dash towards a 'softened' variant of dancehall masculinity which is in direct opposition to the historical imperatives towards the 'tough,' 'rough' and 'hard' variant of hardcore dancehallized masculinity. The tell-tale, glossy sheen of nail hardeners or natural overcoats on manicured and pedicured fingers and toes that was once used as 'incriminating evidence' in Jamaica to identify a *Maama Man* or a *Chi Chi Man* is now openly flaunted by 'hardcore' dancehall men who proudly display this evidence of their appropriation of a ritual of bodily care that purportedly signals wealth, luxury and high status.

Dancehall's fashion culture operates in a cosmopolitan and transnational space that continuously engages the global codes of fashion and style in a constant stream of cross-fertilization. The new millennium's global codes of fashion and style include international fashion culture's retro impulse and its return to the 1970s asexual style of tighter fitting clothes for both men and women, as well as the revolutionary efforts to ungender the colour pink, heralded by the global entertainment industry, and the visibility of prominent men in popular music cultures wearing pink (e.g. American hip hop culture). Consequently, colours originally denoted as feminine or feminized in an earlier era in popular Jamaican culture, including light pastels like peach, and the highly feminized pink, (once taboo and therefore shunned by most men) is a displayed favourite among many dancehall adherents. For many years, the preferred colour of dress for a real, hardcore, dancehall Badman has been the powerful black, with pink its antithesis. For example, Dancehall artiste, Bounty Killer chose black as his signature colour for many years to cement his Warlord, Gladiator, Badman identity in dancehall. The transformation in colour preferences is matched with a displayed fondness for donning close-fitting or skintight pants – an aesthetic choice that also purportedly identified the antithesis of the dancehall's heterosexual masculinity when men wearing tights or tight pants were often identified as homosexual. In contemporary dancehall, the identification of men who favour these aesthetic and fashion choices, as gangster and hardcore creates a truly contradictory and paradoxical variant of masculinity because their re-fashioned bodies simultaneously articulate a gangsterized, hardcore and feminized masculinity that is highly transgressive and revolutionary. The sculpted, costumed and softened Fashion Ova Style men in dancehall simultaneously project a highly feminized aesthetics alongside the behaviours that define a Badman, including the rough, coarse voice, the use of expletives and regular references to violence, as well as the signature Badman slouch and 'screw face'. One can only speculate on whether the only key factor is that fashion and style cues in the international arena may have contributed to the ascendancy and creeping acceptance of these feminized styles and colours within the rigidly guarded spaces of dancehall and inner city masculinities as, in the fashion-conscious space of dancehall culture, fashion and style take precedence over and direct the cues of masculine being and identity in Jamaica. Yet, the primping, preening, styling and sculpting which these men undergo create a contradictory version of dancehallized masculinity that moves away from the early reliance on the traditional, hegemonic standards of Jamaican masculinity constituted at the historical moment of dancehall's ascendancy in the 1980s.

In a late 1990s backlash against the first wave of this propensity to refashion the dancehall male body using feminized and therefore transgressive, codes, dancehall artiste, Elephant Man noted in a popular song, *Dress like Girl*:

> *Badman nuh dress like girl*
> *Wi nuh bore nose and wi nuh bleach face and wi nuh wear drops curls*
> *And some freaky freaky bwoy nuh stop dress like girl.*

[Badmen don't dress like women]
[We don't pierce our noses and we don't chemically lighten our facial skin and we don't wear our hair in (drop) curls]
[(And) some freaky freaky boys won't stop dressing like women]

(c) 2006 The Gleaner

In this song, Elephant Man lyrically distances the Badman from the early re-imaging of dancehall's hardcore male identity and, in so doing, documents several practices that are considered to be precipitously close to the gendered borderline including several aesthetic choices such as the piercing of nose, bleaching (lightening) of the face, wearing drops curls or elabourate hairstyles and dressing in styles that closely resemble those chose by women.

However, as one of dancehall culture's international stars of the

Elephant Man

twenty-first century, Elephant Man's excesses of feminized fashion and style incorporate his signature hair colours, multiple, large earrings and body art. His expensive, brand name costumes and penchant for high fashion pinks and pastels and brilliant neon colours broker on his early status-hungry admonitions for visibility in his signature phrase at dancehall events, 'Shine di light inna mi cute and dainty face' (shine the videolight in my cute and dainty face). In addition, Elephant Man, dancehall's Energy God and Chief Jester has parlayed the late Gerald 'Bogle' Levy's dancing and edgy style of dress into a dancehall character that incorporates the radical aspects of today's 'bling bling' costumes for dancehall men. His success underscores the space that exists for this variant of identity as it flits across dancehall's stages. Indeed, while the late Dance Icon, Bogle, is credited for the development of flashy dance styles, Elephant Man must be credited for the upgrade and transformation of what I refer to as 'Bogle's Progeny' into a variant of dancehall male artistes that has spawned its own successors and carved out is own identity-space.

Since the turn of the new millennium, Elephant Man's signature hair colours, 'up-to-the-minute' colourful costumes, energetic, impish behaviours and promotion of noveau dance styles underwritten by popular songs have driven a new wave of dance in dancehall culture. Dancehall groups like Voise Mail and, more particularly, the dancehall duo RDX (Renegade X and Delomar X), broker on Elephant Man's portrayal of this variant of a successful dancehall artiste/male to expand the repertoire of music, dance and identities that now coalesce in the dancehall. RDX's colourful hairstyles, their cheerful, humorous personalities and their development of a cadre of songs that are brokered on or drive new dance styles in the dancehall speak particularly to this line of succession.

This transition in the presentation of the male body in dancehall has not been without its detractors. For example, the lyrical treatise released in late 2005 by female dancehall artiste Ce'Cile, underscored the hesitation of many dancehall adherents to legitimize the new wave of feminized male Fashion Ova Style as dancehallized masculinity. In her song, *Woman Tings*, Ce'Cile defines and condemns what she perceived as a disturbing trend in men's fashion in Jamaica. In the Intro, she insists that some unidentified entity must leave 'women's things' alone:

Intro:
Let me tell u something
Low woman things, low woman things let me tell u something

[Let me tell you something]
[Leave women's things alone, leave women's things alone, let me
tell you something]

In the chorus of this song, Ce'Cile identifies men as the perpetrators of
this problematic behaviour

Chorus
We can't hot again cause a di man dem
Dem a buy off we blouse and we pants dem
Them thief we pink colour my God then
Dem nu soon start want wear wi thong then

[We (i.e. women) cannot be hot/fashionable anymore because of the
men]
[They are buying out our blouses and pants]
[They have stolen our colour pink, My God]
[Then won't they soon begin to want to wear our thong (panties)
too]

In each subsequent verse she makes particular references to different
behaviours and aesthetic choices that are deemed problematic in their
borderline leanings. For example, in verse 1 she asks youth (i.e. young men)
why their clothing styles must rival those of women and highlights the
scandalous nature of male appropriation of female clothing styles with a
reference to the *X-News*, one of Jamaica's popular tabloids.

Verse 1
My youth why u pants fi tighter than mine
And why u pants no de a you waistline?
Hipsters a fi gyal dem design
Me and u nuffi ina di same kind
Go GO WEST cant find no gyal clothes
Whe dem gone only God he knows
U want know read XNews page four
A group a man a buy dem off fi go a dancehall go pose

[My youth, why should your pants be tighter than mine?]
[And why is your pants not at your waistline?]
[Hipsters is designed for girls/women]
[You and I should not be in the same kind (of design)]
[(I) went to Go West (clothing store) and could not find any girls/women's clothing]
[Where have they gone only God knows]
[If you want to know read page four of the X News newspaper]
[A group of men purchased them all so they could go to the dancehall and pose]

In verse two Ce'Cile highlights the paradox of 'gangsters' who are feminine thus:

Verse 2

Gangster youth u nuffi look like Sally
And u nuffi pretty pretty and favour dolly
U fi be Ken u nuffi be di Barbie
From u look feminine boy you cant chat to me
Man all a make mistake call u Shorty
Cause di style a u clothes make u favour Shari
Stop buy di gyal dem clothes nuh Marky
And gi u hipsters dem to u sister Sani

[Gangster youth, you should not look like Sally (a woman)]
[And you should not be pretty and resemble a doll]
[You should be Ken, you should not be the Barbie (doll)]
[Once you look feminine boy, you cannot speak to me]
[Men are even making the mistake of calling you Shorty]¹
[Because the style of your clothing causes you to resemble Shari (a woman]
[Marky, stop buying the girls/woman clothing]
[And give your hipsters (jeans) to your sister Shari]

Ce'Cile pinpoints what she sees as inconsistencies in the presentation of hardcore masculinity as it has been historically defined in popular culture and in dancehall. In verse three of her song she notes that for her (and others), women's clothing, the colour pink, tight pants and 'di wining and di bruk out bruk out' dance styles all constitute markers of femininity which have been selectively appropriated by men in a highly transgressive move. Using select verbal play, Ce'Cile ridicules men who engage in these practices, comparing them to women and denouncing their slippage into femininity as regressive.

Verse 3

Lollypop and tight pants a fi di gyal dem
Pink clothes, bore u nose boy u wrong den
A shave u eyebrow like Sharon dem
And nu see say something wrong boy u condemn
Left di wining to Keiva and Michelle dem
And di crawl up pan di box to Stacey dem
And di bruk out bruk out to Junkoo dem
Who nu like when mi talk try something then

[Lollypop and tight pants belong to the girls/women]
[Pink clothing, pierced nose, boy you are very wrong]
[Shaved eyebrows like Sharon and the others]
[And you don't see that something is wrong, boy you are condemned]
[Leave the 'wining up' (erotic dancing) Keiva and Michelle][2]
[And the crawl up onto sound boxes to Stacey[3] and others]
[And the frenzied dance styles to Junko[4] and others]
[Anyone who does not like what I am saying should try to do something about it]

In this final verse she clearly identifies what are perceived as markers of femininity, such as pierced noses and shaved eyebrows. In the dancehall, these aspects of cosmetic, facial enhancement are often accompanied by another very popular practice, that of skin bleaching or skin lightening.

Skin bleaching has historically been coded as feminine in the dancehall and in the wider Jamaican society. The clarion call of Bembe Thursday's, Kingston's popular Thursday night dancehall gathering, was 'No tight pants bwoy! No bleach out face bwoy!' In an era where male dancers predominate and male posers colonize the centre of dancehall's spaces, Bembe Thursday valiantly attempted to re-centre women in dancehall culture and, thus, is ostensibly demarcated as 'fi di girls dem.' The correlation of bleaching with tight pants suggests a marked transformation in the range of aesthetic rituals that are practiced by men in dancehall. Hardcore dancehall discourses of the twenty-first century project cantankerous debates about the trend towards male bleaching in Jamaica. Dancehall sensation and protégé of Bounty Killer, the Gully Gad, Mavado, in his 2008 treatise, *Nuh Bleach Wid Cream* documents the realities of shottas[5] whose slippery grasp on hardcore heterosexual masculinity is identified by their propensity to bleach. Moving beyond the 'tracing' match with arch rival Vybz Kartel in which he constantly railed at Kartel's lack of male power because of his obvious altering of his epidermis,[6] Mavado documents his concern with the crossing over of hardcore masculinity into the feminized arena of bleaching in violent and derogatory terms:

> *Mi nuh bleach wid cream, mi bleach wid mi M-16*
> *Wid extra magazine, mi alone create mi crime scene*
>
> *You a disgrace, bleaching yuh face*
> *Tru yuh fuckin face yuh marrow drop*
>
> *Yuh bleach wid cream, but mi bleach wid mi M-16*
> *An mi nuh bleach wid team, mi alone step pon mi crime scene aaaay*
> *Shotta nuh bleach wid cream, Wi bleach wid wi M-16*
>
> [I don't use bleaching creams I use my M-16
> [With extra magazines, I create my crime scenes all by myself
>
> [You are a disgrace, bleaching your face
> [Through your fucking face your marrow falls
>
> [You use creams to bleach but I bleach with my M-16
> [And I do not bleach in a team, I step on my crime scene all alone aaaaay
> [Shottas do not use bleaching creams, we bleach with our M-16s

Mavado's double-talk utilizes the Jamaican Creole meaning of the verb 'to bleach.'[7] He suggests that real hardcore badmen, the shottas, endure the long hours of dark(ness) into (day)light with their weapons – without any visible physical deterioration.[8] The response of Rastafari artistes to skin lightening/bleaching (e.g. Queen Ifrica in *Mi Nah Rub* and I-Wayne in *Bleacher*) parallels that of the hardcore dancehall artistes, while simultaneously encoding the socially accepted definitions of bleachers as mentally unstable, traitors to their race and colour, and social deviants and outcasts. Nonetheless, the fashion trends that propel the Fashion Ova Style aesthetic in dancehall continue to gain a foothold and skin bleaching is simultaneously derogated and uplifted. For example, Captain Barkey's *Bleach On* utilizes an understated variation of humor to treat with the aesthetic rituals of women. In *Bleach On* Barkey encourages women to engage in a range of image-altering practices, if they result in enhanced and accepted modes of beauty. His particular focus on skin bleaching, parallels the explosion of bleaching that swept Jamaica at the turn of the millennium and encodes the growing ambivalence to the pervasive practice:

Settle yah mi gyal because you come fi mash it up
Han inna di air cause yuh nuh chop up chop up
Rail up mi gyal you nuh ole an mash up
Wooooeee!
Mi dainty gyal dem!

[Take it easy my girl/s as you have come to
[Wave your hands in the air because/if your skin is free of marks and scars]
[Jump up and prance around my girl/s because you are not old and broken down]
[Woeeeeee!]
[My dainty girls!]

Chorus
If you a bleach an bleaching fit you
Bleach on Bleach on
Yuh have you false hair and false hair fit you
Weave on Weave on
If you a lead and leading fit you
Lead on Lead on
You tek di pace an speeding fit you
Speed on Speed on

[If you are bleaching/lightening your skin and it suits you]
[Continue to bleach/lighten, Continue to bleach/lighten]
[If you are wearing false hair (weaves) and it suits you]
[Continue to weave, continue to weave]
[If you have taken the lead and being in the lead suits you]
[Continue to lead, continue to lead]
[You have set the pace and it suits you]
[Continue to speed ahead, Continue to speed ahead]

Fi all di gyal dem whe a bleach an know say bleaching fit you
Nuh badda go falla nobaddy because you know say Barkey with you
Ah you go buy you tings so none ah dem cyan come box an kick you
An when yuh a bleach it never burn yuh up it never sick you
Dem say you nuh look good but a trick dem a try fi trick you trick you

Dat nah go stop you man from hug you up and kiss you
Dem better get it inna dem head that you ahead Alicia

[For all the women who are bleaching/lightening and know that it suits you]
[Do not listen to anyone as you know that Captain Barkey is in support of you]
[You bought your things/products so no one can box and kick (abuse) you]
[And when you are bleaching/lightening your skin it has not damaged your
epidermis or made you ill]
[They say that you do not look pretty, but they are only trying to trick you]
[That will not stop your boyfriend/partner from hugging and kissing you]
[They had best understand that you have moved ahead (up) Alicia]

Barkey, like many dancehall adherents, projects bleaching as positive, especially when it 'fit you.' This is related to the use of hair extensions (false hair) where he entreats his girls to 'Weave on Weave on,' if the use of these cosmetic props results in aesthetic enhancement. In addition, the idea of capitalist property and ownership is intertwined with these contemporary debates. Your personal expenditure (Ah you go buy yuh tings) suggest ownership and control over the utilization of these aesthetic artifices, regardless of public condemnation of the practice (so nobaddy cyan come box and kick you). This is one popular rebuttal to admonitions about skin bleaching and many bleachers claim that since they purchased their skin products, they are at liberty to use them. In addition, since the epidermis in question is their personal property, they are also at liberty to alter its shade at will, regardless of any dangers, real or imagined. Affirmation by partners, male or female, is also essential, and Barkey underscores not just his support for female bleachers but also the fact that the partner in the mix 'nah go stop hug up and kiss' the woman who bleaches.

The common thread running throughout these debates in dancehall is that skin lightening/bleaching is a feminine activity. In concert with other modes of cosmetic artifice, the superficial application of skin products whether demonized or reified, remained the purview of the female throughout most of the 1990s until its stealthy appropriation by men exploded in working class and dancehall culture. Both I Wayne and Ifrica capture the contemporary modes of bleaching as feminine and masculine and, as Mavado highlights in *Shotta Nuh Bleach wid Cream*, both also signify the paradoxical presentation of shottas (or hardcore men) as bleachers. In his song *Bleacher,* I Wayne speaks to this thus:

> Still wid di guns and bling bling,
> Nuh love demselves so dem bleach dem skin

> [And even while they continue to consort with guns and Bling Bling/ flamboyant aesthetics]
> [They do not love themselves so they have bleached/lightened their skin]

While Queen Ifrica poetically reflects in *Mi Nah Rub* thus:

> See you pon di corner with you thuggy thuggy Ways
> But mi can't understand mek you go bleach Out yo face

> [I see you on the corner with your thuggish/Badman behaviours]
> [But I cannot understand why you have lightened your face/skin].

Yet, while questions continue to be raised this appropriation of feminine aesthetics and dress styles by men is also accompanied by behaviours that overturn accepted male practice. Elephant Man's projection of a refashioned dancehallized self is underscored by his affirmation of the need for dancehall adherents to be 'bling and clean' and his lyrical contributions to the burgeoning wave of male dancing in dancehall culture. This explosive new trend in dancehall dancing is highlighted in the final verse of Ce'Cile's foregoing song, where she entreats dancehall men to leave the erotic, gymnastic and frenzied dance styles to the female Dancehall Queens and Divas. For Ce'Cile, and many other adherents in the dancehall, recasting energetic and erotic dance as masculine in dancehall culture signifies a radical transgression in the embodied codes of hardcore masculinity in the dancehall. This is examined in some detail in the following section.

Recasting Masculine Dance in Dancehall

Real badman nuh wear people pants
We tek dancing to a higher ranks...[9]
Elephant Man, *Pon di River*, 2003

The rise of popularized male dancers in the dancehall is a critical masculine spectacle that points to the re-fashioning and repositioning of the male dancehall body within the spaces of Jamaican dancehall culture. Untamed, ritualistic, stylized and spiritual dance rites form part of the broader practice of dance that has characterized the dancehall since its development in the early 1980s. The drama that infuses any dancehall event is also characteristic of the wider cultural and political anthropology of Jamaica, for example as it unfolds in the African-based religious rites of Kumina and Revival groups or the celebratory ethos of Jonkanoo groups. In the dancehall, a popular dancer is celebrated and lauded to the extent that she (and now he) assumes a god-like aura.[10] Dancehall Queens, modellers and dancers (e.g. the original Dancehall Queen Carlene and others like Stacey, Keiva, Mad Michelle and Junko) have used erotic posing and gymnastic and erotic dancing to claim the status of Queens in the dancehall, based on its earlier propensity to elevate the feminine in the public space of (erotic) display, style and fashion. While the titular 'Queen' implies the existence of a male as the counterpart 'King', the corresponding masculine ethos most popularized in the persona of dancehall's first magnificent male dancer,

(c) 2005 The Gleaner Ltd.

Labba Labba

performer and creator, the late Gerald 'Bogle' Levy, met no such royal appeal. Indeed King Yellowman and Beenie Man have both been crowned Kings of the Dancehall. This reflects the dichotomous split between the word and its use and control as masculine and powerful, and the display and eroticization of the female body as a subsidiary and powerless binary. This is perhaps underscored by a patriarchal reluctance to frame the male body as a desirable object. Other long-standing, popular dancehall male dancers, like the elder Labba Labba, have been immortalized in dancehall song and myth but receive little public accolades beyond the boundaries of local dancehall events in Jamaica.

Dancehall culture coalesced in a society where the historical spaces for men who dance have been cast as middle or upper class (e.g. dance groups like the National Dance Theatre Company), or deeply religious (e.g. Kumina and Revivalism and the spiritual healing profession), or as feminized and homosexual, and therefore taboo. The patriarchal hesitance to pin the male body as desirable object contributed to the reluctance of many Jamaican men to engage in public dance spectacles. All together, these factors negated and ideologically exiled public dancing as routes for masculine expression and ascendancy by hardcore dancehall men in dancehall culture's lower class, secularized and deeply patriarchal space. Over time, it has been common practice for boys and men (particularly those from the inner cities) to avoid formalized careers in dance because of the social and gendered stigma that it carried. Men and boys who 'wear tights' (i.e. dancers) have been ritually denounced in Jamaican life and culture, and often demonized as feminized, 'maama man' and 'battyman'. This convergence of ideas about masculinity with class of origin has meant that many men avoid all forms of contact with 'middle-class' dance groups like the National Dance Theatre Company (NDTC)[11] because of the perception that any such contact will have negative repercussions on their masculine identities. Yet, men and boys often participate in less sensual dances, with their bodies clothed in loose and patently masculine clothing, as opposed to the asexual tights and clinging bodysuits that purportedly project the male body as erotic and sexually desirable.

The spectacle of dancing men in dancehall was also more critically negated in dancehall's heavy focus on sex and sexuality and its propensity to engage with the female body as a source of male empowerment. This masculinist predisposition has been reflected in dancehall's strident anti-male homosexual discourse which has been taken to task by gay lobbyists like GLADD and Outrage! in 1993 and 2004 respectively, which has continued into the current era with Buju Banton's 2009 *Rasta Got Soul* album tour facing protests and cancellations.[12] Consequently, dance, as celebratory performance and spectacle in dancehall has remained historically coded as feminine. Since the turn of the millennium, however, the phenomenon of male dancers has progressively become accepted practice in the spaces of the dancehall and is complemented by escalating male activity, particularly in groups, in the wider sphere of professional, staged dance by groups of young men.[13] Here, men are positioned as objects of desire in a radical challenge to dancehall's propensity to allocate discourses of homosexuality and effeminacy to men who dance.

This explosion of male dancers has created intense competition for space on the dancehall stage, as female dancers and modellers battle to share the centre of the dance and the dancing stage with their male counterparts. Dancehall events provide central spaces for the presentation of self and status for individuals from the marginalized spaces of Jamaica with the omnipresent video cameras and other forms of electronic media that result in visibility, recognition, status and the promise of resources to those whose images are captured in action at these events. In this regard, dancehall stage shows and popular events create a multifaceted, theatrical stage for marginalized men. The feminized, centre of the dance, which is simultaneously the space circumscribed by video cameras at a dancehall event, and once sparsely visited by a few enterprising dancehall men during dancehall's early development, has now been colonized by male dancers, many of whom have brokered their dancing prowess into spaces of social empowerment and wealth creation.[14]

In addition, there is now a distinct separation between male and female dancers on the dance floor and contemporary dancers and dance groups often dance in all-male or all-female groups at most dancehall events, except when there is convergence of space created by the usual intense competition for the space circumscribed by the light of the video cameras. This male/ female separation of the centre space at the dancehall event is a significant departure from accepted dance practices and gendered rituals in dancehall culture. Since the early era of dancehall in the 1980s, the normative practice has been for women to take the stage and publicly perform their dances in the space selected as the centre of the dance, while men remain on the fringes individually or in groups to 'profile' or 'hang out.' The historically accepted practice is for male dancing in the centre of the dancehall to be tolerated only when the man in question is dancing erotically with a female or when the man is particularly skilful and is consequently allowed a moment in time to signify his dance prowess, preferably using a dance coded as hardcore and masculine like the *Cool and Deadly*. Any man who dared to breach this gendered divide and display any prowess in the erotic, sexual and feminized Butterfly dance would find his masculinity questioned and be verbally chastised, booed and even chased from the dance. These gendered boundaries effectively stifled the rise of male dancers and the late Gerald 'Bogle', Levy[15] remained the only highly publicized and popular male dancer in the dancehall for nearly two decades. Bogle's membership in the popular Black Roses Crew helped to distill any aspersions that could have been levelled against his claim to hardcore masculinity as the Black Roses Crew was simultaneously a dancehall sect/ crew similar in constitution to the British Link-Up Crew (discussed in the foregoing chapter), but even more importantly, a ghetto gang, hailing from the tough inner city community of Arnett Gardens and reputed to be involved in illegal gun, drugs and money laundering activities. Thus, Bogle's masculinity enjoyed multiple representations in dancehall's preferred hardcore spaces and could subtly transgress the boundaries of dance without fear of gendered sanctions. Consequently, the phenomenon of myriad young men claiming this once feminized, public space in the centre of the dance as individual dancers or in groups without the intervention of a female or in direct competition with a female dancer signifies an alternative rendering of masculine roles in the dancehall. This phenomenon also highlights dancehall culture's propensity towards duality with increasing levels of homosociality publicly displayed in the choreographed dances and close male-on-male physical contact in the centre of the dancehall, even as dancehall continues its lyrical dis/engagement with male homosexuality.

As one component of this development, male dancers accompany artistes on their tours abroad and often organize their own tours to perform at clubs and other popular cultural sites in the Jamaican diaspora and, as such, creative displays of dance prowess and acrobatic style by men is increasingly being viewed as another useful way to access resources and as a viable route to economic mobility and social visibility. Dancehall's hardcore male dancers use the dancehall stage to parade their popular dance moves and signify their elevated status as they transcend their rigidly bound socio-political spaces by playing to the amorous advances of the ubiquitous high-technology video and camera equipment. Male dancers and dancing crews are now essential components of the rituals and competition for space that characterizes dancehall street dance events like Passa Passa and operate as organic components of the rituals and competition for space, as well as the onstage performance and video productions of many dancehall artistes.[16]

The rise of Fashion Ova Style masculinity is also denoted by the ungendering of dance styles and movements in the dancehall. Dancehall's dance moves have historically been branded with names that encode narratives of cross-fertilization with international media and film, identification with local or global characters or activities, and even body parts. In addition, most dance styles and moves have also been rigidly gendered, with many historically coded as either masculine or feminine and a few as asexual. The *Cool and Deadly* dance style of the early dancehall era was an obviously masculine dance, while the erotic and sexual *Butterfly* of the early 1990s was a patently feminine one and, as Stanley-Niaah (2004, 112) notes, the popular *Bogle* dance was created specifically for men by the late Master Dancer Bogle. Since the late 1990s into the new millennium, however, there has been an explosion of aptly named and genderless dance styles that reflect what I perceive as a creeping 'genderlessness' in the dancehall, or a loosening of the rigid strictures that bound dancehall's masculine stereotypes to the traditional and dated tropes of Jamaican masculinity. These ungendered dance styles include the Blasé, Pon di River, Tall Up Tall Up, Higher Level, Signal Di Plane, Parachute, Zip it Up, Internet and Sweep. This proliferation of new and un-gendered dance styles in the dancehall converges with Elephant Man's rise to stardom and his dissemination of lyrics which are organically driven by (and which drive) the creation of new dances. For example, his songs *Log On*, *Pon di River Pon di Bank*, *Signal di Plane* and *Blasé* are also the names of some popular dances.[17] Other popular songs by Elephant Man in this genre include *Dance di Chaka, Sweep, Dancing Demention, Do the Sponge Bob, Willie Bounce, Gangsta Rock, Fan dem Off, Nuh Linga, Gully Creepa(er)* which are also the names of popular dance styles. The rise to stardom of the duo RDX in 2008 has expanded the proliferation of songs driven by, or which drive popular dances. RDX's popular songs include *Everybody Dance, Bend Over, Daggering, Nuh Linga, Dancers Anthem, Wibble Wabble* and *Dagga Train*. Other dancehall artistes have contributed to the expansion of these dance/songs including Tony Matterhorn with his controversial *Dutty Wine*, Beenie Man's *Row Like ah Boat* and *Swing it Weh,* Ding Dong's *Bad Man Forward Bad Man Pullup* and Mr Vegas featuring Overmars with *Raging Bull/Tek Weh Yuhself.*

Yet, the propensity to create songs which name, describe or are interrelated with popular dance moves is not new in dancehall culture. In the early 1980s several dancehall deejays recorded full songs with dance instructions including *Heel and Toe* by General Trees, *Jump Up, Della Move* and *Butterfly* by Admiral Bailey, and *Water Pumpee* by Johnny Osbourne. In the early 1990s *Bogle* by Buju Banton (named after Master Dancer Bogle) and *World Dance* by Beenie Man were popular dancehall hits and dance tunes. However, the proliferation of dance songs in the new millennium has far outstripped the intermittent forays in this area by early dancehall artistes and points to the opening up of spaces for male energy in dance discourse and activity as a component of the transitions in male activity and identity in dancehall culture. The overlapping of the careers and identities of dancer and artiste also points to the fluidity of boundaries that exist in dancehall which make way for these transformations.

Conclusion

Fashion Ova Style masculinity is brokered on feminine aesthetics, homosociality and the presentation of men as objects of desire in dancehall culture. This arguably reflects the society's responses to challenges and contestations from the underclasses internally, and powerbrokers externally. In dancehall's culturally exalted renderings of masculinity its ultimately hegemonic exemplars, the Badman and the Ole Dawg, have historically been positioned antithetically against the gay male where the Badman and Ole Dawg is everything the gay male is not. However, this paradoxical Fashion Ova Style masculinity tampers with this dichotomy. The Fashion Ova Style male body is clothed in feminized fashions, displays his prowess from a feminized stage, while simultaneously donning the facial expression of the hardcore Badman and disseminating his speech in the harsh, staccato and often coarse language of the Badman. This variant of dancehallized masculinity is projected as aggressively heterosexual while promoting feminized aesthetics and behaviours – a truly borderline version of dancehall masculinity.

This utilization of feminized aesthetic rituals, styles of dress, and dance styles to create a new variant of masculinity in dancehall transgresses the strong hegemonic impulses that have directed dancehall culture's conceptualization of masculinities as hardcore and rigidly heterosexual since its evolution in the early 1980s. It also transgresses dancehall culture's revolt against Jamaica's middle class hegemony by its acceptance of what have historically been defined as a 'middle class' propensity towards energetic, erotic, spectacular, and public dance as an accepted behaviour and practice for lower-class, inner city and dancehall men. Fashion Ova Style masculinity is a dynamic and momentary articulation that bears conceptualization herein because of its radical opposition to the core masculine values that energized the dancehall since its evolution. These core masculine values drew selectively on the constituent facets of Jamaica's hegemonic masculinity by orienting its images around the twin towers of pro-heterosexuality and anti-homosexuality. Yet, with the presentation of Fashion Ova Style, the male homosexual is again rendered invisible, this time by the projection of a masculine exemplar that utilizes a gay aesthetic to hide the male homosexual in full view. This radically transgressive variant of dancehall masculinity expresses dancehall's dualities and inversions, and simultaneously raises questions about the current constitution of Jamaica's hegemonic masculinity from which dancehall culture ultimately draws its strength.

CONCLUSION

The foregoing chapters examined and analysed the process of hegemonic masculinity in Jamaica through the prism of Jamaican dancehall culture and explored the progressive development of a trope of simultaneously traditional and transgressive masculine exemplars in dancehall. What Connell (2001, 39) identified as the historically mobile process of hegemonic masculinity was examined first through four historically prominent masculine exemplars in dancehall culture that are identified as promiscuous/polygamous heterosexuality as masculinity (Ole Dawg with Nuff Gyal), (gun) violence and aggression as masculinity (Badman/Shotta), the use of anti-feminine paranoia and the policing of male boundaries as masculinity, exemplified in the anti-male homosexual or Chi Chi man discourse, and the use of conspicuous consumption and masculine pose as masculinity (Bling Bling). A fifth version of dancehallized masculinity, identified as the most contemporary is labelled Fashion Ova Style, and defined as the use of feminine aesthetics, fashion and style along with the engagement in homosocial, stylistic, spectacular and exhibitionist dance to project a variant of masculinity in dancehall culture. I have argued that these five dancehallized masculinities moved progressively from being patently hegemonic to being simultaneously transgressive and hegemonic and then to being patently transgressive and perhaps newly hegemonic. In this regard, the fifth and most contemporary exemplar of masculinity in the dancehall, Fashion Ova Style, displayed a greater propensity to transgress the early traditional readings of hegemonic Jamaican masculinity and inscribe alternative and transgressive modes of masculinity across the male dancehall body.

Dancehall is the popular space where DJs, dancers and other male adherents of the dancehall act out and play with and against their own ambivalent masculine fantasies as they simultaneously strive towards and transgress against the superordinate standard of traditional, hegemonic

Jamaican masculinity. Here, dancehall culture's cultural hegemony from below tackles traditional middle class hegemony from above in the clash of the ideologically powerful variations of dancehall masculinities that gain prominence at various points in dancehall's development and performance. To this end, the male adherents of dancehall culture, many of whom inhabit the marginalized and dispossessed spaces of Jamaican life, are encouraged to and often do articulate their masculine ethos by inflating, ritualizing and conspicuously performing particular heterosexual masculine characteristics encoded in the traditional, hegemonic masculine ideals of Jamaica. As a result, these predominantly ritualistic, and sometimes empty, practices are elevated to the status of preferred masculine roles which are articulated across the male body of the dancehall and receive wide appeal, adulation and accord as dancehallized masculinities.[1] In this instance, these black male bodies are transformed into what Stuart Hall refers to as 'canvasses of representation' (1996, 470). The re-imaged versions of dancehallized masculinities examined in this work exemplify creative refashionings of gendered selves that are discoursed in popular Jamaican dancehall culture and articulated across the dancehall body. The concurrent operation of Jamaica's rigid class structure with the society's patriarchal guarantee produce extreme, and often ambivalent, manifestations of Jamaican masculinities in dancehall where, as Collier and Rosaldo posit, these cultural representations of gender are not simply *reflections* of a social reality but are 'functioning aspects of a cultural system through which actors manipulate, interpret, legitimize and reproduce the pattern of cooperation and conflict that order their social world' (1981, 311). Dancehallized masculinities are both affect and effect of the wider terrain of Jamaica's rigid hierarchal socio-economic and gendered structures and reflect 'aspects of wider conceptual systems that arise from, and contribute to, social action' (Collier & Rosaldo 1983, 311).

The ambivalence in dancehall's masculine 'play' simultaneously draws from, reinforces and simultaneously transgresses against the overarching hegemonic patriarchal constructs that exist in the wider Jamaican society. Accordingly, dancehall culture represents a dynamic clash of hegemony, class and ideology where members of the most subordinate and powerless classes have successfully accessed an important site of power-making that has gained national, regional and international appeal. Drawing organically from inner city culture, dancehall culture appropriates elements of Jamaica's hegemonic masculine trope and inflates these to masculine roles that are ideologically and culturally manipulated to bestow status and privilege on the bodies of subordinated and marginalized Jamaican men. Dancehall's articulations code a real man as a promiscuous Ole Dawg, an aggressive, violent and powerful Badman or Shotta, a patently anti-male homophobe, or a conspicuously wealthy Bling Blinger. On this continuum of masculinities, the trope of Shotta or Badman has historically been the most revered and this category generally subsumed all other manifestations of masculinity in dancehall culture. This represented an early shift from the accepted hegemonic tradition where economic wealth and class of origin were (and are) explicitly coded as the most empowering facets in the hegemonic articulation of Jamaica's masculinities, and emphasizes dancehall culture's continuous re-scripting of the norms of personhood and identity from within its public/private marginalized spaces. Yet, one must be cautious in advocating that any one individual male can be identified as representing any one model of these masculinities in isolation of the others. What is common is for one form of dancehallized masculinity to predominate with other dancehallized male identity roles operating concurrently. For example, the identity of 'real badman' is balanced with the identity of 'family man' or 'violently anti-homosexual' usually revolving between the public/private spheres, or on an on-demand basis.

As debates about dancehall's various transgressions dominate media and social discussions in Jamaica, the lack of true civic engagement throughout all social, political, economic and other domains which has been created by the growing apathy and ambivalence of the Jamaican middle classes, has encouraged the society to rely heavily on the cultural output of the dancehall griots to define and identify Jamaican culture and lifestyle locally, regionally and internationally. Meeks's (1996, 124–43) concept of hegemonic dissolution in Jamaica proved particularly useful in theorizing the rise of dancehall culture from below as a challenge to hegemony from above in an era where the hegemony of these middle classes is in a state of flux. In this sphere of hegemonic dissolution, the passivity and reactivity of Jamaica's state, civil society and its citizens empower the dancehall as a space where gendered and classed modes of being proliferate, and where gendered revisions of a dancehallized identity can be negotiated, represented and subtly rescripted.

Consequently, dancehall's exemplars are inextricably bound up with the production and reproduction of fantasized images of Jamaican men in a Utopian sphere of pure patriarchy on the one hand, and a real life stage bounded by Jamaican classism and market capitalism, on the other.

This work also underscored the exploitation of a gendered predilection by contemporary dancehall masculinities, where the historical activities of female erotic dancers and modellers in dancehall culture highlighted the propensity of dancehall femininities to widen feminine boundaries. Notions of feminized costuming and masculine activity have been recast in dancehall culture to fabricate a highly transgressive dancehallized masculinity that is brokered not only on conspicuous consumption but indisputably on what has been historically coded as feminized practices, including spectacular dancing and a focus on bodily aesthetics and clothing styles by hardcore men, labelled Fashion Ova Style. Fashion Ova Style is enhanced with the growing numbers of Bogle's Progeny – an explosion in public, stylistic and spectacular dancing by groups of hardcore dancehall men who claim centre stage at dancehall events, and pander feverishly to the whims of the video light, which I refer to as the Videolight Syndrome.[2] The implosion of Bogle's Progeny within the centre/stage of dancehall symbolizes the gendered dislocations that are at work in Jamaica where the rigid patriarchal boundaries are experiencing incremental loosening and the hegemonic masculine tropes of the 1980s have been progressively reconstituted and incarnated in the Fashion Ova Style male body. It is evidenced in the spectacular exhibition of men claiming feminine aestheticization through dance, and the homoerotic dalliance and display in dancehall, all in a ritual denunciation of the rigid patriarchal structures that denied 'hardcore' dancehall and inner city men access to this magnificent and glorified arena of self promotion, homo-social engagement, and identity-creation as Dancehall Kings. The continued maturation and explosion of dancehall music and culture authorize the flamboyant, spectacular and stylish Dancehall Kings who continue to cement their position at dancehall's centre/stage. The celebratory and public dance moves of Bogle's Progeny, the popularized male dancers, on the centrestage of dancehall culture underscores the appropriation of feminized aesthetics and ritual practices by hardcore dancehall men as a part of their quest for male ascendancy, status and power in the dancehall. Even more importantly for the scope of this work, these Dancehall Kings co-opt dancehall's propensity for liminality and boundarylessness (Stanley Niaah 2004b) in traversing the increasingly porous and permeable gendered ramparts to traffic in a creative version of dancehallized masculine duality.

The ideological transgressions that early variants of dancehallized masculinities made in their re-articulations of Jamaican masculinity are identified as elements of the 'correct' representations of hegemonic masculinity as exemplified, for example, in the extreme forms of anti-male homosexual discourse in dancehall culture that effectively masks the symbiotic and necessary relationship between this form of dancehall masculinity and its antithesis, the homosexual male. These renderings of masculinities in dancehall signal a corresponding elucidation of ambivalent masculinities in dancehall culture which constitutes alternative spaces for the coding of dancehallized masculinities, while simultaneously cleaving to the primary markers of traditional, hegemonic masculinity in Jamaica. Indeed, the renderings of the Fashion Ova Style variant of dancehall masculinity embody the more transgressive elements of dancehall's masculine typologies. Yet, while it is brokered on transgressive, and often feminized behaviours, aesthetics and practices, Fashion Ova Style is projected as hardcore, heterosexual and even violent in that it incorporates elements of Badman, Ole Dawg and anti-Chi Chi Man masculinity. This paradoxical rendering of Fashion Ova Style is positioned at the nexus of dancehall's traditional and transgressive masculinities, and it is at this nexus that dancehall's ambivalent duality is incarnated and highlighted. Consequently, it is here in the embodiment and incarnation of a highly feminized and transgressive form of dancehallized masculinity on the stage of dancehall culture, that dancehall finds its own resolution to the inherent tensions in its ambivalent projections.

Thus, Fashion Ova Style signals both the creation of a new and highly transgressive variant of masculinity in dancehall culture, and temporally captures the dynamic modification of Jamaica's hegemonic masculinity in the face of growing challenges to the hegemonic order. Hegemonic masculinity must of necessity consistently modify itself to maintain its hegemony and often these modifications are reflected in a shift in the cultural meanings of masculinity without an accompanying shift in social structural arrangements (Hanke 1990, 244–45) as has occurred in Jamaican dancehall culture and

Jamaican society. This is signalled, for example, in the progression of the type of 'spontaneous consent' that is characteristic of hegemonic processes, where the reconstitution of the accepted codes of hegemonic masculinity in Jamaica is reflected in the ambivalence and/or acceptance of dancehall culture's hardcore adherents to the burgeoning spectacle of feminized male dancers as normative and normal. This highly feminized version of dancehallized masculinity, Fashion Ova Style, now holds currency and legitimacy in both dancehall culture and traditional Jamaican culture, in the context of the dated Victorian conservatism of Jamaica.

In the final analysis, Fashion Ova Style dancehallized masculinity also represents the current reconstitution of Jamaica's middle class hegemonic masculinity within dancehall culture. It is simultaneously a hardcore, polygamous and aggressive Badman or Shotta, and a patent heterosexual, who displays a softer, feminized aesthetic and actively engages in what have been coded as feminine and almost homosexual displays and behaviours in dancehall culture. Fashion Ova Style as dancehallized masculinity incorporates elements of older hegemonic imperatives with the radically newer inversions that together constitute the most contemporary version of hegemonic Jamaican masculinity in dancehall culture and points the way forward to wider social engagement with the hardcore machismo that has imprisoned many Jamaican men in its sway. Yet, as Jamaica progresses to its undefined future, defining and performing masculine personhood and citizenship in terms of the penis and sexual behaviour, the gun and violent behaviour, conspicuous consumption, 'flossing,' and narcissistic posing becomes more redundant and questionable. The corruption and stagnation of social and gendered power structures that encourage Jamaican men (particularly from the lower classes and Kingston's inner cities) to ritualize and perform these often empty and extreme patriarchal fantasies of penile, phallic and consumptive power, demand radical transformation. Even while the foregoing masculine exemplars provide cathartic release from the traumas forged in the crucible of Jamaican life, masculinities that are oriented towards the behaviours and activities of fatherhood, parenting, protection and real self development are the ones that hold greater social, political and gendered routes to empowerment for Jamaica's future men and women.

NOTES

INTRODUCTION

1. Jamaica National Census 2002, Statistical Institute of Jamaica. http://www. statinja.com

2. See Carolyn Cooper's feminist-influenced treatise on the dancehall in 'Erotic Play in the Dance Hall' (Pts. 1 & 2) in *Jamaica Journal* Vol. 22 Nos. 4 & Vol. 23 No. 1 (1990) p. 14–50 and her essay 'Slackness hiding from Culture: Erotic Play in the Dancehall' in *Noises in the Blood: Orality, Gender, and the "vulgar" Body of Jamaican Popular Culture*. Warwick University Caribbean Studies Series. London, Macmillan, 1993, pp. 136–73.

3. In other work, I define the *Videolight Syndrome* as 'the insatiable desire of many dancehall patrons to have their presence duly documented at the dances, stage shows and other dancehall events that they attend' where '...many of these individuals will go to great lengths to ensure that their images are captured on camera. This includes the wearing of elabourate and expensive jewellery and regalia, conspicuous purchase and consumption of expensive, brand name beverages like Moet & Chandon and Alizé, together with the wearing of erotic, revealing clothes and performance of erotic, x-rated dances by women.' (Hope 2006a, 127–8).

4. I have been conducting research on dancehall culture since the mid-1990s and have been a participant since the early 1980s.

5. See for example Errol Miller's (1987 and 1991) academic work on this crisis particular in the educational sector; as well as Albuquerque & Ruark 1998, and Figueroa 2004. Additionally there are numerous and ongoing discussions in the Jamaican newspapers, in particular the *Gleaner*. See for example Melville Cooke's critical article on fathering practices in the *Gleaner* of June 3, 2004; Peter Espeut's three-part article on the masculinity crisis in the *Gleaner* on February 16 & 26 and March 2, 2005; and Nyron Burke's letter to the Editor (named Letter of the Day) issuing a challenge to males on the education crisis in the *Gleaner* of February 23, 2005.

CHAPTER 1

1. Male interviewee at dancehall event, January, 2005.

2. Sexton, 1969, p. 15 quoted in Carrigan, Connell and Lee 1987, 148.

3. See Christine Barrow's discussion in the Introduction in Barrow 1998b (ed.), particularly pages xiii–xv.

4. Alexander, M. Jacqui, 1994, pp. 11–12.

5. The body of work undertaken by Carl Stone in the late 1970s and early 1980s on the composition and structure of Jamaica's class hierarchy now demands intense social science scrutiny to analyse how the economic and social mobility of the individuals from the inner cities and lower classes have impacted on transitions in the class formations since the 1980s.

6. In Hope 2001 the term dis/place refers to the overlapping sociocultural, political and economic discourses that characterize the space of the dancehall and draws on a multilayered etymology to construct a working definition: 'this disrespectful place where we have been placed; this place where we are consistently disrespected and mistreated; this place where we are consistently denied our legitimate human rights'; 'this place where we are denied access to resources'; 'this place where our identities are negated' and even more importantly, 'this place from within which we are forced to recreate and claim our resources, identities, personhood and self-esteem by any means.'

7. 'Donmanship' refers to the political structures that are raised on the interplay between community Dons and other constituents in political constituencies. Don is a title of distinction afforded to men who are considered to be of high social, political and economic status in Jamaica and the term is used, more particularly, to denote status among men from the lower socio-economic levels and in the inner city context. The Jamaican definition of Don draws significantly from the distinctive label given to Mafia overlords of the kind immortalized in the movie *Godfather;* however it is oriented around indigenous symbols of the 'ghetto gunman' who may sometimes have political and/or narco-political linkages. See Chapter 4 for a detailed description and analysis of the Don and his links to community control and gun violence.

8. For a discussion on Passa Passa in Jamaica see Hope, Donna P. 'Passa Passa: Interrogating Cultural Hybridities in Jamaican Dancehall.' *Small Axe: A Caribbean Journal of Criticism*, No. 21, October 2006, pp.119–33.

9. See a discussion on the seminal value of specific brand name cars in according higher levels of status to male identity in dancehall in Chapter 5.

CHAPTER 2

1. The term Ole Dawg wid Nuff Gyal is loosely translated to mean Old Dog with Many Women. I credit Beenie Man's two popular songs 'Ole Dawg,' and 'Nuff Gal' with the idea for this chapter title.

2. 'Fenky fenky' is a Jamaican Creole colloquialism which means shy, weak or reserved.

3. Batty is a Jamaican Creole colloquialism for 'bottom' or 'anus'. The 'batty business' refers to male homosexuality.

4. The anti-male homosexual discourse that is an integral part of male socialization, inner city culture and dancehall discourse in Jamaica is more extensively discussed and analysed in Chapter 4 of this work.

5. 'Boom off him fist' refers to the symbolic form of male-male salute that involves the touching of clenched fists in a symbolic gesture of acknowledgement or respect.

6. This passage is a composite extracted from several interviews with male respondents from an inner city community in West Kingston.

7. See a related discussion in my book *Inna di Dancehall*, 2006, pp. 48–52.

8. See my article 'Love Punaany Bad: Negotiating Misogynistic Masculinity in Dancehall Culture.' In *Caribbean Culture: Soundings on Kamau Braithwaite,* Annie Paul, ed. Kingston: University of the West Indies Press, 2007, pp. 367–80.

9. Other synonyms for the Punaany include: Punash; Pum pum; Pums; Punny; Renkin' meat; Ten ton; Tight an' good; Tight underneath; and Vagi.

10. At the time of coining this song, Rema and Jungle were politically polarized communities in the same political constituency of St Andrew Southern, held by the People's National Party with Minister Omar Davies as its Member of Parliament. Rema was aligned to the Jamaica Labour Party and Jungle to the People's National Party. Beenie Man's exhortations then meant that one should have women from various communities, regardless of political affiliation. Since 2005, Rema has begun to demonstrate more allegiance to the ruling PNP.

11. My navel string/umbilical cord was buried at the root of a coconut tree on my paternal Grandfather's property. As a child I recall how my mother (now deceased) would visit my Grandfather's farm and check on the status of this tree. When her visits became sparse, she would inquire about the health and well-being of the tree from my aunts and uncles. When I grew older she would remind me about the need to ensure that 'my tree' was watered and fed with relevant agricultural

products during my summers at my Grandfather's property. I do believe the tree is still alive and doing well.

12. *Mumma* is a honorific title bestowed on women considered senior, authoritative and powerful in traditional Jamaican parlance – a Jamaican Creole synonym for Matriarch. Its relation to chronological age is minimized by its emphasis on the high regard in which these women are held and the high levels of respect which they are accorded.

13. The Ouch Crew faded from the dancehall scene at the end of the 1990s and is reputed to have migrated to the USA.

14. Elephant Man is noted for his propensity to engage in simulated sex-behaviour (in particular the popular doggy style or 'back shot' position) with female patrons on stage during his live performances.

15. The 'big batty ooman', 'strong body ooman', and 'feisty ooman' are prominently discussed in dancehall myths of this nature.

16. A 2009 study conducted by the University of the West Indies and spearhead by the author targeted youths 15–24 years of age. The study revealed that at Vybz Kartel was perceived as the Most Popular Artiste and identified as the Most Favourite Artiste out of the 300 respondents targeted in the survey at that time.

17. 'The dancehall speaks many truths about women and men and about life. For example, look at how they regularly disrespect the (deviant) politicians and male homosexuals.'

18. 'Nyamming off,' 'Eating out' or 'eating off' women are all synonyms for cunnilingus.

19. I use the words 'grilled up' from conversations with a male interviewee. His use of the term refers to 'caged' or 'webbed', where, as he explains it, many young men follow the route of sexual posturing and become fathers to several children by the time they are in their early 20s. However, many often realize, too late, that this was not in their own, or their children's best interest.

20. See 'Musical Dads' in the Sunday Feature section of the *Sunday Observer* on Fathers' Day, June 19, 2005, where dancehall artistes Elephant Man, Mr Lex (formerly Lexxus) and Wayne Marshall shared their views on fatherhood.

21. Elephant Man, '2000 Began,' *Coming 4 You*, 2000.

22. In my earlier work on dancehall culture and sexuality (Hope 2001) I examine how multiple representations of femininity are narrated in dancehall culture. The role of Mother is invested with positive connotations and is greatly revered. This is in direct contestation to other representations of Woman that are either

perceived as threatening to the maintenance of masculinities; or as routes by which masculinities can be negotiated and/or achieved.

CHAPTER 3

1. Murder them, murder them, we are going to murder them in (lyrical) competition.
2. See for example Henry's (2002) treatise on the Shaft films which tackles the duality of race and masculinity and its conjunction with violence.
3. The representations of Jamaican badman, gangsta or Shotta as folk hero or anti-hero are performed in films like *The Harder They Come* (1972); *Dancehall Queen* (1997); *Third World Cop* (1999) and *Shottas* (2002).
4. 'I will stab any man who discusses peace here.'
5. 'Those boys up the road must die!'
6. See Annie Paul's discussion on this renaming in her blog on the Gully/Gaza phenomenon at: http://anniepaulactivevoice.blogspot.com/2009/09/eyeless-in-gaza-mi-deh-pon-di.html.
7. In a related discussion, David Scott (1999) uses the Fanonian concept of colonization/decolonization and then transcends with the Foucaultian concept of the body's role in examining the creation of spaces of liberty within a repressed context. In this refashioning he analyses the ruud bwai phenomenon described by Garth White in his 'Rudie oh Rudie' essay (over three decades ago). Scott then projects this forward and also touches on the concept of violence, which is extremely central to discourses on the cultural/political/sociological mixture existing in the popular culture of contemporary Jamaica.
8. Cooper's (1994) discussion on lyrical and metaphorical gun play in dancehall culture also tackles this point, noting that 'Badmanism' is a theatrical pose that has been refined in the complicated socialization processes of Jamaican ghetto youth who learn to imitate the sartorial and ideological style of the heroes and villains of imported American films.

    See also discussions in the Jamaican *Daily & Sunday Gleaner* about the 'crisis of Jamaican masculinity, in particular Chang, Cooke, Mills, Mitchell and Simms (all 2004).
9. Babylon as used here refers to the individual policeman but also refers to the collective body of security forces. This usage draws on the ideology of Rastafari where the Biblical reference to the symbolic whore of Babylon was taken and invested with further negatives that are used to impute collusion with/

representation of oppressors which include the State and its agents, market capitalism and so on.

10. Ratty refers to the character played by Mark Danvers in the Island Records film, *Third World Cop*. Ratty was murdered because of his underhanded and traitorous activities.

11. Elephant Man, 'Bad Man', *Good to Go*, Atlantic Records, 2003.

12. See Chapter 5 for an in depth discussion and analysis of this fear of male feminizing as expressions of an anti-male homosexual ethos.

CHAPTER 4

1. A line from an anti-male homosexual treatise by Elephant Man & Ward 21 (2000).

2. In Jamaica, the term batty is Jamaican creole or slang for buttocks. Battyman is a pejorative term for men who have sex with men, as anal sex is perceived as the act which defines them.

3. Author's CD collection.

4. See the 2004 Human Rights Watch Report on Jamaica titled 'Hated to Death: Homophobia, Violence and Jamaica's HIV/AIDS Epidemic' and in particular Section IV – 'Homophobia in Jamaica and its role in driving the HIV/AIDS epidemic.'

5. See Atluri's (2001) paper for a more extensive discussion on the structure of homophobia in four Anglophone Caribbean countries, Barbados, Trinidad & Tobago, Jamaica and The Bahamas.

6. As discussed in Chapter 2, in the dancehall, fellatio or cunnilingus is referred as 'bowing' and men or women who perform these acts are referred to as 'bow cats' or 'bow seed'. The word 'bow' as disseminated in the dancehall, signifies the low status assigned to the act where one must stoop 'down low' to show deference or respect for a higher authority figure, in effect willfully accepting and participating in one's own subservience and subjugation.

7. For related discussions on the legislative terrain of Caribbean and Jamaican heterosexist ideology see Atluri 2001 (in particular pp. 26–32); and Hron 2003 (in particular pp. 4–5).

8. Laws of Jamaica, Volume XIX. See also discussion in Hron 2003.

9. See Stephens, Gregory. Transcript of Radio Interview 'A Culture of Intolerance: Insights on the Chi Chi Man Craze and Jamaica Gender Relations with Julius Power of JGLAG.' Spring 2002 at http://www.jahworks.org/music/interview/jflag_interview.html.

10. For example, he was identified as the uncle or older brother who was overly effeminate, had never married, had no children and kept an unusually neat and tidy house. For some interviewees, he was usually educated and self sufficient, holding a steady job and paid unusual attention to his personal aesthetics, including the wearing of 'good' clothing that was well coordinated. Interviewees noted that this man usually had very good relationships with 'the women' but did face the occasional verbal accusation/condemnation and slurs.

11. Interview conducted December 2004.

12. This outline is the result of a series of in depth interviews with men from inner city and poor communities.

13. Literally translated this means 'they are not more than me/we.' The phrase actually means 'their status level is not higher than mine/ours.' In the class and status driven crucible of the country, Jamaicans are quite adept at leveling the status-driven playing field by identifying various traits or behaviours of another individual or group, as deviant and therefore a marker of lesser status.

14. See Gutzmore, Cecil. 'Casting the First Stone!: Policing of Homo/Sexuality in Jamaican Popular Culture,' in *Interventions: International Journal of Postcolonial Studies* Special Issue on Jamaican Popular Culture co-edited by Carolyn Cooper and Alison Donnell 6.1: April, 2004, pp. 118–34.

15. '(The) homosexual men are becoming too visible.' Interview with male dancehall adherent, December 2004.

16. 'They have even formed (a) group and are appearing on television.' Interview with male dancehall adherent, December 2004.

17. These programmes include *Will and Grace, Queer as Folk* and *Queer Eye for the Straight Guy.*

18. Visit www.jflag.org for information on this group.

19. Alozade, 2000. Chi Chi Crew. From Author's CD collection.

20. In the dancehall and in Jamaica this notion of male superiority versus female inferiority and the resultant privileging of heterosexual masculinity is often countered by the high value placed on womanhood as mothers and wives, which arguably incorporate similar notions of the privileging of heterosexual masculinity, as women in these roles provide support and sustenance for these male identities.

21. For a broader discussion of dancehall's lyrical discussions on gun, see Carolyn Cooper's discussion of the metaphorical and lyrical discussions of the gun in Jamaican dancehall in her chapter 'Lyrical Gun: Metaphor and Word Role-Play in Dancehall Culture' in her *Sound Clash.* 2004. pp.145–78.

22. Note that dancehall is the contemporary strain of Jamaica's popular music culture and, as such, is not a source of the society's anti-male homosexual discourses. Rather, it is an extreme representation of Jamaica's views and values. For example, in Jamaica, I was first introduced to anti-male homosexual discussions as a child in Sunday school, more than two decades before these debates coalesced in the dancehall.

23. See 'AIDS in Jamaica: The fear that spreads death,' *Economist*, 24 November 2005.

24. See 'New Push for gay rights debate – Rhodd's committee wants discussion on legalizing homosexuality, prostitution' in *Jamaica Observer*, 31 July 2005.

25. See, for example, 'Golding talks about policing, gays on the BBC' in *Jamaica Gleaner*, May 21, 2008 at http://www.jamaica-gleaner.com/gleaner/20080521/lead/lead3.html; a set of (seven) Letters to the Editor with varying views on the issue published under the heading 'The gay debate' in *Jamaica Gleaner*, May 23, 2008 at http://www.jamaica-gleaner.com/gleaner/20080523/news/news3.html; and Ian Boyne's column entitled 'Golding and the gays' in *Sunday Gleaner*, May 25, 2008 at http://www.jamaica-gleaner.com/gleaner/20080525/focus/focus1.html.

26. See for example 'PNP lashes Ernie Smith on stance against gays' in *Daily Gleaner*, February 19, 2009 at http://www.jamaica-gleaner.com/gleaner/20090219/lead/lead4.html; Letter to the Editor from Yvonne Mcalla Sobers 'Gaps in discourse on sex' in *Jamaica Gleaner*, 20 February 2009 at http://www.jamaica-gleaner.com/gleaner/20090220/letters/letters8.html; and Garth Rattray, 'No Accountability for Smith' in *Daily Gleaner*, 23 February 2009 at http://www.jamaica-gleaner.com/gleaner/20090223/cleisure/cleisure2.html; and Lloyd B. Smith's 'Would lawyer Ernie Smith refuse to represent gays' in the *Jamaica Observer*, 17 February 2009 at http://www.jamaicaobserver.com/columns/html/20090216T220000-0500_146329_OBS_WOULD_LAWYER_ERNIE_SMITH_REFUSE_TO_REPRESENT_GAYS_.asp.

27. See 'Buggery laws firm: PM Says Life or 15 years for some sex-offences breach' in *Jamaica Gleaner*, 4 March 2009 at http://www.jamaica-gleaner.com/gleaner/20090304/lead/lead1.html.

CHAPTER 5

1. Interview conducted January, 2003.

2. For works on fashion, style and identity, see for example, Benstock & Ferriss (eds.) *On Fashion*, 1994; Finklestein, *Chic Theory,* 1997; Leitch, *Costly Compensations*, 1996; Wilson & Ash (eds.), *Chic Thrills*, 1992.

3. According to Merton (1938) identifies ritualism as one of the responses to the disparity between goals and means. He expands his discussion and definition in his 1949 paper, which is significantly reproduced in the Chapter titled 'Continuities in the Theory of Social Structure and Anomie' his 1957 book, *Social Theory and Social Structure.*

4. See for example the discussion in Stone (1992) on the role dress plays in defining status in Jamaica.

5. See for example Chapter 4 in Carolyn Cooper's *Sound Clash*, 2004, titled 'Mama, is that You?: Erotic Disguise in the films *Dancehall Queen* and *Babymother*'; and Bibi Bakare-Yusuf's 'Fabricating Identities: Survival and Imagination in Jamaican Dancehall Culture,' *Fashion Theory*, Vol 10, Issue 3, 2006, pp. 1–24.

6. Heavy gold jewellery was favoured by both men and women as a signal of wealth. During the 1980s to 1990s the 'Peace and Love' jewellery store on Harbour Street in downtown Kingston was very popular and frequented by many dancehall adherents as it catered to the desire for heavy and flamboyant gold pendants, bracelets, earrings, necklaces and anklets, often adorned with colourful stones. Large earrings shaped like bunches of grapes and the flowers from the hibiscus plants were very popular among women. Large rings shaped like Africa were popular among men. Many people could not afford to purchase real gold and so 'Peace and Love' and other jewellery stores provided an alternative in the form of gold plated jewellery popularly known as 'Enciz' or 'Encees'.

7. The locally-owned Jamaica Telephone Company changed hands to become the British-owned Telecommunications of Jamaica, which then changed its name to Cable and Wireless. This company re-imaged and rebranded in 2009 to become known as LIME, an acronym for Land, Internet, Mobile and Entertainment. The obvious challenges with this name and Jamaican culture were seemingly overlooked in the thrust to have a regional mode of identification. For example, in Trinidad, the term lime or lyme means to chat and socialize with good friends. In Jamaica the term lime refers to the sour citrus fruit that is used to make beverages. In Jamaican culture the term 'sour like lime' is used in a negative sense to connote harshness, distasteful and unfit for pleasurable consumption. Thus, in Jamaica, the telecommunications giant continues to display that it is not fully cognizant of Jamaican culture and has earned a culturally appropriate moniker from ordinary Jamaicans thus: 'sour LIME.'

8. See for example, Digicel's price list at: http://www.digiceljamaica.com/en/phones/phones_list.php. In addition, Jamaicans purchase these phone instruments from individual retailers who import them from abroad and may

sell them approximately ten per cent cheaper than the prices quoted by Digicel. Others may receive them as gifts from family or friends at home and abroad.

9. For example, during the height of its popularity, Vybz Kartel and Spice's controversial song *Ramping Shop* was a very popular ring tone among my students at the University of the West Indies, Mona.

10. Research shows that while they do cost less at liquor stores and other outlets, the going rate for these beverages at dancehall events and popular clubs are/were as follows:- Alizé – J$7,000 to J$8,000 per bottle; Cristal – J$14,000 to J$18,000 per bottle; Moet and Chandon – J$7,000- J$8,000 per bottle;, Hypnotic – J$7,000 per bottle and Henessey J$7,500 to J$10,000 per bottle. On the other hand, the minimum wage in Jamaica as at the time of this paper was J$3,700.00 per week.

11. PNP Money was apparently on full display at the Nomination Day (celebrations) on Monday, September 30, 2002, as recorded by the *Jamaica Gleaner* reporter who covered the proceedings. The effort made by members of different political persuasions to be identified not only by their partisan colours and clothing was also augmented by their need to be part of the hype. 'PNP Money' also known as the 'Joshua' (a popular name given to the late Michael Manley in his political heyday) was the legal tender chosen by several People's National Party candidates to pay the J$3,000.00 nomination fee. While the article did not speak to the type of bills used by the Prime Minister, it clearly stated that National Democratic Movement's Leader, Hyacinth Bennett used the $500 bills (the 'Nanny) because 'they carry the face of Jamaica's lone female national hero,' Nanny of the Maroons. The nomination fee for the then Leader of the Opposition Jamaica Labour Party, Edward Seaga, was paid with thirty J$100.00 bills, which bear the image of the late Sir Donald Sangster, former Prime Minister and member of the JLP.

12. These identity groups demand further research and analysis which are not the focus of this work.

13. See discussion in Chapter 3 on the importance and pertinence of symbolic and real violence in denoting traditional status and personhood to young men, particularly from inner city communities.

14. The Caribbean's most dramatic example of this cathartic carnivalesque is the annual staging of Carnival in Trinidad & Tobago.

15. The Rolex watch is an internationally recognized symbol of personal wealth.

16. 'Those men have everything under control,' meaning they are perceived as successful and powerful.

17. 'A man has to be expensively attired to denote his high status.'

CHAPTER 6

1. Here, 'Shorty' reflects the cross-fertilization with American hip-hop culture in its affectionate and diminutive reference to a woman.

2. Keiva and Mad Michelle are both popular female dancers in the dancehall. Mad Michelle was crowned Dancehall Queen 2003 at the annual Dancehall Queen contest held in Montego Bay, Jamaica.

3. Stacey is another popular female dancer in the dancehall who was crowned Dancehall Queen 1999 at the annual Dancehall Queen contest held in Montego Bay. Stacey is popularized for her gymnast-like feats including the propensity to jump up onto the top of sound system boxes at dancehall events and use this vantage point to display her dance prowess to the dancehall audience.

4. Junko 'Bashment' Kudo is a Japanese woman who was the first non-Jamaica to be crowned Dancehall Queen 2002 at the annual Dancehall Queen contest held in Montego Bay. Junko subsequently became a popular staple at dancehall events in Jamaica and was featured in several dancehall events. She opened a school to teach Jamaican dance in Tokyo, Japan.

5. The literal translation of 'shottas' is shooters. The term refers to gunmen or 'real badmen' who epitomize the type of violent heterosexual masculinity that is lauded in dancehall.

6. For example in Mavado's song *Mr Palmer (New Name fi Informa)*, 2008.

7. 'To bleach' in Jamaican Creole also means to stay awake all night without sleep until day lights, i.e. from darkness to light. It is often associated with staying out at parties, dances, wakes or similar events. Thus, people who work night shifts will not usually say that they 'bleach' but someone who attended a party or a wake will claim to have 'bleached' all night. A good 'bleacher' is someone who can stay up all night and then conduct their regular daylight duties at work or school without any visible effects of having missed a night's sleep.

8. Dancehall's daily calendar incorporates ample opportunities for this type alternative notion of 'bleaching' as regular dancehall activities usually get underway close to midnight and taper off after daybreak, oftentimes close to 8:00 a.m.

9. 'Really bad men do not wear pants that belong to other people. We take dancing to a higher level.' Elephant Man, '*Pon di River,*' 2003.

10. See Stanley-Niaah (2004a) for a discussion on this, in particular pages 112–13.

11. The National Dance Theatre Company was pioneered over 40 years ago by University of the West Indies intellectual, dancer and choreographer, the late Professor Rex Nettleford. The NDTC remains one of Jamaica's most prominent dance groups. Others include L'Acadco, The Company, and the University Dancers.

12. See Chapter 4 for a discussion of the role of extreme and often violent anti-male homosexual discourses in creating alternative discourses of dancehall masculinity.

13. In her *Sunday Gleaner* article of July 3, 2005, Tanya Batson-Savage discusses the increase in male dancers in professional dance ensembles like the National Dance Theatre Company (NDTC) which seemingly indicates an erasure of the homosexual and feminized stigma that haunted this activity.

14. Popular Male Dancers include: Bogle (R.I.P.), Willie Haggart (R.I.P.), Labba Labba, Bruk Up, Shelley Belly, Overmars, Ding Dong, Bwoysie, John Hype, Ice (R.I.P.), Craigy Dread, Tippa, Sick in Head, Sadiki; and Popular Male Dance Crews include: Black Roses, Ravers Clavers, M.O.B., Black Blingers, Timeless Dancers, Kadillac Dancers, Sample Six, Chef Squad.

15. Popular male dancer and dancehall icon, Gerald 'Bogle' Levy, was murdered in January, 2005.

16. Notably, this phenomenon does not highlight a new wave of dancing among Jamaican men but represents the resurgence of a persistent ethos of male dancing in Jamaican culture that was suppressed and forced underground beneath the pressures of dancehall cultures extreme discourses of anti-male homosexuality and effeminacy, and its projections of the dancehall male as hardcore, violent and unfeminine.

17. Elephant Man's 2003 Album, *Good 2 Go* features a significant number of tracks which have driven the creation and naming of popular dance styles from 2002 onwards.

CONCLUSION

1. Robert Merton's (1938 & 1957) work on anomie and his identification of ritualism as one response to social and economic pressures is relevant to this work. In particular in Chapter 6 where the ritualistic celebration of conspicuous consumption and masculine posing becomes of primary importance in identifying one dancehall discourse of manhood.

2. See Note 3 in the Introduction of this work.

REFERENCES

Adams, Rachel, and David Savran (Eds.). *The Masculinity Studies Reader*. Malden, Massachusetts: Blackwell Publishers, 2002.

Adorno, Theodor. *Introduction to the Sociology of Music*. New York: Continuum, 1968/88.

————. *The Culture Industry: Selected Essays on Mass Culture*. London and New York: Routledge, 1991.

'Adventists won't bury lawbreakers' in *Sunday Observer*, June 19, 2005, pp. 10–11.

Albuquerque, Klaus de and Sam Ruark. '"Men Day Done" Are Women really Ascendant in the Caribbean?' in Christine Barrow (ed.) *Caribbean Portraits: Essays on Gender Ideologies and Identities*: Kingston: Ian Randle Publishers, 1998, pp. 1–13.

Alexander, J. 'The Role of the Male in the Middle-Class Jamaican Family: A Comparative Perspective' in *Journal of Comparative Family Studies* 8, 1977, pp. 369–89.

Alexander, M. Jacqui. 'Not Just (Any) *Body* Can be a Citizen: The Politics of Law, Sexuality and Postcoloniality in Trinidad and Tobago and the Bahamas.' *Feminist Review*. 48, Autumn 1994, pp. 5–23.

Allen, Robert C. (ed.). *Channels of Discourse, Reassembled*. London: Routledge, 1992.

Althusser, Louis. 'Ideology and Ideological State Apparatuses' in *Lenin and Philosophy and Other Essays*. Translated by Ben Brewster. New York: Monthly Review Press, 1971, pp. 127–86.

Appadurai, Arjun. *Modernity at Large: Cultural Dimensions of Globalization*. Minneapolis and London: University of Minnesota Press, 1996.

Attali, Jacques. *Noise: The Political Economy of Music*. Translated by Brian Massumi. Minneapolis, Minnesota: University of Minnesota Press, 1985.

Atluri, Tara L. 'When the closet is a region: homophobia, heterosexism and nationalism in the Commonwealth Caribbean.' Working Paper No. 5, Centre for Gender and Development Studies, University of the West Indies, Cave Hill, Barbados, 2001.

Austin, Diane J. *Urban Life in Kingston, Jamaica: The Culture and Class Ideology of Two Neighborhoods*. New York; London; Paris et al.: Gordon and Breach, 1984.

Ayton, Carl (then Secretary of the Jamaica Federation of Musicians). 'Disgusting Performances.' Letter to the Editor. In the *Daily Gleaner*, Tuesday, August 18, 1987.

Bachrach, C. and F. Sonenstein. 'Male Fertility and Family Formation: Research and Data needs on the Pathways to Fatherhood' in Federal Interagency Forum on Child and Family Statistics (eds.) Nurturing *Fatherhood: Improving Data and Research on Male Fertility, Family Formation and Fatherhood.* www. fatherhood.hhs.gov/cfsforum/front.htm, 1998.

Bailey, B. *Not an Open Book: Gender Achievement and Education in the Caribbean.* Mona, Jamaica: UWI, Centre for Gender and Development Studies, 1997.

Bailey, Wilma; Clement Branche; Gail McGarrity and Sheila Stuart (eds.). *Family and the Quality of Gender Relations in the Caribbean.* UWI, Mona, Kingston: ISER, 1998.

Baird, Vanessa. *Sex, Love and Homophobia: Lesbian, Gay, Bisexual and Transgendered Lives.* UK: Amnesty International, 2004.

Bakare-Yusuf, Bibi. 'Fabricating Identities: Survival and the Imagination in Dancehall Culture' in *Fashion Theory*, Volume 10, Issue 3, 2006, pp. 1–24.

Barriteau, Eudine. 'Postmodernist Feminist Theorizing and Development Policy and Practice in the Anglophone Caribbean: The Barbados Case,' in *Feminism / Postmodernism / Development.* Edited by Marianne Marchand and Jane Plupart. London: Routledge, 1995a.

———. 'Socialist Feminist Theory and Caribbean Women: Transcending Dualisms.' *Social and Economic Studies.* Vol. 44 No. 2 & 3, June, 1995b, pp. 25–63.

———. 'Theorizing Gender Systems and the Project of Modernity in the Twentieth Century Caribbean.' *Feminist Review* Vol. 59 Summer, 1998, pp. 186–209.

———. *The Political Economy of Gender in the 20th Century Caribbean*, Palgrave, Basingstoke, 2001.

———. 'Requiem for the Male Marginalization Thesis in the Caribbean: Death of a Non-Theory.' in *Confronting Power, Theorizing Gender: Interdisciplinary Perspectives in the Caribbean.* Ed. Eudine Barriteau, 322–53. Kingston: University of the West Indies Press, 2004a, pp. 322–53.

Barriteau Eudine (ed.). *Confronting Power, Theorizing Gender: Interdisciplinary Perspectives in the Caribbean.* Kingston: University of the West Indies Press, 2004b.

Barrow, Christine. 'Male Images of Women in Barbados' in *Social and Economic Studies*, Vol. 35, No. 3, 1986, pp. 51–64.

———. *Family in the Caribbean: Themes and Perspectives.* Kingston: Ian Randle Publishers, 1996.

———. 'Caribbean Masculinity and Family: Revisiting "Marginality" and "Reputation"' in Christine Barrow (ed.) *Caribbean Portraits: Essays on Gender Ideologies and Identities*: Kingston: Ian Randle, 1998a, pp. 339–58.

Barrow, Christine (ed.) *Caribbean Portraits: Essays on Gender Ideologies and Identities*: Kingston: Ian Randle Publishers, 1998b.

Barrow, Steve and Peter Dalton. *Reggae: The Rough Guide*. London: Rough Guides Ltd., 1997.

Barthes, Roland. *Mythologies*. New York: Paladin, 1972.

Batson-Savage, Tanya. 'Boys Take to Dance' in The *Sunday Gleaner*, July 3, 2005, pp E1–E2.

Beckles, Hilary. 'Black Masculinity in Caribbean Slavery' in Reddock, Rhoda (ed.). *Interrogating Caribbean Masculinities: Theoretical and Empirical Analyses*. Jamaica, Trinidad & Barbados: UWI Press, 2004a, pp. 225–43.

———. 'Perfect Property: Enslaved Black Women in the Caribbean' in Barriteau Eudine (ed.). *Confronting Power, Theorizing Gender: Interdisciplinary Perspectives in the Caribbean*. Kingston: University of the West Indies Press, 2004b, pp. 142–58.

———. 'Sex and gender in the historiography of Caribbean slavery,' in Bridget Brereton, Barbara Bailey & Verene Shepherd (eds) *Engendering History: Caribbean Women in Historical Perspective*, Kingston: Ian Randle Publishers, 1995, pp. 125–38.

Bederman, Gail. *Manliness & Civilization: A Cultural History of Gender and Race in the United States, 1880-1917*. Chicago and London: University of Chicago Press, 1995.

Bem, Sandra Lipsitz. *The Lenses of Gender: Transforming the Debate on Sexual Inequality*. New Haven, CT: Yale University Press, 1993.

Bennett, Andy. *Popular Music and Youth Culture: Music Identity and Place*. London & New York: Macmillan Press and St. Martin's Press, Inc. 2000.

Bennett, Tony. 'The Politics of the "popular" and popular culture' in *Popular Culture and Social Relations*. Ed. by Tony Bennett, Colin Mercer and Joan Woollacott. Milton Keynes: Open University Press, 1986.

Benstock, Shari and Ferriss, Suzanne (eds.). *On Fashion*. Rutgers University Press, 1994.

Benyon, John. *Masculinities and Culture*. Buckingham; Philadelphia: Open University Press, 2002.

Berger, Maurice, Wallis, Brian and Watson, Simon. (eds). *Constructing Masculinity*. New York and London: Routledge, 1995.

'Big Support for Lockdown: Banks, supermarkets, gas stations among businesses to protest against high crime rate,' the *Jamaica Observer*, Wednesday, May 25, 2005.

Bly, Robert. *Iron John: A Book About Men*. USA, England, Canada, et al: Addison-Wesley Publishing Co. Inc., 1990.

Bordo, Susan. *The Male Body: A New Look at Men in Public and Private*. New York: Farrar, Straus and Giroux, 1999.

Bourdieu, Pierre. (Translated by Richard Nice). *Distinction: A Social Critique of the Judgement of Taste*. Cambridge, MA: Harvard University Press, 1984.

———. *The Field of Cultural Production: Essays on Art and Literature*. (Edited and Introduced by Randal Johnson). Columbia: Columbia University Press, 1993.

Boxill, Ian. 'The Two Faces of Caribbean Music' in *Social and Economic Studies*. Vol 43 No. 2, 1994, pp 494–503.

Boyd, Derick. *Economic Management, Income Distribution, and Poverty in Jamaica*. New York: Praeger, 1988.

Boyd, Todd. *Am I Black Enough For You? Popular Culture From the 'Hood and Beyond*. Bloomington: Indiana University Press, 1997.

Boyne, Ian. 'Decadent Dancehall Mirrors Society' in the *Sunday Gleaner*, January 5, 1997, p. 8A.

———. 'How Dancehall Promotes Violence' in *The Sunday Gleaner*, December 22, 2002, pp. G1 & G3.

———. 'How Dancehall Holds us Back' in the *Sunday Gleaner*, December 29, 2002, pp. G1 & G5.

———. '"Sting": A Disgraced Institution' in *The Sunday Gleaner*, January 4, 2004, pp. E7–E8.

Braithwaite, Edward. *The Development of Creole Society in Jamaica 1770–1820*. Oxford, Clarendon Press, 1971.

Brennan, Teresa. *The Interpretation of the Flesh: Freud and Femininity*. London and New York: Routledge, 1992.

Brereton, Bridget, Verene Shepherd and Barbara Bailey (eds.). *Engendering History: Caribbean Women in Historical Perspective*. Kingston: Ian Randle Publishers, 1995.

Brittan, Arthur. *Masculinity and Power*. Oxford: Basil Blackwell, 1989

Brod. H. (ed.) *The Making of Masculinities: The New Men's Studies*. Boston: Allen & Unwin, 1987.

Brod H. and Kaufman, M. (eds.). *Theorizing Masculinities*. Thousand Oaks, London & New Delhi: Sage, 1994.

Brodber, Erna. *Reggae and Cultural Identity*. Kingston: University of the West Indies Press, 1988.

Brown, Aggrey. *Colour, Class and Politics in Jamaica*. New Brunswick, NJ: Transaction Books, 1979.

Brown, J. 'Findings of the Gender Socialization Project,' Caribbean Child Development Centre, University of the West Indies Jamaica, presented at the annual UNICEF Global Seminar on 'Achieving Gender Equality in Families: The Roles of Males,' 1995.

Brown, Jarrett. 'Masculinity and Dancehall' in *Caribbean Quarterly*, Vol. 45, No. 1, March, UWI, Mona, 1999, pp. 1–16.

Buchbinder, David. *Masculinities and Identities*. Melbourne: Melbourne University Press, 1994.

———. *Performance Anxieties: Re-producing Masculinity*. Sydney: Allen & Unwin, 1998.

Burke, Nyron S. 'Challenge to Males on education crisis.' Letter to the Editor in the *Gleaner*, February 23, 2005.

Burrell, Ian. 'A shift in reggae consciousness?' in the *Sunday Herald*, November 20, 1994.

"Business Lockdown: PSOJ to take decisive action against crime", the *Gleaner*, May 20, 2005.

Butler, Judith. *Gender Trouble: Feminism and the Subversion of Identity*. New York: Routledge, 1990.

———. *Bodies that Matter: On the Discursive Limits of Sex*. Routledge, 1993.

Caplan, Patricia (ed.). *The Cultural Construction of Sexuality*. London & New York: Tavistock, 1987.

Caribbean Child Development Centre. *Men and Their Families: Contributions of Caribbean Men to Family Life*. Jamaica, 1995.

Carrigan, T., B. Connel and J. Lee. 'Hard and heavy: Toward a new sociology of masculinity' in M. Kaufman (ed.), *Beyond patriarchy,. Essays by men on pleasure, power, and change*. New York: Oxford University Press, 1987, pp. 139–92.

Chang, Kevin O'Brien and Wayne Chen. *Reggae Routes: The Story of Jamaican Music*. Kingston: Ian Randle Publishers, 1998.

Chapman R. and J. Rutherford (eds.). *Male Order: Unwrapping Masculinity*. London: Lawrence & Wishart, 1988.

Charles, Christopher. 'Garrison Communities as Counter Societies: The Case of the 1998 Zeeks Riot in Jamaica'. *Ideaz*, Vol. 1, No. 1, 2002, pp. 29–43.

Chevannes, Barry and J. Brown. *Why Man Stay So: Tie the Heifer and Loose the Bull*. Mona, Jamaica: The University of the West Indies, 1998.

Chevannes, Barry. *Rastafari: Roots and Ideology*. Syracuse: Syracuse University Press; and Kingston: The Press, University of the West Indies, 1994.

———. *What we sow and what we reap: Problems in the Cultivation of Male Identity in Jamaica*. Grace Kennedy Lecture Series, 1999.

———. *Learning To be a Man: Culture, Socialization and Gender Identity in Five Caribbean Communities*. Barbados: University of the West Indies Press, 2001.

'Chi-Chi song a no-no', Letter to the Editor in the *Gleaner*, April 6, 2001.

Chin, Timothy. 'Bullers' and 'Battymen': Contesting Homophobia in Black Popular Culture and Contemporary Caribbean Literature. *Callaloo* 20.1, 1997, pp. 127–41.

———. 'Jamaican Popular Culture, Caribbean Literature, and the Representation of Gay and Lesbian Sexuality in the Discourses of Race and Nation' in *Small Axe* No. 5, 1999, pp. 14–33.

Chodorow, Nancy J. 'Gender as a Personal and Cultural Construction' in *Signs* 20:3, 1995, pp. 516–44.

Clarke, Edith. *My Mother Who Fathered Me: A Study of the Families in Three Selected Communities of Jamaica*. Barbados, Jamaica & Trinidad & Tobago: The University of the West Indies Press, 1997.

Clarke, Sebastian. *Jah Music: The Evolution of Popular Jamaican Song*. London: Heinemann Educational Books, 1980.

Clatterbaugh, Kenneth. *Contemporary Perspectives on Masculinity.* 2nd edn. Boulder, Colorado and Oxford: Westview Press, 1997.

Clunis, Andrew. 'Reggae music suffering because of violence' in the *Star*, May 6, 1999a.

———. 'To the Bin with Filthy Lyrics' in the *Gleaner*, August 27, 1999b, p. C1.

———. 'Music Polluting Young Minds' in the *Sunday Gleaner*, May 7, 2000, p. 1E.

Cohan, S. *Masked Men: Masculinity and the movies in the fifties.* Bloomington, IN: Indiana University Press, 1997.

Connell, R. W. *Gender and Power: Society, the Person and Sexual Politics.* Cambridge: Polity Press, 1987.

———. 'An Iron Man: The body and Some Contradictions of Hegemonic Masculinity,' in M. Messner and D. Sabo (eds.). Sport, Men and the Gender Order. Champaign, IL: Human Kinetics Books, 1990.

———. *Masculinities.* Berkeley & Los Angeles: University of California Press, 1995.

———. 'The Social Organization of Masculinity' in Whitehead, Stephen and Barrett, Frank J. (eds.). *The Masculinities Reader.* Cambridge & Oxford, UK and Malden, MA: Polity and Blackwell, 2001, pp. 30–50.

Conyers, James L. (ed.). *African-American Jazz and Rap: Social and Philosophical Examinations of Black Expressive Behaviour.* North Carolina: McFarland & Company, Inc., 2001.

Cooke, Mel. 'The "babyfather" privilege – Me a de bes' babyfaada inna Jamaica.' the *Gleaner*, June 3, 2004.

———. 'Story of the Song: General Trees calls for the "$50 Bill"'. The *Sunday Gleaner*, May 31, 2009.

Cooper, Carolyn. 'Erotic Play in the Dance Hall' (Pts. 1 & 2) in *Jamaica Journal* Vol. 22 Nos. 4 & Vol. 23 No. 1, 1990, pp. 14–50.

———. 'Slackness hiding from Culture: Erotic Play in the Dancehall' in *Noises in the Blood: Orality, Gender, and the "vulgar" Body of Jamaican Popular Culture.* Warwick University Caribbean Studies Series. London, Macmillan, 1993, pp. 136–73.

———. 'Lyrical Gun': Metaphor and Role Play in Jamaican Dancehall Culture. *The Massachusetts Review*, Vol. 35, Iss. 3–4, Autumn 1994, pg. 429–47.

———. "Punany Power", *Black Media Journal*, 2, 2000, pp. 50–52.

———. *Sound Clash: Jamaican Dancehall Culture from Lady Saw to Dancehall Queen.* Palgrave Macmillan, 2004.

Dann, Graham. *The Barbadian Male: Sexual Attitudes and Practice.* London: Macmillan, 1987.

Davis, Stephen and Peter Simon. *Reggae Bloodlines: In Search of The Music and Culture of Jamaica.* New York: Da Capo, 1992.

———. *Reggae International.* New York: Rogner & Bernhard 1982.

Dent, Gina, (ed.). *Black Popular Culture.* Seattle: Bay Press, 1992.

Donaldson, Mike. 'What is Hegemonic Masculinity?' in *Theory and Society*, Vol. 22, No. 5, Special Issue: Masculinities, Oct. 1993, pp. 643–57.

Douglas, Mary. *Purity and Danger: An Analysis of Concepts of Pollution and Taboo.* London: Routledge and Kegan Paul, 1966.

Edwards, Tim. *Men in the Mirror: Men's Fashion, Masculinity and Consumer Society.* London: Cassell, 1997.

Emmanuel, Patrick, A. M. *Elections and Party Systems in the Commonwealth Caribbean: 1944–1991.* St. Michael, Barbados: Caribbean Development Research Services, 1992.

'Emotional Farewell for "Haggart"' in the *Gleaner*, Wednesday, May 9, 2001, p. A1.

Espeut, Peter. 'The Crisis in Masculinity (Part 1).' the *Gleaner*, February 16, 2005.

———. "The Crisis in Masculinity (Part III)." the *Gleaner*, February 26, 2005.

———. "The Crisis in Masculinity (Part III)." the *Gleaner*, March 2, 2005.

'Extortionists Sow Fear in May Pen,' the *Gleaner*, Tuesday, May 17, 2005.

Farrell, Warren. *The Liberated Man, Beyond Masculinity: Freeing Men and their Relationships with Women.* New York: Random House, 1974.

Featherstone, Mike, Hepworth, Mike and Turner, Bryan. (eds). *The Body: Social Process and Cultural Theory.* London: Sage, 1991.

Figueroa, Mark. 'Male Privileging and Male "Academic Underperformance" in Jamaica,' in Reddock, Rhoda E. (ed.). *Interrogating Caribbean Masculinities: Theoretical and Empirical Analyses.* Jamaica; Barbados; Trinidad & Tobago: University of the West Indies Press, 2004, pp. 137–66.

Figueroa, Mark and Amanda Sives. 'Homogenous voting, electoral manipulation and the "garrison" process in post-independence Jamaica.' *Journal of Commonwealth and Comparative Politics,* 40:1, March 2002, pp. 81–108.

Finkelstein, Joanne. 'Chic Theory', *Australian Humanities Review,* March, 1997, http://www.lib.latrobe.edu.au/AHR/archive/Issue-March-1997/finkelstein.html.

Fiske, John. *Understanding Popular Culture.* Boston: Unwin Hyman, 1989a.

———. *Reading the Popular.* Boston: Unwin Hyman, 1989b.

———. *Media Matters: Everyday Culture and Political Change.* Minneapolis: University of Minnesota Press, 1996.

Flood, Michael. 'Fatherhood and Fatherlessness,' Discussion Paper No. 59, The Australia Institute, November 2003.

———. *The Men's Bibliography* (for a comprehensive online bibliography of writing on men, masculinities, gender and sexualities) at http://www.xyonline.net/mensbiblio/.

Flügel, J.C. *The Psychology of Clothes.* London: Hogarth P., 1930.

Forbes, John D. *Jamaica: Managing Political and Economic Change.* Washington: American Enterprise Institute for Public Policy Research, 1985.

Forman, Murray. *The 'Hood' Comes First: Race, Space and Place in Hip-Hop.* Middletown, Connecticut: Wesleyan University Press, 2002.

Foucault, Michel. *Power/Knowledge: Selected Interviews and Other Writings*. New York: Pantheon Books, 1980.

———. *The History of Sexuality, Vol. 1: An Introduction*. New York: Vintage Books, Random House, Inc., 1990a.

———. *Politics, Philosophy, Culture: Interviews and Other Writings 1977–1984*. Edited and with an Introduction by Lawrence D. Kritzman. New York and London: Routledge, 1990b.

Frank, Blye. 'Hegemonic Heterosexual Masculinity,' in *Studies in Political Economy*, Vol. 24, Autumn 1987, pp. 159–70.

Freud, Sigmund. *Three Essays on the Theory of Sexuality*. Basic Books, 2000.

Frith, Simon. *Performing Rites: On the Value of Popular Music*. Cambridge Mass: Harvard University Press, 1996.

———. (ed.). *Facing the music: A Pantheon guide to popular culture*. New York: Pantheon Books, 1988.

Gardiner, Judith Kegan (ed.). *Masculinity Studies and Feminist Theory: New Directions*. New York: Columbia University Press, 2002.

Geertz, Clifford. *The Interpretation of Cultures*. New York: Basic Books, 1973.

George, Nelson. *Hip-Hop America*. New York: Viking Books, 1999.

Ghoussoub, Mai and Sinclair-Webb, Emma (eds.). *Imagined Masculinities: Male Identity and Culture in the Modern Middle East*. London: Saqi Books, 2000.

Gilroy, Paul. *The Black Atlantic: Modernity and Double Consciousness*. Cambridge: Harvard University Press, 1993a.

———. *Small Acts: Thoughts on the Politics of Black Cultures*. London: Serpent's Tail, 1993b.

Giroux, Henry A. *Disturbing pleasures: Learning Popular Culture*. New York: Routledge, 1994.

Goffman, Erving. *Gender Advertisements*. New York, NY: Harper and Row, 1976.

———. 'The Arrangement Between the Sexes' in *Theory and Society,* No. 43, 1977, pp. 301–31.

Golden, Thelma (ed.) with a preface by Henry Louis Gates, Jr. *Black male: representations of masculinity in contemporary American art*. New York: Whitney Museum of American Art and distributed by H.N. Abrams, 1994.

Gordon, Derek (1987). *Class, Status and Social Mobility in Jamaica*. University of the West Indies, Mona, Kingston, Jamaica: ISER, 1987.

Gordon, Derek, Patricia Anderson and Don Robotham. 'Jamaica: Urbanization during the Years of Crisis' in Portes, Alejandro et al. (eds.). *The Urban Caribbean: Transition to the New Global Economy*. Baltimore, USA: The Johns Hopkins University Press, 1997, pp. 190–223.

Gramsci, Antonio. 'Hegemony, Relations of Force, Historical Bloc' in *The Antonio Gramsci Reader: Selected Writings 1916–1935*. Edited by David Forgacs. New York: New York University Press, 2000, pp. 189–221.

————. 'Popular Culture' in *The Antonio Gramsci Reader: Selected Writings 1916–1935*. Edited by David Forgacs. New York: New York University Press, 2000, pp. 363–78.

Gray, Ann and Jim McGuigan (eds.). *Studying Culture: An Introductory Reader*. London & New York: Edward Arnold, 1993.

Gray, Obika. 'Discovering the Social Power of the Poor' in *Social and Economic Studies* 43, No. 3, September 1994.

————. *Demeaned but Empowered: The Social Power of the Urban Poor in Jamaica*. Jamaica, Barbados, Trinidad & Tobago: University of the West Indies Press, 2004.

Grossberg, Lawrence. *Dancing in spite of myself: essays on popular culture*. Durham, NC: Duke University Press, 1997.

Grossberg, Lawrence et al. *Mediamaking: mass media in a popular culture*. Thousand Oaks, California: Sage Publications, 1998.

Gunst, Laurie. *Born Fi' Dead: A Journey Through the Jamaican Posse Underworld*. New York: Henry Holt, 1995.

Gutmann, Matthew C. *The Meanings Of Macho: Being a Man in Mexico City*. University of California Press, 1996.

Gutzmore, Cecil. 'Casting the First Stone!: Policing of Homo/Sexuality in Jamaican Popular Culture,' in *Interventions: International Journal of Postcolonial Studies* Special Issue on Jamaican Popular Culture co-edited by Carolyn Cooper and Alison Donnell 6.1: April, 2004, pp. 118–34.

Habekost, Christian. *Verbal Riddim: The Politics and Aesthetics of African-Caribbean Dub Poetry*. Amsterdam and Atlanta GA: Rodopi, 1993.

Halberstam, Judith. *Female Masculinity*. Duke University Press, 1998.

Hall, Stuart and Tony Jefferson (eds.). *Resistance Through Rituals*. London: Hutchison, 1976.

Hall, Stuart. 'What is this "black" in Black Popular Culture?' in Morley, David and Kuan-Hsing Chen (eds.). *Stuart Hall: Critical Dialogues in Cultural Studies*. London: Routledge, 1996, pp. 465–75.

Hall, Stuart and Paul du Gay (eds.) *Questions of Cultural Identity*. London and Thousand Oaks, California: Sage, 1996.

Hall, Stuart (ed.) *Representation: Cultural Representations and Signifying Practices*. London; Thousand Oaks, California: Sage, 1997.

Hanke, R. 'Hegemonic Masculinity' in *thirtysomething* in *Critical Studies in Communications*, Vol. 7, 1990, pp. 231–48.

———— . 'Redesigning Men: Hegemonic Masculinity and Transition.' in S. Craig (ed.), *Men, Masculinity and the Media*. Newbury Park, CA: Sage, 1992, pp. 185–89.

————. 'Theorizing Masculinity With/In the Media' in *Communication Theory*, Vol. 8: 2, May 1998, pp. 183–203.

Harper, S. 'Subordinating Masculinities/Racializing Masculinities: Writing White supremacist discourse on men's bodies.' *Masculinities* V. 2, 1994, pp. 1–20.

Harrington, C. Lee and Denise D. Bielby. (eds.). *Popular Culture: Production and Consumption.* Malden, Mass.: Blackwell Publishers, 2001.

Harriott, Anthony. *Police and Crime Control in Jamaica: Problems of Reforming Ex-Colonial Constabularies.* Kingston: University of the West Indies Press, 2000.

Hatty, Suzanne E. *Masculinities, Violence, and Culture.* Thousand Oaks; London; New Delhi: Sage, 2000.

'Head of crack cocaine empire convicted' *Guardian Unlimited* Special Reports. June 12, 2004.

Hebdige, Dick. *Subculture: The Meaning of Style.* London & New York: Routledge, 1991.

———. *Cut n' Mix: Culture, Identity and Caribbean Music.* London: Methuen & Co., 1987.

Henry, Krista. Blackberry's 'ping' Entertainment Industry, the *Jamaica Star*, May 5, 2009.

Henry, Matthew. 'He is a "bad mother *$%@!#": Shaft and contemporary black masculinity' in *Journal of Popular Film and Television*, Summer 2002, pp. 114–19.

Henry, Tricia. *Breaking all the Rules: Punk, Rock and the Making of a Style.* London: U.M.I. Press, 1989.

Hope, Donna P. 'Sting 2003: Performing Violence and Social Commentary.' *Sunday Gleaner*, January 4, 2004a, pp. A10–A11. http://www.jamaica-gleaner.com/gleaner/20040104/cleisure/cleisure5.html.

———. '*Ninja Man* the Lyrical Don: Embodying Violent Masculinity in Jamaican Dancehall Culture,' in *Discourses in Dance*, 2:2, 2004b, pp. 27–43.

———. 'The British Link-Up Crew – Consumption Masquerading as Masculinity in the Dancehall' In *Interventions: International Journal of Postcolonial Studies* Special Issue on Jamaican Popular Culture co-edited by Carolyn Cooper and Alison Donnell 6:1, April, 2004c, pp. 101–17.

———. *Inna di Dancehall: Popular Culture and the Politics of Identity in Jamaica.* Kingston: University of the West Indies Press, January 2006a.

———. 'Dons and Shottas: Performing Violent Masculinity in Dancehall Culture,' *Social and Economic Studies*, Special Issue on Jamaican Culture, Vol 55: 1 & 2. UWI, Kingston: SALISES, 2006b, 115–31.

———. 'Passa Passa: Interrogating Cultural Hybridities in Jamaican Dancehall' in *Small Axe: A Caribbean Journal of Criticism*, No. 21, October 2006c, pp.119–133.

———. 'Love Punaany Bad: Negotiating Misogynistic Masculinity in Dancehall Culture.' In *Caribbean Culture: Soundings on Kamau Braithwaite,* ed. Annie Paul. Kingston: University of the West Indies Press, 2007, pp. 367–80.

Hopkins, Patrick D. 'Gender Treachery: Homophobia, Masculinity and Threatened Identities' in May, Larry and Strikweda, Robert (eds.). *Rethinking Masculinity: Philosophical Explorations in Light of Feminism*. Lanham, Maryland: Rowman & Littlefield, 1992, pp. 111–31.

Horrocks, Roger. *Male Myths and Icons: Masculinity in Popular Culture*. New York: St Martin's Press, 1995.

Horst, Heather A., and Daniel Miller. *The Cell Phone: An Anthropology of Communication*. Oxford and New York: Berg, 2006.

Hron, Anthony (Programme Director of Jamaica Forum for Lesbians, All-Sexuals and Gays). *Report on Persecution of Sexual Minorities in Jamaica*. With contributions from Phillip Dayle, Ian McKnight, Robert Carr and Jamaica AIDS Support. May 2003 – http://www.laccaso.org/pdfs/impunidad_jamaica_glbt.pdf.

Human Rights Watch. "Hated to Death: Homophobia, Violence and Jamaica's HIV/AIDS Epidemic, 2004."

"JAMAICA-POPULATION: Condom Distribution Proposal Sparks Riots", *InterPress News Service (IPS); 22 August 1997* -http://www.aegis.com/news/ips/1997/IP970807.html.

Jones, Hedley H.G (then President, Jamaica Federation of Musicians). 'Music and its Effects.' Letter of the Day to the Editor in the *Daily Gleaner*, August 19, 1989, p. 7.

Jones, Simon. *Black Culture, White Youth: The Reggae Tradition from JA to UK*. London Macmillan Education Ltd., 1988.

Kaplan, E. Ann. *Rocking Around the Clock: Music Television, Postmodernism and Consumer Culture*.

Kaufman, Michael (ed.). *Beyond Patriarchy: Essays by Men on Pleasure, Power and Change*. New York: Oxford University Press, 1987.

Kellner, Douglas. 'Madonna, Fashion, and Identity,' in Shari Benstock and Suzanne Ferriss (eds.) *On Fashion*. Rutgers University Press, 1994, pp. 159–82.

Kimmel, Michael. 'Masculinity as Homophobia' In Whitehead, Stephen M. and Barrett, Frank J. (eds.). *The Masculinities Reader*. Cambridge & Oxford, UK and Malden, MA: Polity and Blackwell, 2001.

———. *Manhood in America: A Cultural History*. New York & London: The Free Press,1996.

Kimmel, Michael S. and Michael Messner (eds.). *Men's Lives*. 6th edn. Boston, New York, London et al.: Pearson Education, Inc./Allyn & Bacon, 2004.

Lancaster, Roger N. *Life is Hard: Machismo, Danger, and the Intimacy of Power in Nicaragua*. Berkeley and Los Angeles: University of California Press, 1992.

Lancaster, Roger and Micaela di Leonardo (eds.). *The Gender/Sexuality Reader*. New York and London: Routledge, 1997.

Le Franc, Elsie. *Consequences of Structural Adjustment: A Review of the Jamaican Experience*. Kingston, Jamaica: Canoe Press, 1994.

Leitch, Vincent B. 'Costly Compensations: Postmodern Fashion, Politics and Identity,' *Modern Fiction Studies*, 42, Spring 1996, pp. 111–28.

Lent, J.A. *Caribbean Popular Culture*. Bowling Green: Bowling Green State Popular Press, 1990.

Leo-Rhynie, Elsa. 'Socialisation and the Development of Gender Identity: Theoretical Formulations and Caribbean Research' in Barrow, Christine (ed.) *Caribbean Portraits: Essays on Gender Ideologies and Identities*. Kingston: Ian Randle Publishers, 1998, pp. 234–51.

Levitt, Kari Polanyi. *The Origins and Consequences of Jamaica's Debt Crisis 1970–1990* (revised). Kingston: Consortium Graduate School of Social Sciences, University of the West Indies, 1991.

Lewis, Linden. 'Caribbean Masculinity: Unpacking the Narrative,' in Lewis, Linden (ed.). *The Culture of Gender and Sexuality in the Caribbean*. Florida: University of Florida Press, 2003a, pp. 94–125.

Lewis, Linden (ed.). *The Culture of Gender and Sexuality in the Caribbean*. Florida: University of Florida Press, 2003b.

Lewis, Lisa A. *Gender Politics and MTV: Voicing the Difference*. Philadelphia: Temple University Press, 1990.

———. (ed.) *Adoring Audience, The: Fan Culture and Popular Media*. London; New York: Routledge, 1992.

Lindsey, Linda. *Gender Roles: A Sociological Perspective*. 2nd edn. Englewood Cliffs, New Jersey: Prentice Hall, 1994.

Lipsitz, George. *Dangerous Crossroads: Popular Music, Postmodernism, and the Poetics of Place*. London; New York: Verso, 1994.

Mac an Ghaill, Mairtin (ed.). *Understanding Masculinities. Social Relations and Cultural Arenas*. Buckingham and Philadelphia: Open University Press, 1996.

Majors, Richard G. and Mancini, Janet. *Cool Pose: The Dilemmas of Black Manhood in America*. New York: Lexington Books, 1992.

Manley, Michael. *The Politics of Change: A Jamaican Testament*. London: Deutsch, 1974.

———. *Jamaica: Struggle in the Periphery*. London: Third World Media, 1982.

Manuel, Peter et al. *Caribbean Currents: Caribbean Music from Rumba to Reggae*. Philadelphia: Temple University Press; Kingston: Ian Randle Publishers, 1995.

May, Larry and Strikweda, Robert (eds.). *Rethinking Masculinity: Philosophical Explorations in Light of Feminism*. Lanham, Maryland: Rowman & Littlefield, 1992.

McRobbie, Angela, (ed.). *Zoot Suits and Second-hand Dresses: An Anthology of Fashion and Music*. Boston: Unwin Hyman, 1989.

Merton, Robert K. 'Social Structure and Anomie,' *American Sociological Review* 3: 1938, pp. 672–82.

———. 'Social Structure and Anomie: Revisions and Extensions' in *The* Family. Edited by Ruth Anshen. New York: Harper Brothers, 1949, pp. 226–57.

———. *Social Theory and Social Structure.* Revised edn. Glencoe: Free Press, 1957.

Messerschimdt, J. *Masculinities and Crime: Critique and Reconceptualization of Theory.* Lanham, MD: Rowman and Littleman, 1993.

Messner, M. 'The Meaning of Success: The Athletic Experience and the Development of Male Identity' in Brod. H. (ed.) *The Making of Masculinities: The New Men's Studies.* Boston: Allen & Unwin, 1987, pp. 193–210.

Middleton, Richard. *Studying Popular Music.* Milton Keynes: Open University Press, 1990.

Mill, John Stuart. *The Subjection of Women.* Edited and with an Introduction by Susan Moller Okin. Indianapolis: Hackett Publishing Co., 1988.

Miller, Errol. *Marginalization of the Black Male: Insights from the Development of the Teaching Profession.* ISER, UWI, 1987.

———. *Men at Risk.* Kingston: Jamaica Publishing House, 1991.

Millett, Kate. *Sexual Politics.* Urbana and Chicago: University of Illinois Press, 2000.

Mirzoeff, Nicholas (ed.). *The Visual Culture Reader.* 2nd edn. London & New York: Routledge, 2003.

Mitchell Damion. 'Rescue the Boys! – Special Intervention mooted for Schools.' *Sunday Gleaner,* May 30, 2004.

Mohammed, Patricia. 'Nuancing the Feminist Discourse in the Caribbean' in *New Currents in Caribbean Thought, Special Issue of Social and Economic Studies* Ed. Brian Meeks. Vol. 43, No.3, 1994.

—————. 'Writing Gender into History: The Negotiation of Gender Relations' in *Engendering History: Caribbean Women in Historical Perspective.* Ed. Bridget Brereton, Verene Shepherd and Barbara Bailey. Kingston: Ian Randle Publishers, 1995, pp. 20–47.

———.(ed.). 'Rethinking Caribbean Difference Special Issue.' *Feminist Review No. 59.* New York: Routledge, Summer 1998.

———. (ed.). *Gendered Realities: Essays in Caribbean Feminist Thought.* Kingston: University of the West Indies Press, 2002.

Morais, Richard. 'Popular Culture blamed for boys' poor grades' in the *Gleaner,* Friday January 21, 2000.

Morley, David. *Television, Audiences, and Cultural Studies.* London, New York: Routledge, 1992.

Morley, David and Kuan-Hsing Chen (eds.). *Stuart Hall: Critical Dialogues in Cultural Studies.* London: Routledge, 1996.

'MPs Turn out for Funeral,' the *Gleaner,* May 9, 2001, p. A2.

Muggleton, David. *Inside Subculture: the Postmodern meaning of style.* Oxford and New York: Berg, 2000.

'Musical Dads,' Sunday Feature section in the *Sunday Observer,* June 19, 2005.

Neal, Mark Anthony. *What the Music Said: Black Popular Music and Black Public Culture.* New York and London: Routledge, 1999.

Nelson, Barbara. 'The Church speaks on vulgar lyrics and gun violence' in the *Sunday Gleaner*, January 30, 1994.

Nelson, Cary and Lawrence Grossberg (eds.). *Marxism and the Interpretation of Culture*. Urbana: University of Illinois Press, 1988.

'Ninja Man hands over gun to Adams.' *Jamaica Observer,* December 28, 2002.

Nixon, Sean. 'Exhibiting Masculinity.' In Hall, Stuart. (ed). *Representation: Cultural Representations and Signifying Practices*. London: Sage, 1997, pp. 291–330.

'No plans to issue condoms in prisons - Health Ministry,' *Jamaica Gleaner*, Thursday, May 10, 2001– http://www.jamaica-gleaner.com/gleaner/20010510/news/news1.html.

———. 'Adams, "Ninja Man" deny gun hand-over at Sting staged.' *Jamaica Observer,* January 6, 2004.

Ortner, Sherry B and Whitehead, Harriet (eds.). *Sexual Meanings: The Cultural Construction of Gender and Sexuality*. Cambridge: Cambridge University Press, 1981.

Parry, O. 'In One Ear and Out the Other: Unmasking Masculinities in the Caribbean Classroom.' *Sociological Research Online*, Vol. 1, no. 2, 1996 http://www.socresonline.org.uk/socresonline/1/2/2.html.

Pease, Bob. *Men and Gender Relations*. Melbourne: Tertiary Press, 2002.

———. *Recreating Men: Postmodern Masculinity Politics*. London: Sage, 2000.

Perchuk, A and Posner, H. (eds.). *The Masculine Masquerade: Masculinity and Representation*. Cambridge, MA: MIT Press, 1995.

Pleck, Joseph H. and Jack Sawyer (eds.). *Men and Masculinity*. Englewood Cliffs, NJ: Prentice Hall, 1974.

Portes, Alejandro, Jose Itzigsohn and Carlos Dore-Cabral. 'Urbanization in the Caribbean Basin: Social Change during the Years of Crisis' in *Latin American Research Review,* Vol. 29, No. 2, 1994, pp. 3–37.

'PNP Bigwigs Mourn Slain Don,' Headline article in the *Daily Observer*, Wednesday, May 9, 2001.

Portes, Alejandro, Carlos Dore-Cabral, and Patricia Landolt (eds.). *The Urban Caribbean: Transition to the New Global Economy*. Baltimore, USA: The Johns Hopkins University Press, 1997.

Price, Charles. 'What the Zeeks Uprising Reveals: Development Issues, Moral Economy and the Urban Lumpenproletariat in Jamaica.' *Urban Anthropology*, 33:1, Spring 2004, pp. 73–113.

'PSOJ leading business closure in crime protest,' the *Jamaica Observer*, May 20, 2005.

Quéniart, Anne. A Profile of Fatherhood Among Young Men: Moving Away from Their Birth Family and Closer to Their Child. Sociological Research Online, vol. 9, no. 3, 2004, http://www.socresonline.org.uk/9/3/queniart.html.

Ramirez, Rafael L., Victor I. Garcia-Toro and Ineke Cunningham (eds.). *Caribbean Masculinities: Working Papers.* Puerto Rico: HIV/AIDS Research and Education Centre, University of Puerto Rico, 2002.

Rapley, John. 'Jamaica: Negotiating Law and Order with the Dons.' NACLA *Report on the Americas*, Vol. 37:2, Sept/October, 2003, pp. 25–29.

Reddock, Rhoda. 'Primacy of Gender in Race and Class' in J. Edward Greene (ed.) *Race, Class and Gender in the Future of the Caribbean.* Mona, Kingston: ISER, 1993, pp. 43–73.

————.(ed.). *Interrogating Caribbean Masculinities: Theoretical and Empirical Analyses.* Kingston: University of the West Indies Press, 2004.

Rose, Tricia. *Black Noise: Rap Music and Black Culture in Contemporary America.* Hanover, NH: University Press of New England, 1994a.

————. 'Rap music and the demonization of young Black males.' In Golden, Thelma (ed.) with a preface by Henry Louis Gates, Jr. *Black male: representations of masculinity in contemporary American art.* New York: Whitney Museum of American Art and distributed by H.N. Abrams, 1994b, pp 149–58.

Ross, Andrew. *No Respect: Intellectuals and Popular Culture.* New York: Routledge, 1989.

————. 'The gangsta and the diva.' In Golden, Thelma (ed.) with a preface by Henry Louis Gates, Jr. *Black male: representations of masculinity in contemporary American art.* New York: Whitney Museum of American Art and distributed by H.N. Abrams, 1994, pp. 159–66.

Ross, Andrew and Tricia Rose (eds.). *Microphone Fiends: Youth Music & Youth Culture.* New York: Routledge, 1994.

Rutherford, J. 'Who's That Man?' in Chapman R. and Rutherford J. (eds.). *Male Order:*

Unwrapping Masculinity. London: Lawrence & Wishart, 1988, pp. 21–67.

Saunders, Patricia J. 'Is not Everything Good to Eat, Good to Talk: Sexual Economy and Dancehall Music in the Global Marketplace' in *Small Axe*, No. 13, March 2003, pp. 95–115.

Scott, David. *Refashioning Futures: Criticism After PostColoniality.* Princeton, New Jersey: Princeton University Press, 1999.

Scott, Joan. *Gender and the Politics of History.* New York: Columbia University, 1988.

Segal, Lynne. *Slow Motion: Changing Masculinities, Changing Men.* New Brunswick and New Jersey, Rutgers University Press, 1990.

Segree, Clifton. 'Too much disposable music' in the *Gleaner*, February 9, 2000a, p. C2.

———— . 'Put some decency into dancehall dress' in the *Sunday Gleaner*, February 27, 2000b, p. 3E.

Seidler, Victor J. *Man Enough: Embodying Masculinities.* London; Thousand Oaks, California: Sage, 1997.

Shilling, Chris. *The Body and Social Theory.* London: Sage, 1993.

Simpson, Mark. *Male Impersonators: Men Performing Masculinity*. New York: Routledge, 1994.

Simpson, Trudy. 'Are Jamaican Women too Aggressive?' the *Gleaner*, November 3, 2003.

Skelton, T. 'I Sing Dirty Reality, I am out there for the Ladies,' Lady Saw: Women and Jamaican ragga music, resisting patriarchy. *Phoebe*, 7 (1/2) 1995, pp. 86–104.

Smith, Germaine. Female Dancers Make Strides, the *Sunday Gleaner*, May 29, 2005, E1 & E4.

Smith, Paul (ed.) *Boys: Masculinities in Contemporary Culture*. Boulder, Colorado and Oxford, UK, 1996.

Smith, R. T. *The Negro Family in British Guiana: Family Structure and Social Status in Villages*. New York: Grove Press, 1956.

———. *Kinship and Class in the West Indies: A Genealogical Study of Jamaica and Guyana*. Cambridge: Cambridge University Press, 1988.

Spicer, Andrew. *Typical Men: The Representation of Masculinity in Popular British Culture*. I B Tauris & Co Ltd., 2001.

Stacey, J. 'Dada-ism in the 1990s: Getting Past Baby Talk about Fatherlessness' in C.R. Daniels (ed.), *Lost Fathers: The Politics of Fatherlessness*. London: Macmillan, 1998, pp. 51–84.

Stanley-Niaah, Sonjah. 'Kingston's Dancehall: A Story of Space and Celebration' in *Space and Culture*, V. 7, No. 1, February, 2004a, pp. 102–18.

———. 'Making Space: Kingston's Dancehall culture and its philosophy of "Boundarylessness"' in *African Identities*, V. 2, No. 2, 2004b, pp. 117–32.

Stearns, Peter N. *Be a Man! Males in Modern Society*. New York: Holmes and Meier, 1979.

Stephens, Evelyne Huber, and John D. Stephens. *Democratic Socialism in Jamaica: The Political Movement and Social Transformation in Dependent Capitalism*. London: Macmillan, 1986.

Stephens, Gregory. Transcript of Radio Interview 'A Culture of Intolerance: Insights on the Chi Chi Man Craze and Jamaica Gender Relations with Julius Power of JGLAG.' Spring 2002 at http://www.jahworks.org/music/interview/jflag_interview.html.

Stewart, Kingsley. 'So Wha, Mi Nuh Fi Live To?': Interpreting Violence in Jamaica Through the Dancehall Culture,' in *IDEAZ*, Vol. 1 No. 1: University of the West Indies, Mona, May 2002, pp. 17–28.

Stolzoff, Norman. 'Murderation: The Question of Violence in the Sound System Dance,' *Social and Economic Studies*, Vol. 47 no. 1, March, 1998.

———. *Wake the Town: Dancehall Culture in Jamaica*. Durham and London: Duke University Press, 2000.

Stone, Carl. *Class, Race, and Political Behaviour in Urban Jamaica*. Mona, Jamaica: Institute of Social and Economic Research, University of the West Indies, 1973.

————. *Democracy and Clientelism in Jamaica*. New Brunswick and London: Transaction Books, 1980.

————. *Class, State, and Democracy in Jamaica*. New York, Connecticut & London: Praeger, 1986.

————. 'Values, Norms and Personality Development in Jamaica'. Presented at the National Consultation on Values and Attitudes. Mona, Kingston Jamaica: ISER, 1992.

Stone, Carl and Aggrey Brown (eds.). *Essays on Power and Change in Jamaica*. Kingston: Jamaica Publishing House; distributed by Teachers Book Centre, 1977.

Storey, John. *Cultural Studies and the Study of Popular Culture: Theories and Methods*. Athens, Georgia: University of Georgia Press, 1996.

————. *An Introduction to Cultural Theory and Popular Culture*. 2nd edn. Athens, Georgia: University of Georgia Press, 1998

————. *Cultural Consumption and Everyday Life*. London: Arnold; New York: Co-published in the U.S.A. by Oxford University Press, 1999.

————. (ed). *Cultural Theory and Popular Culture: A Reader*. 2nd edn. London, New York, Toronto, Sydney et al: Pearson Education Limited, Prentice Hall, 1998.

Sullivan, Robin, Fathering and Children, *Family Matters* No. 58, Autumn 2001, pp. 46–51.

Tafari, Imani. 'Lady Saw…Dancehall Donette' in *Sistren* 16(1/2), 1994.

Tasker, Y. *Spectacular bodies: Gender genre and the action cinema*. London: Routledge, 1993.

Tate, Greg. *Flyboy in the Buttermilk*. New York: Simon and Schuster, 1992.

'There's no stopping "Chi Chi Man"' in the *Gleaner*, Saturday, March 31, 2001.

Thorne, Barrie. *Gender Play: Girls and Boys in School*. New Brunswick, NJ: Rutgers, 1994.

Thornton, Sarah. *Club Cultures: Music, Media and Subcultural Capital*. Cambridge: Polity, 1995.

Thornton, Sara and Ken Gelder (eds.). *The Subcultures Reader*. London, New York: Routledge, 1997.

'Tok defends "Chi Chi Man"' in the *Sunday Gleaner*, March 4, 2001, p. 3E.

Tong, Rosemarie Putnam. *Feminist Thought: A More Comprehensive Introduction*. 2nd edn. Colorado & Oxford: Westview Press, 1998.

Torres, S. 'Melodrama, masculinity and the family: *Thirtysomething* as therapy.' *Camera Obscura*, 19, 1989, pp. 86–106.

Waters, Anita. Race, Class, and Political Symbols: Rastafari and Reggae in Jamaican Politics. New Brunswick and London: Transaction Publishers, 1989.

Weeks, Jeffrey. Coming Out: Homosexual Politics in Britain from the Nineteenth Century to the Present. London: Quartet, 1977.

————. *Sexuality*. London & New York: Routledge, 1986.

Wernick, Andrew. 'From Voyeur to Narcissist: Imaging Men in Contemporary Advertising' in Kaufman, Michael (ed.), *Beyond Patriarchy: Essays by Men on Pleasure, Power, and Change.* Toronto & New York: Oxford University Press, 1987, pp. 277–97.

West, Candace, and Don H. Zimmerman. 'Doing Gender' in *Gender and Society* 1(2), 1987, pp. 125–51.

West, Candace, and Sarah Fenstermaker. 'Doing Difference' in *Gender and Society* 9(1), 1995, pp. 8–37.

Whitehead, Stephen M. *Men and Masculinities: Key Themes and New Directions.* Cambridge: Polity Press, 2002.

Whitehead, Stephen and Barrett, Frank J. (eds.). *The Masculinities Reader.* Cambridge & Oxford, UK and Malden, MA: Polity and Blackwell, 2001.

Whiteley, Sheila, Andy Bennett and Stan Hawkins (eds.). *Music, space and place: popular music and cultural identity.* Burlington, VT: Ashgate, Forthcoming 2004.

Wignall, Mark A. 'Politicians and Dons,' in the *Daily Observer*, May 10, 2001, p. 7.

'Willie's final rites,' the *Star*, May 9, 2001, p. 3.

Wilson, Claude. 'Mobay artiste stokes "shotta" controversy,' in the *Gleaner*, August 8, 1999.

Wilson, Elizabeth and Juliet Ash (eds.). *Chic Thrills: A Fashion Reader.* Berkeley: University of California Press, 1992.

Wilson, Peter J. 'Caribbean Crews: Peer Groups and Male Societies,' *Caribbean Studies* 10:4, 1971, pp 18–34.

———. Crab Antics: The Social Anthropology of English-Speaking Negro Societies of the Caribbean. New Haven: Yale University Press, 1973.

———. 'Reputation and Respectability: A Suggestion for Caribbean Ethnology,' *Man*, New Series, 4:1, 1969, pp. 70–84.

Witter, Michael. 'The Role of Higglers/Sidewalk Vendors/Informal Commercial Traders in the Development of the Jamaican Economy.' Paper presented to symposium on informal commercial importers, University of the West Indies, Mona Jamaica, May, 1988.

———. 'Music and the Jamaican Economy.' Report prepared for UNCTAD/ WIPO, February 2002. http://www.wipo.int/about-ip/en/studies/pdf/ study_m_witter.pdf.

Young, Richard (ed.). *Music, Popular Culture, Identities.* Amsterdam : Rodopi By Editions, 2002.

DISCOGRAPHY

Alozade. *'Chi Chi Crew'*. Personal CD Collection, 2000.

Assassin. *'How We Roll'*. *Personal CD Collection.* 2000

———. *'Idiot Ting Dat,'* Renaissance, 2004.

BabyCham. '*Another Level*' (featuring Bounty Killer), Track 9, Disc 2 (*Another Level*), *Wow…The Story*, Madhouse/Artists Only! Records, 2000.

———. '*Babylon Boy,*' Track 10, Disc 1 (*The Beginning*), *Wow…The Story*, Madhouse/Artists Only! Records, 2000.

———. '*Boom/Can I Get a,*' Track 6, Disc 1 (*The Beginning*) *Wow…The Story*, Madhouse/Artists Only! Records, 2000.

———. '*Many Many,*' Track 2, Disc 1 (*The Beginning*) *Wow…The Story*, Madhouse/Artists Only! Records, 2000.

Beenie Man. '*Crazy Notion,*' Track 5, *Art & Life,* Virgin, 2000.

———. '*Ole Dawg,*' Track 11, *The Best of Two Badd DJS*. V.P. Records, 3105, 1997.

———. '*Nuff Gal,*' *Best of Beenie Man*. V.P. Records, 2000.

Bounty Killer. '*Benz &Bimmer,*' *My Xperience*, TVT Records, 1996.

———. '*Cellular Phone,*' Track 7, *Down in the Ghetto,* VP Records, 1995.

———. '*Down in the Ghetto,*' Track 1, *Down in the Ghetto*, V.P. Records, 1403, 1995.

———. '*Mama,*' *My XPerience*, TVT Records, 1996.

———. '*New Gun,*' *Nah no Mercy: The Warlord Scrolls*, Disc 1, VP Records, 2006.

———. '*Spy fi Die,*' *Roots Reality and Culture*, VP Records, 1994.

Buju Banton. '*Boom Bye Bye,*'1992.

———. '*Dickie,*' Track 7, *Mr. Mention*, Fader/Pgd., 1993

———. '*Massa God World ah Run*'/How the World ah Run, Penthouse, 1992 (& *Ultimate Collection*, Hip-O Records 2001).

———. '*Stamina Daddy,*' Track 1, *Stamina Daddy*, Techniques/V.P. Records, 1992.

Capleton. '*Bun out di Chi Chi*', Personal CD Collection, 2000.

Captain Barkey. '*Bleach On,*' *Mud Up,* Greensleeves, 2001.

Ce'cile. '*Do it to me,*' Kings of Kings, 2003.

_____. '*Woman Tings,*' Richard Browne, 2005.

Cobra. '*Not this Face,*' Track 38, *100% Master Mix Volume 1*, undated.

Cutty Ranks. '*Grizzle,*' Dancehall Classics, circa 1991.

Elephant Man. '*Bad Man,*' Track 5, *Good 2 Go*, Atlantic, 2003.

———. '*Bow City,*' Track 16, *Coming 4 You*, Greensleeves, 2000.

———. '*Headache*' (featuring Delly Ranks), Track 18, *Coming 4 You*, Greensleeves, 2000.

———. '*Log on,*' Track 1, *Log On*, Greensleeves, 2001.

———. '*Never Bow,*' Track 20, *100% Master Mix Volume 1*, undated.

———. '*1000 Dollar Bill,*' Madd Dawgz, 2000.

———. '*Pon di River, Pon di Bank,*' Track 1, *Good 2 Go*. Atlantic, 2003.

———. '*Signal di Plane,*' Track 3, *Good 2 Go*, Atlantic 2003.

———. '*2000 Began,*' Track 7, *Coming 4 You*, Greensleeves, 2000.

Elephant Man & Ward 21. 'Rush Hour (Medley)'. Personal CD Collection, 2000.

Flippa Mafia. '*Foundation Ova Hype.*' Di Genius, 2009.

Frisco Kid. '*Doggystyle.*' Personal Collection (circa 1991).

Gaza Kim and Lisa Hype. '*Bill,*' Russian, 2009.

General Trees. '*50 Dollar Bill.*' Black Scorpio, (circa 1984).

I-Wayne. '*Bleacher,*' *Lava Ground* (Black Shade Riddim), 2005

Lady Ann. '*Informer,*' Joe Gibbs Music, 1983.

Lecturer. '*Punaany Too Sweet,*' Jammys, 1987.

Lexxus (Mr. Lex). '*Ring Mi Cellie,*' Track 4, *Lexxus AKA Mr. Lex,* VP, 2000.

Lovindeer, Lloyd. '*Light a Candle,*' *Best of Lovindeer,* The Sound of Jamaica, TSOJ9200, 1993.

Mavado. '*Mr Palmer,*' Black Chiney, 2007.

———. '*Nuh Bleach wid Cream,*' Big Ship Records, 2008.

Macka Diamond. '*Chase Money ,*' *Money-O*, Greensleeves, 2005.

———. '*Lexus and Benz,*' *Money-O*, Greensleeves, 2005

Merciless. '*Ole Gallis.*' *Vol. 2-East Coast.* East Coast Records, 1997.

Mr. Vegas. '*Heads High,*' Track 1, *Heads High,* Greensleeves, 1998.

Ninja Man. '*My Weapon*'. *Anything Test Dead. Reggae Anthology* – Ninja Man. V.P. Records, 2001.

Nuclear. '*Single Mother,*' 2009.

Queen Ifrica. '*Mi Nah Rub,*' Downsound Records, 2007.

Red Dragon/Flourgon & Sanchez. '*The Agony/Dungle Lover.*' Techniques (Ja.), WR24, 1989.

Richie D featuring Raine Seville and Leftside. '*What's Your Pin.*' Leftside, 2009.

Shabba Ranks. '*Best Babyfather,*' Personal CD collection, undated.

———. '*Dem Bow,*' Track 7, *Caan Dun,* CD1, VP Records, 1450, 1995.

———. '*Love Punaany Bad,*' Track 7, *Caan Dun,* CD1, VP Records, 1450, 1995 originally released as a single by King Jammys, 1995.

Spragga Benz. '*Jack it Up,*' Track 3, *Jack it Up,* V.P. Records, 1348, 1994.

———. '*Coulda Deal,*' Track 1, *Jack it Up,* V.P. Records, 1348, 1994.

Supercat. '*Don Dada,*' Track 6, *Don Dada,* Sony, 1992.

———. '*Trash and Ready.*' Jammys Records, 1984.

Tiger. '*Don is Don.*' Personal Collection (undated).

Timberlee. '*Bubble Like Soup,*' 2007.

TOK '*Chi Chi Man*'. Personal CD Collection, 2000.

Toots and the Maytals. '*Peeping Tom,*' Trojan Records, 1970.

Tony Rebel. '*Chatty Chatty,*' Penthouse, 1992.

Wayne Wonder. '*Informers,*' Xtra Large, 1998.

Wayne Wonder/Frisco Kid. '*Dreamland,*' Xtra Large, undated.

Vybz Kartel. '*Tek Buddy,*' 2003.

———. '*Mama,*' 2009.

VIDEOGRAPHY

Bloise, Garfield (Producer/Director). *Thug Life.* 2000.

Browne, Christopher (Director). *Third World Cop.* Palm Pictures, 1999.

Elgood, Rick (Director) and Don Letts(Director). *Dancehall Queen*. Island Jamaica Films, Island Digital Media, 1997.

Henzell, Perry (Director). *The Harder They Come*. Island Records, 1973.

Katz, Jackson and Jeremy Earp (Producer) and Jhally, Sut (Director). *Tough Guise* (Videotape). Media Education Foundation, 1999.

Ninja Man, Ce'cile and Donna Hope. Interviewed by Cliff Hughes on 'Impact' aired on CVM Television August 17, 2003.

Passa Passa Volume 1, (DVD) Reggaesound, 2004.

Roy Fowl and Donna Hope. Interviewed by Cliff Hughes on 'Impact' aired on CVM Television April 28, 2002.

Silvera, Cess (Exec. Producer & Director) & Massenberg, Kedar (Co-Executive Producer). *Shottas*, Access Pictures, 2002.

INDEX

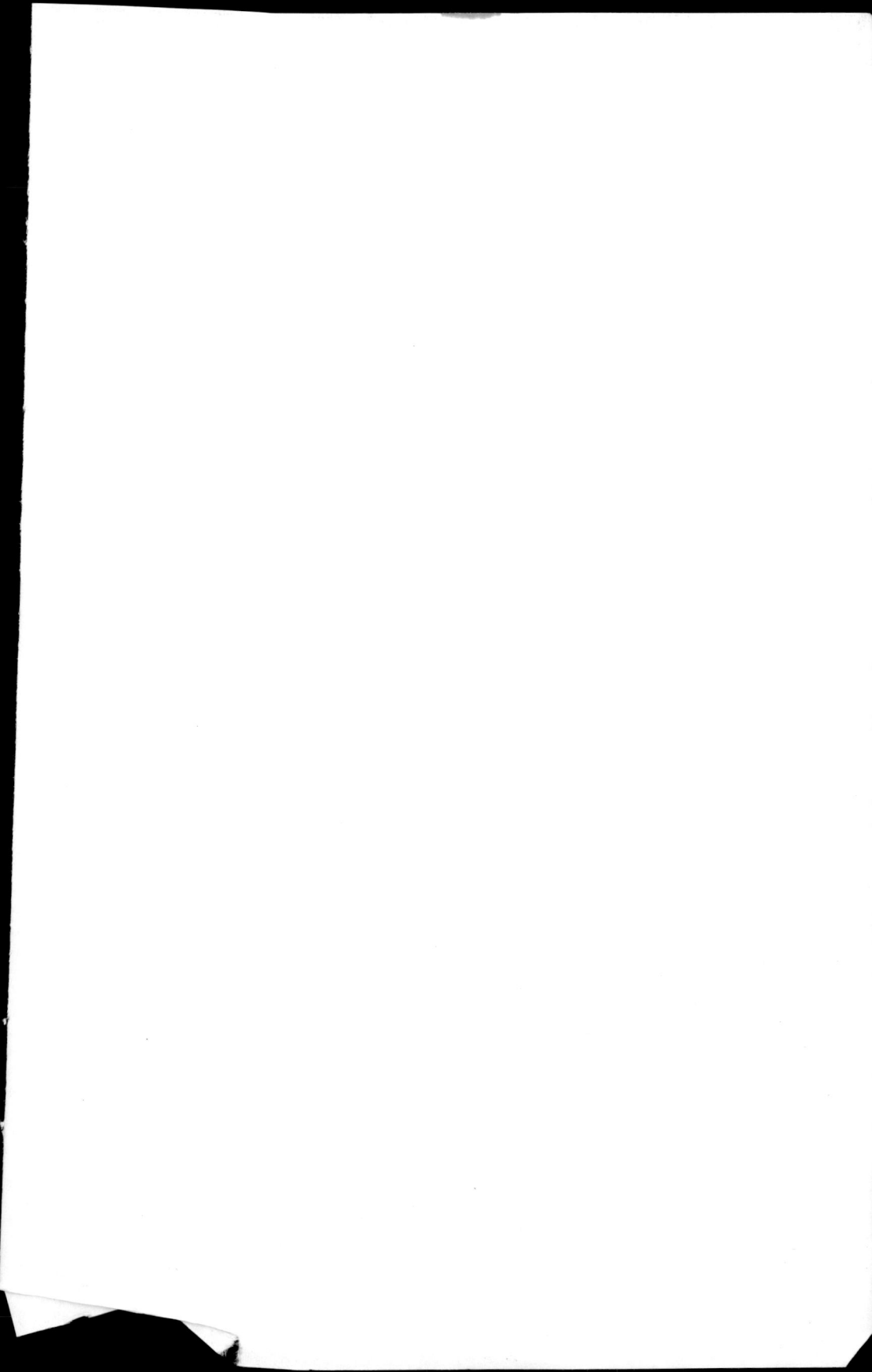

Lightning Source UK Ltd.
Milton Keynes UK
02 July 2010
156400UK00002B/10/P